Travels in Greeneland

Travels in Greeneland

The Cinema of Graham Greene

Quentin Falk

Quartet Books
London Melbourne New York

First published by Quartet Books Limited
A member of the Namara Group
27/29 Goodge Street, London W1P 1FD

Copyright © 1984 by Quentin Falk

British Library Cataloguing in Publication Data

Falk, Quentin
    Travels in Greeneland.
    I. Greene, Graham—Film adaptations
    1. Title
    791.43   PR6013.R44Z/

    ISBN 0-7043-2425-3

Typeset by MC Typeset, Chatham, Kent
Printed and bound in Great Britain
by Mackays of Chatham Ltd, Kent

To Anthea

Contents

Acknowledgements

My grateful thanks to many people who have helped me with this book: David Hovatter for his tireless library research, Harvey Mann for his picture research, the British Film Institute, the National Film Archive, Janet Spooner for typing the manuscript, Val Sillery for my index, *Film Literature Quarterly*, *Sight and Sound*, Gene D. Phillips S.J. and Sophia Waugh.

For their generous recall: Ken Annakin, Sir Richard Attenborough, John and Roy Boulting, Richard Broke, Peter Duffell, Guy Elmes, Sir Alec Guinness, Lady Gardiner (Muriel Box), Norma Heyman, John Mackenzie, Tom Stoppard and, of course, Graham Greene. For the use of photographs: Thorn EMI Films Ltd, Twentieth Century-Fox, Paramount Pictures, Columbia Pictures, Wheel Productions, MGM-UA, Warner Brothers, London Films, Rank Film Distributors, Flamingo Pictures, Thames Television, Consolidated Productions, Michael Korda and the Kobal Collection.

For granting permission to quote from their books, I wish to thank the following authors, their executors and publishers: the Bodley Head, William Heinemann Ltd and Gerald Pollinger of Laurence Pollinger Ltd for various works by Graham Greene; Martin Secker & Warburg for *The Long View* by Basil Wright and *Crime Movies – An Illustrated History* by Carlos Clarens; Jonathan Cape Ltd for *By Myself* by Lauren Bacall and *The Life of Noël Coward* by Cole Lesley; Weidenfeld (Publishers) Ltd for *Up in the Clouds, Gentlemen Please* by John Mills; Hutchinson Publishing Group for *Mind's Eye* by Basil Dean; Teacher's College Press for

Graham Greene — The Films of His Fiction by Gene D. Phillips S.J.;
Arbor House for *Ladd* by Beverly Linet; W.H. Allen & Co Ltd for
An Autobiography by Veronica Lake; Consolidated Press, Sydney
for *The Celluloid Muse* by Charles Higham and Joel Greenberg;
Penguin Books Ltd for *Charmed Lives* by Michael Korda; Blake
Friedmann for *The Man Who Could Work Miracles* by Karol Kulik;
Frankfurt, Garbus, Klein & Selz for *Memo from David O. Selznick*,
edited by Rudy Behlmar; the Putnam Publishing Group for
Encountering Directors by C.T. Samuels; Don Congdon Associates
for *Otto Preminger*, *An Autobiography* (copyright 1977 by Otto
Preminger); Angus & Robertson (UK) Ltd for *Peter Finch* by
Trader Faulkner; Macmillan Publishing Company for *The Moving
Image* by Robert Gessner; Plexus for *About John Ford* by Lindsay
Anderson.

Introduction

The great muted chromium studios wait . . . the novelist's Irish sweep: money for no thought and the inhuman romance: money for forgetting how people live: money for 'Siddown, won't yer' and 'I love, I love, I love' endlessly repeated. Inside the voice goes on 'God . . . I pray . . .' and the writers, a little stuffed and a little boozed, lean back and dream of the hundred pounds a week – and all that's asked in return the dried imagination and the dead pen. – 'Film Lunch', 1937

Graham Greene has been translated to the cinema more than any other major novelist this century. More than Maugham, Conrad, Hemingway, D.H. Lawrence, Fitzgerald, Steinbeck, Faulkner and Waugh. More even than Alistair Maclean or Harold Robbins. With and without his connivance there have been twenty three films of his published works, including eighteen of the novels, over six decades. Film-makers of the calibre of John Ford, Fritz Lang, Joseph Mankiewicz, the Boultings, Carol Reed, George Cukor and Cavalcanti have been attracted to his work. He has also adapted other writers for the cinema, been a playwright, journalist, perceptive critic and essayist on film, and now, in his eightieth year, while claiming 'not to be very interested in films these days' remains knowledgeable and, despite his much publicized concern about shady Riviera politics, ever-courteous with those who will descend on his Antibes eyrie to pick his brains for business or pleasure.

The extent of the adaptations tends to take people by surprise.

1

Everyone remembers *The Third Man*, *The Fallen Idol* and *Brighton Rock*. Television, in the past year alone, has scheduled, on various channels – and at various times of o'clock, from afternoon to late-night – *This Gun for Hire*, *Ministry of Fear*, *Our Man in Havana*, *The Comedians* and *The Human Factor*. Nevertheless, it is all too easy to mislay *The Confidential Agent*, *The End of the Affair* or *Across the Bridge* in the monochrome past. As with any great body of work, the quality of their translation has been extremely variable – both in terms of fidelity to the original and/or in any innate merit as pieces of celluloid. In fact, it is likely that inferior adaptations considerably outnumber successful ones for reasons I will suggest later. But Greene's own blanket dismissal that 'my books don't in fact make good films',[1] even taking into account the exceptions he is prepared to make for the handful with which he has been personally involved, is more the justly prejudiced cry of a tampered author than the rational observer of a prolific filmography that is ripe for reassessment.

'Born a child of the film age' is how film-maker and historian Basil Wright has described Greene, and even on the very first page of his first volume of autobiography, Greene is found evoking, in loving detail, his home town Berkhamstead's High Street cinema with 'its green moorish dome'. His father, who was headmaster of Berkhamstead school – where Greene agonized with divided loyalties and increasing traumas through a troubled adolescence – once gave permission for some of his senior boys to see Tarzan 'under the false impression that it was an educational film of anthropological interest and ever after he regarded the cinema with a sense of disillusion and suspicion';[2] two emotions which Greene himself would probably admit to in varying degrees over the ensuing years. The first film he ever saw is indelibly printed in his memory – a silent version of the Anthony Hope adventure, *Sophy of Kravonia*; that was in about 1911 and now, more than seventy years later, 'I can hear still the rumble of the Queen's guns crossing the high Kravonian pass beaten hollowly out on a single piano'.[3] Barely surviving teenage, with visits to the psychiatrist's couch and a flirtation with Russian roulette, all set against a backcloth of boredom (which would for ever continue to dog him), he went up to Oxford at eighteen and after graduating in 1926, joined *The Times* as a sub-editor. In that same year he enjoyed an extremely brief attraction to the Communist Party and was received into the Catholic Church. The following year, he married Vivien Dayrell-Browning; the marriage produced two children.

Between 1929 when his first novel, *The Man Within*, was published and 1935 when he started a four-and-a-half-year stint film reviewing for the *Spectator* and the short-lived magazine *Night and Day*, (at Oxford he had been critic for a university magazine) five more novels appeared as well as a short story, *The Basement Room* (later to be turned into *The Fallen Idol*).

Greene adopted the role of film critic 'from a sense of fun' and for ulterior motives too – 'those films were an escape – escape from the hellish problem of construction in Chapter Six, from the secondary character who obstinately refused to come alive, escape for an hour and a half from the melancholy which falls inexorably round the novelist when he has lived for too many months on end in his private world'.[4] Greene was, all seem agreed, one of the finest critics of the thirties and revisiting his reviews today is as fresh an experience as it must then have been for all but the most regular recipients of his critical whiplash – British cinema in general and Korda and Hitchcock in particular. He admired René Clair, Lang's *Fury*, Wyler's *These Three*, Duvivier, Pabst and Capra but his praise was never unqualified.

Whether it can be said that he established a set of critical principles to guide his reviewing and his own subsequent work at first hand in the cinema, is a little hard to discern. Championing the 'frankly commercial' he nevertheless would reiterate 'life as it is, life as it should be', which he believed was too often missing within the green, moorish domes of the Odeons, Empires and Essoldos. He perhaps came closest to a personal affirmation when, in December 1935, he wrote: 'The cinema, as much as poetry in the eighteenth century, needs patrons. Little good work can come from the commercial companies under the pressure of popular taste . . . the modern commercial picture has not merely learned nothing in the last six years, it has even forgotten what it once seemed to be learning from the Russian cinema . . .' Later though, in the same review, he rightly warns: 'I doubt if the best work has ever been produced in complete independence of a public . . . popular *taste* makes a thoroughly bad dictator, but the awareness of an audience is an essential discipline for the artist.'[5] This, and his regular sentiments about the British Board of Censors – 'a curious body . . . rumoured to consist of retired Army officers and elderly ladies of no occupation'[6] would find considerable sympathy in a British film industry today, seduced by the success of *Gandhi* and hog-tied by an ever-stifling system of cinema exhibition and distribution. *Plus ça change.*

The most notorious moment during this distinguished period of reviewing should also be mentioned – the successful libel action brought by Miss Shirley Jane Temple (then aged only nine) and Twentieth Century-Fox against Greene and *Night and Day* magazine for his remarks on the moppet's proto-sexual appeal in a review of *Wee Willie Winkie*. The settlement caused the magazine to grind to a halt after a six-month run.

During this time, the first film adaptation of his work by another writer (*Stamboul Train*, which he labelled an 'entertainment' to distinguish it from his more serious work) had come and, rather rapidly, gone and he too had slipped into screen-writing for no more relevant reason than that he needed the money. His books were not earning enough to support his family and any profits remained obstinately obscured by the constant debt to publishers on account of advances. It was not until *Brighton Rock* (1938) which sold 80,000 copies that he was able to clear the debt – 'and the war was a salvation too; I was able to get a job'.

A child of the film age and a writer, said Basil Wright, who always

> had a built-in filmic style; nor was it by chance that he became one of the acutest and best film critics of the 1930s. Indeed his experience as a critic may have helped him intensify his cinematic approach until it was fined down to the exquisite 'chinese box' flashback technique in a book like *The Quiet American* (1955) which, in a sense, becomes more elaborate than film, at its present stage, can cope with.[7]

Greene readily acknowledges the influence of the moving camera as opposed to the frozen image of the photographer's eye. He told me: 'When one describes something, it is in moving terms, as if one were going down the street in a taxi, looking from one side to the other. That's the way I've been influenced just as Victorian novelists like Scott were influenced by paintings or, later, Henry James by the theatre.' Evelyn Waugh, noting

Greene's camera eye in *The Heart of the Matter*, concluded, a little waspishly: 'Now it is the cinema which has taught a new habit of narrative. Perhaps it is the only contribution the cinema is destined to make to the arts.'[8]

Yet the apparent perfection of a writer–director collaboration – as manifested in *The Fallen Idol* (1948) and *The Third Man* (1949) – with Carol Reed – and even the confession some years after this that 'my own experience of screen-writing has been fortunate and happy'[9] was to lead to a clear disillusionment with the medium by the end of the 1950s. By then, he had also acted as co-producer on a film twice in *The Stranger's Hand* (1954) and *Loser Takes All* (1956) – 'the wrong actors, the wrong director, the wrong colour process, won't come together and produce a lucky accident' – and endured the revisionist version of *The Power and the Glory* by John Ford and the 'treachery' of Joseph Mankiewicz's adaptation of *The Quiet American*, with neither of which he was directly involved. In his memorable essay 'The Novelist and the Cinema' (1958) he is perhaps as much ventilating his fury at the very nature of film's bowdlerization as at his own sporadic role in that process:

> even if a script be followed word by word, there are those gaps of silence which can be filled by a banal embrace; irony can be turned into sentiment by some romantic boob of an actor. No, it is better to sell it outright and not connive any further than you have to at a massacre . . . a writer should not be employed by anyone but himself. If you are using words in one craft, it is impossible not to corrupt them in another medium under direction . . . This is the side of my association with films that I most regret and would most like to avoid in future if taxation allows me to.[10]

The disillusionment was either momentary or the demands of the taxman too pressing for he went on to write two more movies. And today, though he has not written a screenplay since *The Comedians* (1967), he is still sought out and responds with varying degrees of helpfulness in the continuing adaptations of his work.

Greene, who settled in the South of France in 1966, denies that he wishes to use literature for political or religious ends – 'even if my novels happen incidentally to be political books, they're no more written to provoke changes than my so-called "Catholic"

books are written to convert anyone'.[11] It is, though, 'the
theology that gives the tone that attracts people to buy the stuff to
film in the first place', asserts Guy Elmes, who has adapted two of
the films. 'Then,' he goes on,

> they actually have to script it and it becomes rather frightening
> and a concern whether mass audiences will be able to take this
> internal agony thing he's trying to externalize all the time. It's a
> constant battle between commercial considerations and trying
> to be honourable and decent to the writer's concept. Incidental-
> ly, I once asked Graham why he was perverted to the Catholic
> faith. He told me, 'Well, I looked at them all and the only one
> that measured up to my evil was the Catholic faith.'

Elmes tells another nice story of his collaboration with Greene,
on *The Stranger's Hand*.

> We'd be sitting together in the Piazza in Venice and we'd come
> to a halt in the writing. First I'd ask him to stop twitching his
> pencil as he flicked at flydirts on the edge of the paper (it made
> me terribly nervous) and then I'd say, 'You're a bit like a British
> documentary. When they are in any doubt, they cut to seagulls;
> in your case, you cut immediately to God. Can we please avoid
> cutting to God?'

Elmes's point about the inevitable conflict between com-
merce and original conception and attempting to reconcile the
two as honourably as possible is not only the eternal problem of
literary adaptation but may be, paradoxically, at the core of the
often less than successful efforts to translate Greene's filmic style
to film itself.

The writer-director Peter Duffell who has adapted and
directed one Greene film, *England Made Me*, and made his own
abortive attempt to film another, *The Honorary Consul*, claims
that the apparent ease of adaptation serves only to deceive:

> His novels are cinematic, but deceptively so. What he's in fact
> doing is producing objective correlatives for states of mind; if
> you don't get that over, you fail. In a sense, I think it is
> nonsense to get a writer of quality in his own right to adapt

another major writer like Greene. Rather, it takes a film-maker's mind to translate his work, to honour the spirit of what he's doing, not necessarily the letter.

Greene himself believes that adapting the novel must, inherently, result in a flawed production. Unlike a short story which can be enlarged, the process of cutting down a novel must detract from aspects of all-important characterization:

It may be just that the man takes mustard with his fish; now this seems unimportant to the scriptwriter, he decides to cut it out and suddenly you find the character has no character at all and, finally, you end up with a narrative without characters. A successful film depends on believing and being interested in characters. A story without characters cannot succeed.

Sir Richard Attenborough, who has appeared in three of the adaptations – most memorably as Pinkie in *Brighton Rock* – told me: 'You'd think that Graham had been an actor himself for so much of his dialogue is a joy to speak. At one time, I was going to make *England Made Me* and when we were putting the screenplay together, one felt one could lift whole bits straight from the page.'
Many critics have averred that while Greene's entertainments tend to make good films, his serious novels, from *The Power and the Glory* to *The Honorary Consul* continue to resist filmic treatment. Is it that deepest Greeneland, a word he hates and one whose attachment to this book's title is intended in its widest possible context, simply defies adjustment from verbal imagery to celluloid flesh?
'White men going to seed in outlandish places. Unshaven, guilt-ridden, on the bottle.' These are the fictional inhabitants of Greeneland as Greene reluctantly defines it; and it is fundamentally these characters that have fascinated, though more often than not flummoxed, film-makers since 1933.
In the final analysis however, it is the range and variety of Greene's filmography that, for me, fascinates perhaps even more than the mere perpetuation of the author's characters and ideas; it encompasses everything from wide-screen spectacles to film *noir*, from Hollywood studio star 'vehicles' to rural olde Englande. The cinema of Graham Greene is a microcosm of cinema itself.

PART ONE

The Thirties

1
Writer for Hire

Alexander Korda summoned Greene to see him at the Denham Film Studios in 1937. This was on the principle that he would rather be joined by the writer than continue to be attacked by him in the consistently withering reviews of Korda and his films which appeared in the *Spectator*. The 'usual Denham mouse' was a regular epithet.

June 5th, 1936 – England, of course has always been the home of the exiled; but one may at least express a wish that *émigrés* would set up trades in which their ignorance of our language and culture was less of a handicap: it would not grieve me to see Mr Alexander Korda seated before a cottage loom in an Eastern country, following an older and better tradition. The Quota Act has played into foreign hands, and as far as I know, there is nothing to prevent an English film unit being completely staffed by technicians of foreign blood. We have saved the English film industry from American competition to surrender it to far more alien control.
September 4th, 1936 – (*The Man Who Could Work Miracles*) The direction and the production are shocking . . . the slowness, vulgarity, over-emphasis are typical of Mr Korda's production . . . a publicity man of genius who has not yet revealed a talent for the films, [he] casts his pictures with little regard for anything but gossip paragraphs . . .
November 20th, 1936 – Reverence and a good cameraman are not enough . . . [*Rembrandt*] is ruined by lack of story and continuity: it has no drive.[1]

In a masterpiece of understatement, Greene hazards that Korda was perhaps 'curious' to meet his enemy.

When we were alone he asked if I had any film story in mind. I had none, so I began to improvise a thriller – early morning on Platform 1 at Paddington, the platform empty, except for one man who is waiting for the last train from Wales. From below his raincoat a trickle of blood forms a pool on the platform.
    'Yes? And then?'
    It would take too long to tell you the whole plot – and the idea needs a lot more working out. I left Denham half an hour later to work for eight weeks on what seemed an extravagant salary, and the worst and least successful of Korda's productions thus began.[2]

Four Dark Hours – 'and seldom have four hours seemed so long' said one critic – was how the project started out, with Greene's story and preliminary scenario worked up into a final screenplay by Ted Berkman and Arthur Wimperis and a new release title, *The Green Cockatoo*. The whole action takes place between one and five in the morning and it is worth a close look at the story for even in this sixty-five-minute Quota Quickie are echoes of many of Greene's recurring themes – for example, innocence threatened in an alien landscape. It could also almost have served as a 'trailer' for *Brighton Rock*, which would be published the following year.
    Eileen, a naïve, young West Country girl is visiting London for the first time. On the train a kindly, but eccentric, old man advises her to ring Whitehall 1212 (Scotland Yard) on arrival. Obediently, Eileen tries to telephone from a call box but is interrupted by Dave Connor, who politely but firmly grabs the telephone in an urgent and vain attempt to make a call of his own. He persuades the bewildered Eileen to let him show her a dingy hotel where she can get a room for the night. She is unaware that Dave is dying from stab wounds he received back at the station from racetrack gangsters whom he had double-crossed. It was to his brother Jim he'd been trying to phone an SOS. As he dies, he mutters 'find Jim Connor at the Green Cockatoo' to a horrified Eileen who has picked up a dagger which had fallen out of the wound in Dave's side. Discovered thus by the landlady who accuses her of murder, Eileen flees remembering just one thing – Dave's dying message.

Eventually she finds the Green Cockatoo, a shady Soho night-club where Jim turns out to be the resident song-and-dance man.

Jim chivalrously shields her when the police swoop on the club looking for the fugitive from the hotel. Terrell, leader of the gangsters, has also followed Eileen to the club fearing that she will put Jim on their track. Eileen's ordeal increases as Jim gets suspicious of her and Terrell starts putting on pressure. When the gang tries repeatedly to silence Jim, he fights back with a vengeance and eventually has Terrell and his associates arrested.

No longer suspicious of Eileen, Jim has, of course, fallen in love with the hapless rustic miss and determines to take her back west so he can marry her.

There seems to be a little confusion about who actually perpetrated the direction of the film. Though listed as 'A William K. Howard Production' with William Cameron Menzies credited as director, it is likely that, in practice, the two Korda faithfuls actually co-directed *The Green Cockatoo*. Menzies was better known as a production designer (he designed and co-directed Korda's *Things to Come* as well as later winning the second of his Oscars for his work on *Gone with the Wind*) while Howard had a string of directorial credits, including Korda's *Fire Over England*.

John Mills, who played Jim Connor, had it clear in his mind that it was Howard at the helm, if none too firmly.

[*Green Cockatoo*] was directed by a charming American, William K. Howard, who, although no one suspected it at the time, was happily hitting the bottle. I discovered this quite by accident. During the mid-morning break I noticed that the property man always brought a pot of tea and two cups to our director on the set. It was his habit during this fifteen minutes to discuss the previous day's work with his editor, whom he had brought with him from the States.

On one occasion the editor was absent. I had missed the tea-trolley and asked Bill Howard if I could have a cup of his tea. He hesitated for a second and then said, 'Sure, Johnnie, black or with milk?' 'Milk please,' I said, and took a large gulp. It was neat whisky.

Bill smiled at me as I choked. 'Heart-starter time,' he said. 'We don't have tea-breaks in the studios back home. Great idea.'

Bill Howard had made some excellent movies in America, but
by the time we caught up with him he was, I'm afraid, slightly
over the hill . . .[3]

When the film was eventually released in 1940 the critics were
pretty unanimous in their condemnation – a reaction underlined
by Greene who had also found the whole experience 'terrible'.
Today's Cinema wrote: 'Melodramatic possibilities of plot are
nullified by unconvincing behaviour on part of heroine and mass
of far-fetched detail involving inept police, bloodthirsty racecourse gang and cabaret-singer hero – existing entertainment
being familiar matter of vigorous surface action, varied with songs
from hero and Shakespearean quotations from naïve heroine . . .'

The *Kinematograph Weekly* found Mills 'not bad' as Jim, but
'René Ray is a colourless Eileen. Charles Oliver, Bruce Seton and
Julian Vedey trying to look like members of a racecourse gang
seldom meet with success.' Greene's connection with the production fortunately appears not to have been noticed.

If nothing else, the experience had sparked off between Greene
and Korda a friendship which endured until the latter's death in
1956. Greene wrote: 'There was never a man who bore less
malice, and I think of him with affection – even love– as the only
film producer I have ever known with whom I could spend days
and nights of conversation without so much as mentioning the
cinema.'[4]

Writing scripts for Korda and reviewing the mogul's work
unfavourably actually coincided with his adaptation of John
Galsworthy's short story 'The First and the Last'. Greene recalls
that he was still not earning enough with his books to make a
living for his family and therefore almost any assignment was
welcome at the time. Made in 1937, the film sat around on the
shelf for two years before being released. With that two-year
perspective Greene, as critic, unleashed his own brand of bile in
the 12 January 1940 *Spectator*. He rightly declared an interest:

perhaps I may be forgiven for noticing a picture in which I had
some hand, for I have no good word to say of it. Galsworthy's
story was peculiarly unsuited for film adaptation, as its whole

point lay in a double suicide (forbidden by the censor), a burned
confession, and an innocent man's conviction for murder
(forbidden by the great public). For the rather dubious merits of
the original, the adaptors have substituted incredible coinci-
dences and banal situations. Slow, wordy, unbearably sentimental, the picture reels awkwardly towards the only suicide
the censorship allowed – and that, I find with some astonish-
ment, has been cut out. I wish I could tell the extraordinary
story involving a theme-song, and a bottle of whisky, and
camels in Wales . . .[5]

That final observation is so tantalizingly cryptic that it bears some
investigation. The screen story revolves around Keith Durrant
(Leslie Banks) a brilliant lawyer who is poised to become a judge.
His younger brother Larry (Laurence Olivier) is a wastrel. One
evening, Larry takes Wanda (Vivien Leigh), a working girl with
whom he is in love, back to her flat.

There he is confronted by her vicious husband Walenn (Esme
Percy) who attempts to blackmail Larry and is then accidentally
killed by him. After dumping the corpse in a lonely spot, Larry is
accosted by a seedy, drunken ex-priest Evan (Hay Petrie). Larry
fobs him off with a cigarette but unwittingly drops his gloves
which Evan picks up. Larry makes a clean breast to his brother
Keith who, desperately anxious to avoid any kind of scandal in
view of his impending judgeship, begs Larry to leave the country.

Meanwhile Evan is arrested for the crime and Larry refuses to
let an innocent man suffer. To complicate things, Evan had
robbed the dead man and his sense of shame, heightened by a
deranged mind, drives him to plead guilty. He is remanded for
twenty-one days. Larry decides to enjoy himself with Wanda
during this period and then will give himself up. Poor Keith, still
thinking about his own career, once again implores Larry to get
out of England. At this point a convenient twist, represented by
Evan's sudden death from heart failure, leads to the inevitable
happy ending.

Such melodrama and, as Greene says, 'there was little of
Galsworthy's plot left when I had finished'. The film was directed
by Basil Dean who had produced Galsworthy's own stage
adaptation of the tale some fifteen years earlier at the Aldwych
Theatre with the legendary Meggie Albanesi, 'of unforgettable

memory', as Wanda. More recently Dean, who divided a prolific
career between screen and stage, acquired the film rights:

> with the intention of making the girl's lover the central figure so
> as to provide Clive Brook, already working with us at Ealing,
> with the star part. Graham Greene was at work upon the
> scenario. Unfortunately Clive took a dislike to the subject, so I
> was forced to abandon it. Matters remained at a standstill until
> Alex (Korda) rang me up one morning offering to take over the
> project. Mrs Galsworthy, my long-standing friendship with
> J.G. in mind, was adamant that I must retain general supervi-
> sion . . . and that is how I found myself working at Denham.

Korda agreed to Dean's casting of Olivier and Leslie Banks as
the judge but for the Albanesi role

> he brushed aside all other suggestions to announce that Vivien
> Leigh was to play the part. I had my doubts about this because
> of her obvious lack of experience, but Alex was adamant . . .
> By the second or third day's shooting I knew I was in for a
> difficult time for Vivien and Larry were in the first stages of
> their love affair. Their joyous awareness of each other took the
> form of much laughter and giggling on the set. It was
> impossible for them to take the film seriously. In the general
> hilarity, even the gentlest remonstrance was brushed aside. I
> was nicknamed 'Sugar' for what reasons I know not but the
> soubriquet pleased them mightily for they burst into laughter
> whenever they used it. What J.G. would have thought of this
> approach to his sombre story of love and conscience, it is
> difficult to imagine. Certainly I found it embarrassing.[6]

Greene agrees there were

> great production problems. Our producer was taken off the
> film because he had to get a lot of camels – or was it elephants? –
> to Wales because they were making *Elephant Boy*. Then there
> was this scene where the Lord Chief Justice is giving a dinner
> party and it was being done with a high crane shot above the
> table. Shooting started but then was almost immediately
> stopped by Basil who, after checking the table setting, declared:

'You haven't got coffee sugar, you've got lump sugar' (which seems to be the giveaway clue for Olivier–Leigh's 'Sugar' reference).

All shooting was halted until a car had been sent down to London to fetch the right form of sweetener. Greene goes on:

> I had a collaborator on the film and we were sitting up until about two o'clock one morning trying to finish the film which then had to go to Lajos Biro (one of Korda's creative entourage) to be judged. Dean wanted it as a full shooting script and we got a little bit drunk while putting on the crew directions. And I said. 'Let's put in a theme-song' – no, I can't remember the words – and so we wrote alternate lines and this was inserted in the Southend sequence. Lajos Biro accepted the script and Dean seemed satisfied but not a word had been said about the theme-song. Then we went down to Southend – it was out of season – to see where to do the shooting and suddenly, while we were walking around the empty funfair, Basil said to me: 'Graham, I don't quite understand that theme-song.' At that precise moment, the cameraman shouted: 'Hey Mr Dean, please come over here!' and he never mentioned it again. And the song didn't turn up in the film.

All of which accounts for the reference to 'camels in Wales' and 'theme-song' in Greene's withering critique. As for the 'bottle of whisky', that remains a mystery.

Despite its compromised content, *The First and the Last* was shot with some style. A typical London street-market was reconstructed on Denham's Stage 5 and Basil Dean arranged with real stallholders to bring their barrows to the studios to help authenticate the sequence. It was part of a set which covered the whole stage and which showed another Soho street with its public houses, delicatessens, wine shops and cafés.

Three cameramen worked on the set under the supervision of Jan Stallich. One of the cameras was situated forty feet above street level so it could shoot down through one of the windows to the busy street. The other cameras, at various points, picked up Laurence Olivier as he wended his way through the crowds followed by Vivien Leigh.

There was also filming on the Thames pleasure steamer, the *Royal Eagle*, and the locations in Southend including the Kursaal pier.

Meanwhile Korda was giving Basil Dean a tough time. The elaborate Old Bailey Number One Court was built and then swiftly dismantled after just a single shot when the director was planning for four days of filming. Korda had other plans for the space and dispatched his crew to shoot exteriors. When the Old Bailey set was rebuilt, the director ran into problems with actor Robert Newton as counsel for the defence. He had to make a long, impassioned speech to the jury:

> Alas! That fine actor was far gone in alcoholism . . . Poor Bob had been struggling for days to memorize the speech. On the set he would manage to electrify the whole courtroom with a sentence or two before his memory vanished. Then he had to be led into a quiet corner while a sympathetic secretary fed him relentlessly with the forgotten lines. Finally, we came to the end of the painful episode by filming the speech in short sketches and using the breaks to cross-cut reactions in the courtroom . . . Alex did not understand the essential 'Englishness' of Galsworthy's writing. He decided to insert an additional sequence directed by himself. He further insisted that the title should be changed to 'Twenty-one Days' which Mrs Galsworthy thought pointless. I was not asked to see a 'rough cut' of the resulting hotch-potch, nor did I even see the finished picture.[7]

Clearly the film's box-office potential was not considered very great as it lay unused for two years until Columbia bought it in 1939. For those two years, Korda had been able to claim the film as an asset and in the end it was Columbia who had to bear the brunt of the film's financial failure. It was eventually released in the wake of Vivien Leigh's worldwide success and acclaim in *Gone with the Wind*, presumably with the hope that some of MGM's blockbusting achievement might rub off on it. A forlorn hope, it transpired.

Reviews were mixed, from *Faulkners Film Review* of April 1939, 'An unusual drama, well off the beaten track. Those who like strong, holding dramatic fare will appreciate this film . . .' to the *Monthly Film Bulletin* from 31 May 1939 which declared, 'this telling Galsworthy story is not equally effective on the screen. This is partly because the tempo is very slow, and partly because the acting is extremely uneven . . . the supporting players are noticeably good, Hay Petrie as Evan being outstandingly effective.' And it was only Hay Petrie who escaped the main brunt of Greene's own criticism: 'The brilliant acting of Mr Hay Petrie as a decayed and outcast curate cannot conquer the overpowering flavour of cooked ham.'

Greene later made further public acknowledgement of his apprentice effort by saying it was 'suffered with good-humoured nonchalance by Laurence Olivier and Vivien Leigh, who had much to forgive me'. His review concluded with the humiliating *mea culpa*: 'Let one guilty man, at any rate, stand in the dock, swearing never, never to do it again.'[8]

To research *Stamboul Train*, his fourth book and his first 'entertainment', Greene simply could not afford to leave his cottage in the Cotswolds. 'I'd got a baby coming, only about £20 in the bank and I was receiving a total of just £600 a year from my English and American publishers. This was to be the last book on the contract. The previous two books had sold, at the most, about two thousand copies so I thought I really must get on with it.' For the first and last time in his life, Greene has recorded, he 'deliberately set out to write a book to please, one which with luck might be made into a film'.[9] Train movies were all the rage at the time – Paramount had made *Shanghai Express*, which was directed by von Sternberg, with Marlene Dietrich and Clive Brook; Britain's effort was *Rome Express*, a Michael Balcon production with Conrad Veidt and Gordon Harker, and even the Russians had followed the fashion with *Turksib*.

Greene had started writing *Stamboul Train* a year earlier, in 1931, and recalls both the Dietrich and the Veidt films being discussed and indeed even possibly appearing while he was still finishing his book. 'Anyway I remember thinking then that my last chance had gone because there was surely no way they were going to do a third – but they did.' 'They' was Twentieth Century-Fox (who six years later would successfully sue Greene for libel in the Shirley Temple case). Fox bought the rights for £2,000, a sale which enabled Greene to go on writing without seeking other employment until Paramount bought *A Gun for Sale* four years later.

Stamboul Train is a stimulating read, funny, exciting, sad and annoying in almost equal parts with a colourful set of characters interacting in claustrophobic settings – the ingredients of instant drama, if not melodrama. The dramatis personae are a young dancer Coral Musker, who is an early and less gutsy incarnation of *Gun for Sale's* Anne Crowder; Carleton Myatt, a merchant obsessed with his Jewishness in what appears to be a climate of rampant anti-Semitism; Mabel Warren, a blowsy lesbian journalist with a pretty friend, Janet; Dr Czinner, a Balkan communist leader in constant danger of arrest; Josef Grunlich, a murderous crook on the run; the censorious Peters couple; Quin Savory, a home-spun English novelist (J.B. Priestley read this portrait as a slur upon himself and so sued Greene with the result that about twenty pages of the book had to be reprinted); Mr Opie, a cricket-obsessed clergyman.

Curiously, it took four screen-writers, including the film's producer-director Paul Martin and pianist-comedian Oscar Levant (later so memorable in *An American in Paris* and *The Band Wagon*), to work on material which Gene Phillips is right to point out was so essentially cinematic in the first place: 'Greene wrote the book as if he was in effect moving a camera from compartment to compartment on the train, developing the story on the way.'

The result of all those hands was, said *Picturegoer*, 'an ambling and somewhat incoherent' narrative and a film, according to *Kinematograph Weekly*, 'astonishingly destitute of clear, dramatic purpose'. Greene himself caught up with the film – retitled *Orient Express* with stunning originality – a couple of years after its general release, while he was in Africa, writing *Journey without Maps*: 'It was a bad film, one of the worst I had ever seen; the direction was incompetent, the photography undistinguished, the story sentimental. If there was any truth in the original it had been carefully altered, if anything was left unaltered it was because . . . it was cheap and banal enough to fit the cheap and banal film.'[10]

Not surprisingly, the film had pared away the book's ultimately rather tiresome preoccupation with anti-Semitism, and the colourful depiction of lesbian jealousies and lusts, not to mention some of the jollier characters like Opie and Savory. The much-flawed Coral and Carleton of the book became simply, according to a florid blurb, 'two youthful hearts fleeing from life, crashing across Europe on the wheels of fate', impersonated by the pretty expatriate British actress, Heather Angel, and Norman Foster, who later switched from acting to directing movies like *Journey into Fear*, with rather more success.

Thirty years later the BBC produced its own version of *Stamboul Train*, which was summarily dismissed by Greene as even worse than Fox's feeble effort. The BBC's adaptation was more explicitly sexual – there was a seduction scene and another scene showing Mabel's proclivities – and caused a howl of protest from the public. So much so that the corporation actually admitted it was wrong to screen the play.

Replying to one protester programme controller Stuart Hood wrote, in best hair-shirt fashion: 'I also consider that *Stamboul Train* offended against taste and against the standard of writing I expect for TV plays. I am afraid it is not possible to offer any excuse for the programme but I am sure you will understand if I say the matter is being dealt with internally.' Apparently the advertising had led viewers, like Reverend Donald Plumley of St James, Tunbridge Wells, Kent, to expect something 'in the nature of an Agatha Christie mystery play'. The problems of delinquency and lower moral standards were, he said, 'large enough today without their being complicated by this effort which we imagine is either meant to shock us or to stimulate the present-day unhealthy obsession with sex'. And all Greene had originally wanted to do thirty years earlier was to make money!

PART TWO

The Forties

2
Propaganda War

Ealing Studios produced about twenty films between 1939 and 1945 dealing with aspects of the war, from Will Hay comedies, light-heartedly exposing traitors in high places, to semi-documentary-style tributes about the various fighting services (for example the Royal and Merchant Navies in *Convoy*, Fleet Air Arm in *Ships with Wings*, and the Army in *Nine Men*. Essentially, they were all propaganda films – stirring, stiff upper lip and ultimately flagwaving. Above all, comfortable.

Among this wartime Ealing folio there were, in particular, two distinctly uncomfortable, indeed positively threatening, films – Thorold Dickinson's *Next of Kin* and Cavalcanti's *Went the Day Well?* They were both cautionary tales; the first, in a cleverly constructed suspense-and-spy format, vividly explored the heavy cost to human, and above all British, life that could be caused by 'careless talk'; the second, even more chilling in its portent, centred on a question – what would happen if Germans were to invade British soil.

Collier's Magazine published a short story by Greene in June 1940 called 'The Lieutenant Died Last'. The old village poacher is away from his community pursuing his business when a small group of Germans parachute in, fooling the villagers into thinking they are British soldiers on manoeuvres, when in fact they are an advance-guard of a proposed Nazi invasion. They take over the village and round up the locals. The poacher, realizing by now what has happened and fortified by Dutch courage, stalks the Germans one by one and picks them off with his shotgun. Hazily

25

he thinks of them as Boers, since his last memories of battle were in the Boer War. The community is liberated and the poacher is a hero who, nevertheless, feels a pang of regret when he finds a family photograph clutched in the hand of the invaders' leader, who was shot last.

Brazil-born Alberto Cavalcanti, a friend of Greene's and a considerable figure in documentary film, made his full-length feature debut with Angus MacPhail, John Dighton and Diana Morgan's adaptation of Greene's story – MacPhail and Dighton, both Ealing 'in-house' writers, had also been responsible for *Next of Kin* two years after *Collier's* publication. Greene had by this time been posted to West Africa. Made swiftly and inexpensively, the film caused considerable controversy when it was released in October 1943.

The film opens with a poetic caption: 'Went the day well?/We died and never knew/But well or ill,/Freedom, we died for you.' This refers to the villagers who were killed fighting the Germans, whose names we are shown inscribed on a headstone in the church's graveyard. As a prologue, we are shown the after-events of the story and the elderly church sexton tells us of the mysterious names who 'wanted England, and this is the only part of English soil they got'. He then begins to narrate the events that led up to that epitaph.

Troops purporting to be a unit of the Royal Engineers turn up in truckloads and billet themselves in the village ostensibly as part of an exercise. The villagers' suspicions are gradually aroused when the soldiers start making slips like writing the number 'seven' with a continental crossbar and misspelling words like 'chocolate'. All attempts at getting messages out are frustrated; when the vicar tries to summon help by bells he is shot dead, even the village squire turns out to be a quisling; local Home Guarders, outside the village on their own exercise, are ruthlessly cut down in an ambush.

Greene's poacher now comes on the scene and, with the help of one of the village lads, manages finally to get a message out. Up at the big house the squire, seemingly with his cover not yet blown, aims for one final betrayal only to be shot by the vicar's plucky daughter: 'the whole scene, with the house functioning diagrammatically as a map of "England" under attack, is one of the most intense in all British war films'[1] remarks Ealing Studios' historian,

Charles Barr. One also has to agree with him that the casting, particularly of the two leaders (Basil Sydney as the occupying officer, Leslie Banks as the squire) is 'artful'. It was like, he says, 'an exorcizing of the kind of thirties leadership they represent (its reactionary quality underlined by the fact that Banks's most celebrated role of that decade was as *Sanders of the River*)'.

Greene has never seen the film – 'I was in Africa when it came out. My sister saw it on television recently and didn't like it at all' – and, unfortunately, seems to feel (obviously from what he has been told about the adaptation) that the original idea contained in his story is a better one than the film's: 'the whole story is practically done through the eyes of the old poacher as he stalks them with his shotgun'. Greene also, not surprisingly, prefers his original title.

'Why,' says Basil Wright, 'this film aroused such passionate feelings, pro and con, is difficult to say. Perhaps the divisions of opinion were caused by the reactions of different people, at that particular crisis, to the very idea of showing invasion actually in progress . . . it would be interesting to revive it today.'[2]

Considering that it combined the functions of a timely propaganda exercise with starring 'vehicle' for an attractive contract actress, the Hollywood treatment of *A Gun for Sale* is remarkable for retaining so much flavour of the original, even with the changes necessarily wrought by virtue of its significant switch of milieu.

Paramount bought the book when it was first published in the States under the title *This Gun for Hire* in 1936 but did not actually film it until five years later, by which time the world was at war and Pearl Harbor was almost at hand. The film was rushed into production mainly to capitalize on the burgeoning reputation of petite blonde Veronica Lake, whose two preceding roles in *I Wanted Wings* and *Sullivan's Travels* had transformed her from a $75-dollar-a-week contract player into a $350-dollar-a-week studio star.

Fourth on the credits (after Lake, Robert Preston and Laird Cregar) was the twenty-nine-year-old Alan Ladd. Up until 1941 Ladd had passed virtually unnoticed in a whole host of bit roles, for example a reporter in *Citizen Kane*. But that year he progressed to seventh billing on a stirring wartime tale, *Joan of*

Paris, and was about to marry Sue Carol, a former actress turned agent with undisguised ambitions for her new husband-to-be. Ladd was to play Raven, the bitter, unsmiling, hare-lipped killer – seminal in the book but, in film terms, a mere satellite to the top-credited couple, the cop and his girl, played by Preston and Lake – until the end of just the first day's shooting, that is, when the director Frank Tuttle, after viewing the rushes, realized he had something really rather special with Ladd's characterization.

From that moment on the whole emphasis of the film was shifted on to Ladd's Raven, with more close-ups than the script demanded and extra touches added to heighten his effect. This shift also helped to bring the film partly back in line with Greene's original, and even its working title on the Paramount lot had the sort of spiritual ring of which Greene might have approved – *The Redemption of Raven*.

Elements of *A Gun for Sale* could almost serve as a prequel to *Brighton Rock*, published two years later. Raven, Greene recalls now, was a prototype for the later Pinkie – 'a Pinkie who has aged but not grown up. The Pinkies are the real Peter Pans – doomed to be juvenile for a lifetime.' One of Raven's victims is the racecourse gangleader, Kite, who was succeeded by Pinkie. The flavour of the novel was aimed deliberately as a kind of antidote to Buchan-style melodrama. This hunted man was to be no Hannay, instead 'a man out to revenge himself for all the dirty tricks of life, not to save his country'. It was no longer, Greene rightly points out, a Buchan world: 'patriotism had lost its appeal, even for a schoolboy, at Passchendaele . . . the hunger marchers seemed more real than the politicians.'[3]

Although written in the mid-thirties, the book has the aura of imminent war. Raven is hired to shoot a minister whose violent death Raven's employers hope will help plunge the country into the conflict, earning them a fortune on the way. Raven works for a giant steel combine. Raven is paid in stolen notes and the police are tipped off, which means that the normally anonymous killer has to go on the run. As far as Raven is concerned, this is the last straw in a life full of ugliness, loneliness and bitterness – his father was hanged, his mother killed herself and he grew up in a home with his hare lip a daily reminder of his alienation. The hunted turns hunter as he aims to wipe out the employers who had double-crossed him. With some help from a spunky showgirl,

Anne Crowder, whose boyfriend Mather just happens to be leading the police hunt for Raven, he kills the Midland Steel chief and henchmen in a final act of what is a violent expiation for his own stormy life. He, in turn, is cut down by the police.

It is a tale that really would translate very easily to an American setting – unscrupulous big business, an assassin that could have been plucked from Capone's Chicago streets, gun-happy cops and a feisty female.

The book's re-evaluation in American film terms was in the hands of screen-writers W.R. Burnett and Albert Maltz. Burnett had evoked some of the very best tough-guy portrayals to date with his scripts for *Little Caesar, Scarface* and *High Sierra*. Maltz, here at the beginning of his Hollywood career, would go on to write top film *noir* like *Cloak and Dagger* and *The Naked City*, before falling from grace as one of the black-listed Hollywood Ten in the fifties. Their Raven was to have no hare lip, a cause of great concern to some critics who felt, like Gene Phillips, that depriving Raven of a hare lip would be robbing him of the outward signs of 'the spiritual deformity of his personality' which in turn led one to 'understand the morbid loneliness that has driven him to become an embittered assassin'.[4] In other words, the hare lip was motivation and without it we are unable to understand Raven, let alone pity him.

This, I feel, is merely lip-picking and instead I go along with Carlos Clarens when he writes:

> In the original, Raven was a hare-lipped virgin of a man, loquacious and bigoted, haunted by one specific murder in his career, that of the minister's secretary who fought for her elderly life with a passion that left its mark on the hardened killer. The picture substituted a monosyllabic gunsel in a raincoat – the first emblematic use of that garment – and removed the hare lip. In the film Raven is obsessed by a recurring dream in which he re-enacts the stabbing of an aunt who beat him as a child and once branded him with a red-hot iron. Metaphysical anguish had been displaced by a psychic disturbance. The effect was roughly the same: Raven's as sexless as the angel of death.[5]

Burnett and Maltz provided motivation enough; we can

understand Raven, though I doubt, just as with the book, whether one can pity him.

Tuttle's eleventh-hour reassessment of Ladd's potential is apparent from the very first frame in which the character gets the star build-up.

> Shooting in near darkness, the camera catches a fleeting glimpse of Raven's mutilated hand taking in milk for a pet cat. Then it pans and lingers on an unshaven face, catching the cold fanaticism behind the eyes. For what seems an interminable time, still under low-key lighting, Raven prepares for his assignment and slowly the viewer becomes aware that it is an assignment to kill.[6]

When he is out of the room for a moment, a sluttish cleaner comes by to tidy up, misguidedly shooing away the cat too. Re-enter Raven who rips her dress, smacks her in the mouth and tells her to 'beat it'. The characterization is almost complete – cold, violent, unsmiling, monosyllabic and, by the end of the next sequence, double deadly as Raven dispatches his 'mark', a scientist with a valuable formula, and a secretary who had the misfortune to be present. 'They said he would be alone' Raven mutters by way of apology, as he blasts her through a closed door.

By 1942 war was a fact and not just an imaginary impending scenario so it was not surprising that the screen-writers had to tinker with certain elements to make them more relevant. This meant, for instance, that Midland Steel and its naked opportunism was to become Nitro Chemical Corporation, a hotbed of fifth columnists, supplying poison gas to the Japanese enemy (Pearl Harbor took place during production and so the element of propaganda was stressed as shooting progressed). Lines like Lake's to Ladd: 'This war is everybody's business – yours too' may seem a little shy-making today but must have had the audiences stamping their feet at the time.

In the book, Anne Crowder is some sort of undefined performer on her way to bolster an Aladdin pantomime in Nottwich (Nottingham, a city where Greene had spent three months as a newspaper trainee). We are first introduced to Miss Lake in San Francisco as she auditions for a night-club spot in Los Angeles. She plays no panto hack but clearly a fabulously talented singer–dancer–conjurer called Ellen Graham, whose boyfriend is a top cop. Miss Lake recalls:

> I was all thumbs. Paramount brought in a professional magician, Jan Grippo, to teach me some basics. I didn't learn a thing . . . to compound things, I had to sing and dance besides making eggs disappear. And my singing and dancing ability was as non-existent as my magic ability. Filming dragged on at an agonizing pace especially on those days when my act was in front of the camera . . . if I didn't foul up, it was a crew member. And if we all came through on a take, it was Josephine . . . a mean snippy ape who possessed temperament like no actress on earth. And I was stuck with her as part of my magic act. She'd either whip me with her clipped tail as we did the scene or bite me . . . We did take 52. And 53. And up through 60 and finally, after take 64, called it a day . . . I watched the developed footage the next day. 'All those early takes don't look so bad to me,' I muttered to Frank Tuttle. 'I know,' he agreed, 'I'm using the fourth take . . . it looks great. Don't you agree?'[7]

Miss Lake was never to like Mr Tuttle.

As Ladd's role grew so Miss Lake began to suspect that, though she was nominally the star, the director was anxious not to spend too much time on her solo scenes and those without her and Ladd. If she became merely decorative the other 'star', Robert Preston, became almost non-existent, although he gave Miss Lake her first screen kiss. It was Ladd's show, although he was inevitably given a good run for his money by the splendid Laird Cregar. Cregar plays Johnson *aka* Gates (the book's Cholmondely *aka* Davis) the stout, sweetmeat-loving go-between for the corporation and Raven, first hiring the assassin then betraying him by making the payment in stolen bills.

With a studied faithfulness to the original, Cregar is also a theatrical 'angel' and 'can't stand violence'. In the film's parlance, he backs 'leg-shows' including the show Ellen Graham is auditioning for when we first see her. 'Thank you for digging her up' he tells the agent. 'For ten per cent, I'd dig up my wife's mother' the agent replies laconically. The Americanization now takes its only really false turn when Ellen, successful in her audition and clearly in with the crooked Cregar, is persuaded by the FBI to be a mole in order to help them uncover fifth-column activity.

That and a couple of rather inferior Frank Loesser songs are the only real diversions as film follows book to the 'big finish' at the corporation headquarters. The novel's chief villain, Sir Marcus, has become the wizened Brewster, 'a decrepit double for Henry Ford', as Raven gets into the factory under the cover of an air-raid drill. Brewster escapes the assassin's bullet by taking poison and Cregar is shot dead by Raven before the hired gun, redeemed in the eyes of the film-makers and audience as having effected the ends of enemies of the state, also breathes his last:

> after disposing of the traitors who were involved in selling poison to the enemy, the cold-blooded killer with the newly-acquired patriotic streak, lies full of bullets in solitary splendour on an office couch as Lake stands clutching Preston with romantic fervour. With his last breath, Raven asks for reassurance that she didn't turn him in to the cops. Then, after receiving it, he expires with a heretofore unrevealed, heart-breakingly contrite little-boy smile.[8]

As Ladd's biographer, Beverly Linet, also points out this was 'the imaginative touch that turned a B-film into something more memorable'.

Not that Miss Lake was unduly impressed: 'As I look back on the film, I view it with mixed emotions. It certainly helped perpetuate Veronica Lake as Everyman's mistress which, in turn, assured me further work in subsequent films. But I gave up something in return. I had obliterated any inroads I'd made as an actress in *Sullivan's Travels*. I was right back in the low-cut gowns and wearing the sexy hair.'[9] Greene, perhaps predictably, did not like the film much either (apart from the £2500 Paramount paid for rights): 'I thought it began well and I liked some of the opening shots but then after that it was completely altered. I've always wondered what happened to the cat.'

Two contemporary critics do, however, underline my original contention about the film's fidelity of thought if not of deed.

William Whitebait wrote in the *New Statesman*: 'The routine, and squalor, the bursts of action, the hauteur, the inner necessity of such a life are impressed by a photography that matches the

prose of Greene's novel.' Unfortunately he also goes on to credit
Robert Preston with the characterization of Raven. And Philip
Hartung remarks in *Commonweal*, with no little prescience: 'The
wonderment is that Hollywood hasn't used all of Graham
Greene's stories and clamoured for more. Not that *This Gun for
Hire* is unadulterated Greene. But with all the changes in the story,
the Greene original still survives.'[10]

The choice of Fritz Lang to direct *The Ministry of Fear* was
singularly appropriate: the director might have been handpicked
by Greene himself, had the author been remotely connected with
the project save at source. Not normally given to outbursts of
superlatives, Greene had, in 1936, written of Lang's first American
film, *Fury*, thus: 'Astonishing . . . the only film I know to which I
have wanted to attach the epithet of "great" . . . no other director
has got so completely the measure of his medium and is so
consistently awake to the counterpoint of sound and image.'[11]

Greene was clearly delighted when he learned that Lang had
been signed to turn his own favourite among his 'entertainments'
into a film the same year the book was published, 1943. In fact it
was an extra bonus over and above the very welcome £10,000 he
had received from Paramount for the film rights – 'at the time I
was thankful to sell anything and overjoyed to get the money'. He
had started the book on a cargo ship in 1941 *en route* for his West
Africa posting, finishing it off in the evenings. Carefully typing it
out himself, he was also fearful of sending the manuscript home
by convoy because of the parlous position of British shipping at
the time.

The inspiration for his writing was a piece of Michael Innes
detective fiction he had read and enjoyed on the voyage out. It
was, he felt, a cut above the usual run of a genre he normally
found unrealistic and generally tiresome. 'I developed the ambition to write a funny and fantastic thriller myself. If Innes could do
it, why not I?' The plot he chose appealed to him as grimly comic,
set against a backcloth of blitz-torn London but written in a
climate of growing global conflict: 'a man acquitted of the murder
of his wife by a jury (though he knows his own guilt) who finds
himself pursued for a murder of which he is entirely innocent but
which he believes he has committed'.[12] The title? 'I found "a

Ministry of Fear" in a William Wordsworth poem, one of a
selection of his poetry I had taken out to Africa never having read
much Wordsworth before.' It was a title that, superficially,
reflected perfectly the darkness of the wartime tale.

Arthur Rowe, haunted by guilt at poisoning his sick wife and
having served a short sentence for her mercy-killing – 'Mercy to
her, or mercy to me? They didn't say. Now I don't know' – finds
himself at a charity fête organized by the mysteriously named
Mothers of the Free Nations. He wins a cake in the weight-
guessing competition having been fed the winning information by
Mrs Bellairs, the fortune-teller. The person who was meant to
have won the cake turned up late, and it had gone to Rowe only
because he unwittingly gave Mrs Bellairs the necessary verbal
code. He declines to hand it over and leaves.

Rowe takes the cake back to his digs in war-torn London and
later shares it with a crippled stranger who has moved into the
house. The newcomer not only quizzes Rowe cryptically but is
observed crumbling the cake rather than eating it. He also tries to
ply Rowe with odd-tasting tea. A bomb blast interrupts the
confrontation: Rowe survives intact, the stranger is spirited away
to hospital. A now-worried Rowe decides to employ the services
of a private detective agency to investigate what is going on.
Inquiries lead him first to the offices of the Mothers of the Free
Nations where Austrian brother-and-sister team, Willi and Anna
Hilfe, seem anxious to help. Willi takes Rowe to Mrs Bellairs's
house where they, with a bizarre group of individuals including
Dr Forrester, an elderly psychiatrist, and Mr Cost (whom Rowe
recognizes as the fête latecomer) get embroiled in a seance.

During the seance Rowe is rattled when he is singled out by a
voice – his wife's? – that seems to come from beyond the grave.
When the lights come up and Cost lies dead, apparently murdered
with Rowe's own pocket-knife, Willi helps him make his escape.
On the run, and fearful of being pulled in by the police because of
his 'record', Rowe is fortuitously accosted by an elderly book-
seller, Fullove, lugging a large suitcase ostensibly packed with
books. Fullove enlists the aid of Rowe to take the suitcase to a Mr
Travers's flat. At the block he is told that he is expected and would
he go up and wait for Travers inside the flat. To Rowe's surprise,
he finds Anna waiting for him. Via her veiled references, she
makes it clear that she is part of some sinister plot and that Rowe is

in deep danger. When they decide to open the mysterious suitcase, it explodes.

Rowe is now a man without memory, bearded, known as Digby and ensconced in a mental clinic run by Dr Forrester. Bit by bit, fragments of his memory return. When he tries to leave the home, which is peopled with an odd assortment of lunatics and helpers, he is warned against it by the doctor who tells him that he is a murderer. When he does manage to get away Rowe goes straight to the police to give himself up and learn more of his past. His piecemeal information is just what the police, and then the Special Branch, need to nail a spy network which has been operating with the Mothers etc. as its front. Forrester, with key connections in home security, is clearly part of the ring.

First Rowe and the authorities confront Cost – alive and well and, in reality, a tailor – at his emporium, but he kills himself after first managing to telephone out warning that the spy ring is blown. The scene moves to the clinic where a massacre seems to have taken place with all the inmates dead, including Forrester and the cripple with whom Rowe had shared his cake much earlier. When Rowe telephones the number he had seen Cost dial, it is answered, to his chagrin, by Anna. Tracing the address via the number, he finally confronts Anna and Willi. It seems that Anna has been a passive participant with Willi as the callous ringleader, prepared even to sacrifice his sister to the cause. When Willi tries to shoot Rowe, Anna knocks the gun from his hand and locks her brother in the bedroom. She also hands over part of some crucial top-secret film which had been first secreted in the cake. But it is still only part of the film and Willi, who with his sister's ingenious connivance has escaped out of a window, still has the rest of it. Rowe tracks him down to a train at Paddington Station and leads him away to the lavatories where Willi is persuaded to hand over the remaining film in exchange for his gun. Willi kills himself leaving Rowe and Anna to declare their love for each other.

These bland bare bones do not begin to give an idea of the book's many layers: its undercurrents of treachery, violence, pity and guilt all leavened with a good sprinkling of black comedy. There is a delightfully macabre passage, for instance, when Rowe, on the run and desperately short of money, goes to the home of an old friend to try and borrow cash only to find that the friend is rather more preoccupied with making arrangements to bury his recently deceased hockey-playing wife. The long sequence in the nursing home/asylum is beautifully described as Rowe/Digby tries to fit together the pieces of his past life in a distinctly hostile and sinister environment.

Greene's delight at the swift and profitable sale of a new work should perhaps, in view of his later disappointments, have been tempered by the fact that Paramount had bought the rights on the strength of the title alone. That was ominous enough. And even though Greene happily learned that Lang had become involved, he might have recalled some of his own words on the director just two years after his 1936 eulogy. Writing about *You and Me*, he said: 'Given proper control over story and scenario, Lang couldn't have made so bad a film: the whole film is like an elegant and expensive gesture of despair . . . Everyone has heard of the Hollywood "doghouse" – the practice of ruining a star by providing bad parts. No star has been treated worse than Lang is here by his scenario writers.'[13] The truth of these sentiments would echo in the wake of Lang's accepting *Ministry of Fear* and the director himself would be the first to acknowledge its accuracy in regard to the circumstances of the new project. Lang said:

> Although I didn't know Graham Greene personally, he was one of my favourite writers and I wanted very much to make a film from *The Ministry of Fear*. Accordingly I instructed my agent to buy it for me but he declared it was impossible because Paramount, who were also interested in the book, were outbidding us. Then I went to New York and one day received a cable from my agent containing an offer to make the film for Paramount. I jumped at it but made a big mistake by not specifying in my contract that I wanted to be able to work on the script; I took it for granted, after all the years I'd been accustomed to working on scripts, that my agent would have seen to it that the contract contained some such clause.
>
> When I came back to Los Angeles I found someone in charge of the film who'd never made a picture before and who'd been a trombone player in a band, or something. On top of that I was handed a script which had practically none of the quality of the Graham Greene book. When I wanted to have some changes made in it, the writer resented it deeply. Then, when I wanted to step out of the project, my agent told me that I was

contractually obliged to complete it. So I finished the picture.[14]

I think it is necessary immediately to correct one impression given in this recollection: that Seton Miller the screen-writer and producer was somehow a callow Hollywood newcomer. In fact he was a highly experienced and prolific writer (and also a former silent actor) with a string of impressive credits including *Dawn Patrol*, *The Criminal Code*, *Scarface*, *The Adventures of Robin Hood* and *Here Comes Mr Jordan* (for which he won an Academy Award). Lang was, however, right in one respect: the film did mark Miller's first stint as a producer.

It is easy to see what must have attracted Lang to the original material: a guilt-ridden man released from mental hospital, plunged straight into circumstances beyond his control which lead him to question his own sanity before losing his identity altogether. The novel also has a dreamlike quality which would seem to have been well suited to Lang's use of hallucinations. In addition to all that was its timely undercurrent of Nazi villainy. Lang, with Jewish ancestry, had fled Germany in 1933 after being offered the job as official film director for the Nazis.

This last element, and its superficial evocation in the book's title, is as clear an indication as any to the altogether more superficial route the film would take, bearing in mind the film's own propagandist timing and its initial purchase of rights on title alone. That the movie actually turned out to be something more than just a routine potboiler owes more to Lang's supreme style than any real subtleties in Miller's screenplay.

Arthur Rowe, a dour and uninspiring name, has become Stephen Neale for the film and we meet him first in a darkened room dominated by a wall-clock. Neale is transfixed by the process of passing time. As the clock strikes six, Neale prepares to leave the room. A man who has come into the room says to him:

Man: Not wasting any time, eh?
Neale: Not if I can help it.
Man: Where do you plan to go?
Neale: To London.
Man: It's being heavily bombed these nights. Don't you think some quiet town at first, and get some employment there for a while?

Neale: I want to spend the first months being pushed and
jammed by the biggest crowds I can find. I want to hear people
talk and laugh. After that clock, seeing faces would be a good
tonic.
Man: Well, I don't blame you. I'll walk you to the gate.

This is, to be sure, a rather impressive attempt to establish
place, mood, character and past history without too much
exposition in the shortest possible amount of screen time. Neale's
unspecified incarceration is confirmed as he is led out through a
gate and the camera tracks past a wall-sign which proclaims
'Lembridge Asylum'. Neale is no sooner free than he is drawn into
the nearby fête, for some reason in full swing at what seems like
the dead of night instead of the 'late summer Sunday afternoon' of
the novel. There is passing reference to imminent blackout which
would not be a moment too soon; for with the fête's presently
blazing lights it would surely be the perfect target for a veritable
barrage of German bombs.

Neale leaves the fête with his cake and boards the train for
London. The whole 'digs' encounter with the dark and dwarfish
cripple is replaced by a confrontation on the train between Neale
and an elderly blind man (who we quickly learn is not blind). Like
the grotesque of the book, he crumbles the cake vainly searching
for something and then hits Neale over the head with his stick
when the younger man becomes suspicious. The 'blind' man leaps
out of the train and sets off across country only to be unlucky
enough to receive a direct hit during the ensuing air-raid.

Hiring the services of Rennit and the Orthotex Detective
Agency – but not telling him about his conviction as a
mercy-killer as he does in the book – Neale meets Willi and Carla
(not Anna) Hilfe. The Mrs Bellane (not Bellairs) Willi and Neale
find at the house is extremely glamorous and not at all like the
frumpy fortune-teller of the same name at the fête. At the climax
of the seance, Cost is 'shot' and not stabbed. Neale meets Carla – a
wholly innocent figure in the film as opposed to the knowing, if
passive participant of the book: 'Do you realize,' she blithely tells
the wicked Willi, 'that we have been patriotically slaving for three
years to protect a spy ring?' – in the underground and tells her of
his past. This is a past with a marked difference from that in the
book. The film seeks to make the 'hero' more acceptable by

having him detail a story whereby he bought drugs to help alleviate his wife's pain. She found them on her own and self-administered them, but he nevertheless served a term in hospital/asylum for her mercy-killing. The key element of guilt is therefore removed in the psyche of the central character.

Following the suitcase explosion in Travers's empty flat, the film makes its most serious departure from Greene's original. It completely omits Forrester's clinic and Neale's amnesia, instead having him returning to consciousness in the custody of the police. Greene believes that without that section the whole point of the novel was missing and effectively negated the movie:

> I met Lang just once while I was on a trip to Los Angeles and he excused himself for the film. He said he was short of money and so took a ready-made script – which seemed a terrible come-down for a man of his eminence. The scene in the asylum is the whole centre of the book and so without that the film lost a complete dimension.

There was also, in that section, some explanation of the book's title. Explaining the Germans had a method of putting pressure on key members of the community, Johns, a kindly clinic warder, explains to Rowe/Digby: 'They formed, you know, a kind of Ministry of Fear – with the most efficient under-secretaries. It isn't only that they get a hold on certain people. It's the general atmosphere they spread, so that you feel you can't depend on a soul.'[15] At the end of the book, Rowe comes back to the phrase, imbuing it with an altogether broader, and rather more depressing significance: 'A phrase of Johns's came back to mind about a Ministry of Fear. He felt now that he had joined its permanent staff. But it wasn't the small ministry to which Johns had referred, with limited aims like winning a war or changing a constitution. It was a ministry as large as life to which all who loved belonged. If one loved one feared.'[16] The title remains unexplained in the film.

The search for remains of the cake and its fascinating innards are purely the film's invention. On a painfully studio-bound heath, police officers guided by Neale dig into the bomb-crater, finding bits of the blasted blind man but no cake. As they prepare to leave, now more suspicious than ever of Neale – who while Cost's 'murder' mysteriously remains unreported, is suspected of being linked with foul play in connection with the missing detective Rennit – we hear the twittering of birds in a tree-stump and Neale climbs up to find them feeding on the last crumbs of the cake which also contain top-security microfilm.

After Travers/Cost kills himself, having first managed to telephone out his may-day message, we cut directly to the final encounter with the Hilfes. There is no discovery of a massacre at the mental clinic. Instead Forrester and his fellow conspirators converge on Neale and Carla after Willi has unsuccessfully called her sororial bluff and been shot in the back for his folly. The Special Branch arrive in the nick of time. In a final sequence of quite stunning awfulness, Neale and Carla are driving in an open car before a seafront back-projection. Discussing their impending marriage, Carla squeals: 'We'll have flowers and a big cake . . .' 'Cake?' exclaims a mock-horrified Neale.

It is an ending unworthy even of a stylish potboiler, for apart from its dreadful glibness it also comes with just too much speed and contrivance on top of the shootout with the spies – until one realizes that a rather key sequence has been omitted between front office and paying public. A glimpse in Paramount's publicity synopsis of the time tells that after the Special Branch arrive to deal with the rooftop spies: 'Neale and Carla accompany Prentice (the inspector) to Dr Forrester's office in a private sanitarium where Scotland Yard men have brought in the remaining members of the Nazi band. From a cell where he has been kept prisoner by Dr Forrester is led the trussed-up and gagged Rennit spluttering imprecations on his late captors.'

It had been Rennit's disappearance following discovery of a blood-stained hat and a ransacked office which led to a murder hunt for Neale. In the final print, Rennit's real fate is consigned to the bin and a rather important plot point left unresolved. This cut also accounts for the missing three minutes in running time between the eighty-seven minutes of the synopsis and the eighty-four minutes in the theatres.

Despite its many lapses, not to mention its abysmal end – 'the happy ending is so often a rotten fruit in Lang's work' – film historian David Thomson is an unashamed champion of the film:

> I cannot accept that the screenplay is bad, or the film
> forgettable. Miller eliminated depth, emotional texture and

Rowe's agony from the original and produced a fluent machine for filming in which eventfulness replaces reflection as the mainstream. It lacks subtlety of character and motive, but that places it with Lang's best work.

It is a model screenplay, loaded with incidents that his unrivalled eye will realize on screen. For Lang's quality is a narrow but intense visualization of action conveying fear, claustrophobia and malign fate.

Thomson seems to question the motives attributed to Lang for his initial interest in the material: 'What distinguishes the book is espionage infiltrating an emotional relationship – "they would never know what it was not to be afraid of being found out" – and that is not hinted at in Lang's film. To him, fear is a reaction to bombs, conspiracy and fate; but for Greene, the gravest fear is triggered by one's own feelings and soul.'[17]

While I cannot go along with much of Thomson's thesis – he imbues every camera angle and plot nuance with too much significance for my liking – I am inclined to concur with the judgement that 'the most frightening thing in the film is that unmitigated conception and authority. The film is itself like a product of the ministry it ostensibly hates.'[18] And that may be the most dangerous departure of all from the book and its inherent theme.

3
Men Within

There is a curious anonymity about Greene's structure for his
thriller *The Confidential Agent*. Aside from three of the main
characters bearing mere single-letter handles – D, L and K – there
is a starkness and consistent ambiguity relating to thought and
deed that seems to belong only to the written page. Once
visualized, it surely must become too specific, too melodramatic,
too dissipated. Herman Shumlin's 1945 film, adapted from
Greene's 'entertainment' by the producer Robert Buckner, clearly
suffers from all three defects yet still manages to retain a lot of
dignity and no little degree of sophistication for a Warner Brothers
wartime picture. So much so that Greene himself singles it out as
the one good exception in American-made adaptations of his
work. The rest, he avers, have been 'deplorable'.

Powered by two benzedrine tablets a day – the first and last time
he says he resorted to nerve stimulants – Greene ground out *The
Confidential Agent* in just six weeks during 1938 as opposed to his
normal nine months; two thousand words a day instead of the
regulation five hundred and 'each day I sat down to work with no
idea of what turn the plot might take . . .'[1] *Agent* was just
mornings' activity. The afternoons were reserved for the
altogether slower business of writing *The Power and the Glory*,
which, as far as Greene was concerned at the time, was not likely
to make him and his family any money – therefore the urgent need
to hammer out a swift, saleable 'entertainment'. While Greene
admits it was the Spanish Civil War which provided the
background for the book, there are no such specifics spelt out in

the writing. There is mention of a civil war; D, the central
character – the agent – is pressed into service by the government
(presumably the Loyalists) to come to Britain to make a deal for
coal and thwart the enemies (presumably the Fascists). Greene
calls his rival agents D and L simply because he did not wish to
localize the conflict.

There are no such ambiguities in Buckner's adaptation for the
screen. It is set in October 1937. D becomes Denard, a Republican
agent on a coal-seeking mission for his people though perhaps,
more specifically, aiming to prevent the contract being struck
with L (now Licata) the representative of the Fascists, who will use
the fuel to boost their munitions factories.

The film is generally very faithful to the spirit and story-thread
of the book. Before Denard is thrust into the usual alien
Greenelandscape where he will be beaten up and constantly shot at
before turning from being the hunted to the hunter, he meets Rose
Cullen, who just happens to be the daughter of Lord Benditch, the
coal magnate with whom Denard must deal. Their relationship is
the backcloth of the tale, a difficult relationship emotionally
because he still carries a residue of guilt for the death of his wife
who was shot in the war at home.

The dreary London hotel, with its pathetic fourteen-year-old
in-house slave Else, remains intact. Else's tormentor, known as
'the manageress', 'Marie' and 'Mrs Mendrill' in the book is
substantially fleshed out for the film as Mrs Melandez who in turn
is a cohort of K, now Contreras, a Republican agent-turned-
traitor. Else and Denard become friends and when she is murdered
by Mrs M. protecting his identity papers, the agent vows revenge.
Another of the hotel's residents, Mr Muckerji, a professional
observer, confronts the manageress with her deed and she takes
poison (in the film only) before Denard can get to her. Contreras,
who was not actually in on Else's killing – made to look like
suicide – is cornered by Denard and dies of a heart attack at
gunpoint.

Benditch refuses to deal with Denard as the agent has lost his
papers of authority (which were stolen by the magnate's butler)
and so Denard travels north to put the matter directly to
Benditch's miners. If the contract goes ahead with Licata, the coal
will be shipped to Spain to kill people like themselves, he explains.
The resulting publicity works the trick – 'you couldn't have

advertised the affair better if you'd brought the front page of the *Mail*', Denard is told. 'Already there's been a leading article – about political gangsters and the civil war being fought out on British soil . . . so we cancelled.'[2] Denard is finally spirited out of the country on to an old steamer – which is in the book, flying a Dutch flag, destination unspecified and in the film sailing for Barcelona – and is reunited with a loving Rose.

A splendidly exotic cast was gathered together for the film. Hollywood's favourite Continental, Charles Boyer, who, a year earlier had been menacing Ingrid Bergman in *Gaslight*, was just right as the world-weary Spanish Loyalist with, as Greene had described it, 'worry like a habit on his forehead'. The Greek actress Katina Paxinou, in one of only her handful of Hollywood roles as Mrs Melandez, scourge of Else (played by a then sixteen-year-old Wanda Hendrix) got, as one critic put it, 'to do most of the scenery chewing' and was generally photographed by James Wong Howe looming large in the hallways and on the staircase of her shoddy hotel.

> As Contreras, Peter Lorre got his first chance since *Casablanca* to perform one of his specialities as an actor: the depiction of unrestrained terror. When Denard first meets him at the Language Centre, he is taking large quantities of pills to calm his nerves. Afterwards, when Denard has learned of his duplicity, he is pushed, terrified into a cab and taken to the apartment in which Denard is hiding. Denard calls him a traitor who is also guilty of Else's death, but Contreras protests. 'It's only one girl out of thousands! . . . I was against it.' Denard cocks his gun and Lorre pulls out all stops. His face contorted with fright, Contreras screams, 'I only have six months to live! I didn't want to die in that stupid school! Wait! Hear me out!' Denard's gun jams but Contreras expires of a heart attack. Denard's comment to Rose is cold and blunt. 'He *said* he had a bad heart.'[3]

The most curious piece of major casting was Lauren Bacall as the Hon. Rose Cullen.

Bacall, a Warner contract player, had made a striking debut in *To Have and Have Not* and had followed that up with the as-yet unseen *The Big Sleep* (it was released after *Confidential Agent*). In her autobiography, she gives a revealing assessment of her work and the pressures during the filming.

> Charles Boyer was a marvellous man, a first-class actor, but plagued with insomnia. If he had four hours' sleep, it was a celebration . . . Herman Shumlin (the director) would take no advice from anyone – he even tried to tell Charles, an expert, how to play a love scene. He would not allow me to see the rushes and gave me none of the help which I desperately needed. One would have thought – hoped – that someone, somewhere, would have cared whether I conveyed some sense of the character I was playing, but there was never a suggestion from Shumlin that I alter my speech, change an inflection, convey a particular attitude. From 'You know how to whistle' vamp to British upper-class girl might have been achieved by Lynn Fontanne, but sure as hell not by me. At twenty, I was far removed from either character, but the wry, earthy girl of *To Have and Have Not* had humor, which was always part of me – whereas the British broad was totally straight and dreary. No way – no way possible to deal with her . . . November brought the release of *Confidential Agent*. It was a disaster. The critics said they'd made a mistake – I was not Garbo, Dietrich, Hepburn, Mae West, all rolled into one, as they had thought, I was just terrible me and should be sent back where I came from. As brilliant, exciting and glorious as I had been a few months ago, that's how amateurish, tedious and just plain bad I was now . . . I realized early on how limited the critics' knowledge of actors is, how they do not recognize where an actor's contribution begins or ends. I remember that when *The Big Sleep* was released a year later they said: Ah, that's more like the first Bacall we loved (they hate to be wrong) – she's good in this one – we like her again – let's not judge too quickly – we'll see what happens. What they didn't know, of course, was that *The Big Sleep* was made before *Confidential Agent*. At the time, I didn't realize how much damage had been done, but after *Confidential Agent* it took me years to prove that I was capable of doing anything at all worth while.[4]

The obvious lack of rapport with the director was shared by the cinematographer James Wong Howe who has commented: 'Two pictures of that time I didn't enjoy working on were *The Hard Way* (Vincent Sherman) and *Confidential Agent*; they were both directed by tyros, new men and I wasn't happy with people who in my opinion didn't know the business.'[5]

Quite separately, Wong Howe had received a glittering, unsolicited testimonial five years earlier from Greene, as film reviewer. He wrote: 'Mr Howe is the best cameraman in the industry. He is an incomparable manufacturer of what the industry badly needs. The glittering cellophane packets which give a kind of desirability to the suppressed sobs and the cheeriness and the good hearts you find inside. One can say of Mr Howe's films that, in spite of directors and scenario writers, they are always lovely to look at.'[6]

Agent was one of only two films ever directed by Shumlin, better known as one of Broadway's most distinguished stage directors. His other credit was the award-winning *Watch on the Rhine*, appropriately enough derived from Lillian Hellman's very stagey play.

Bacall's only real champion is, oddly, Greene himself who thought her performance 'very good'. He contends that the reviewers were very 'snobbish' in maintaining that it was absurd for Bacall to be playing an Honourable. 'The woman in the book is the granddaughter of a coalminer; she's not from an aristocratic family. Therefore she was quite right in not giving her any real aristocratic air.'

Not for Greene any concern either that his vividly described London was re-created inadequately in the corner of some foreign field that was forever a Hollywood sound stage – and resonated like one. His only *real* disappointment was that the film-makers didn't use the words of a song he had specially written for a night-club sequence early in the book. It goes:

It was just a way of talking – I hadn't learned.
It was just day-dreaming – but my heart burned.
You said 'I love you' – and I thought you meant it.
You said 'My heart is yours' – but you only lent it.
I don't say you lie: it's just the modern way.
I don't intend to die: in the old Victorian way.
It was just day-dreaming – I begin to discern it:
It was just a way of talking – and I've started to learn it![7]

Greene says: 'When I saw the film I thought well now they're actually going to hear a song of mine, set to music – but they substituted another! I suppose they felt that if they took the song from the book, they'd have to pay me copyright . . .' *The Confidential Agent* is one of the few books of his which he says he has wanted to reread. He also confessed to me that he would 'rather like to see the film again'.

The Man Within, Greene's third novel but his first published, in 1929, had instant success, indeed the sort of success that would lure him into a false sense of security as the real struggle to establish himself began in the succeeding years. 'Young', 'very sentimental' and 'embarrassingly romantic' is how Greene recalls the novel today – 'if I had been a publisher's reader, which I became many years afterwards, I would have turned it down unhesitatingly'.[8] Greene is maybe, with considerable hindsight, a little too self-critical bearing in mind that he was only twenty-two when he started *The Man Within* and just twenty-five when it was published. That said, his tale of pursuit, guilt, betrayal and retribution set against a backcloth of eighteenth-century Sussex is pretty heavy going – densely written and unsatisfactorily re-solved.

The novel begins with young Francis Andrews on the run from a gang of smugglers he has 'shopped' to the authorities. He takes refuge in a cottage whose sole occupier is Elizabeth. Andrews tells Elizabeth of his past – how his dominating father was the leader of the smugglers' gang and how, after first getting a good education, Francis was drawn into the gang's activities, always though in the giant shadow of his father.

When his father died, Carlyon became top dog as well as being a sort of substitute father-figure for Francis. Elizabeth tells him he must follow up his 'betrayal' of the gang by testifying against them at their coming trial. He does so, but they are acquitted and so he has to go back on the run again. The smugglers pursue him to Elizabeth's cottage and while he keeps out of harm's way, she kills herself rather than give Francis away. Carlyon, who has retained a kind of paternal interest in the boy, tells him that as long as he keeps out of the gang's way in future, they will not keep up their pursuit of him. When the revenue officers arrive, Francis tells them that he killed Elizabeth – it was, in fact, his knife she had stabbed herself with – as a sort of penance for abandoning her to the smugglers. As the officers take him away, we are meant to suppose that Francis snatches his knife back and does himself in too.

It took eighteen years for the novel to reach the screen – runner-up in tardiness to the altogether finer *England Made Me* which took thirty–five – and its route into eventual production was fairly circuitous.

Greene sold the rights for between £200 and £300 to Ralph Keene, a documentary film director friend of his with whom he had worked on a propaganda film for Imperial Airways. Greene says: 'He told me that with this book he had the chance of making his first feature film.' Keene in fact had no success trying to set up a production – although, in the interim, some of Greene's subsequent books had been successfully translated into film – and in February 1944 he sold the rights, for a small profit, to the film-making team of Sydney and Muriel Box (now Lady Gardiner). She told me:

> Ralph, being a documentary producer, had found it extremely difficult to set up and finance a feature production since this required special experience and knowledge in this particular field that he did not possess. Sydney and I felt the novel was unusual and although the first work of an author, it showed an original talent and powerful characterization strong enough to justify a successful translation into film.
>
> I started to write the first draft screenplay in June 1944 but owing to other studio commitments, it did not go into production until 1946. We began casting it in March of that year. Michael Redgrave had just given a brilliant performance in our film *The Years Between* and we thought he would give an equally fine interpretation of Carlyon. As Francis, we chose Richard Attenborough because he had sensitively portrayed the young sailor in *In Which We Serve* for Noël Coward. Joan Greenwood had just starred in our own picture *A Girl in a Million* and seemed absolutely right for Elizabeth (Dilys Powell later confirmed this, praising her performance as 'a cool, charming piece of acting'). Jean Kent was under contract to Gainsborough when we arrived at Shepherd's Bush studios to

make the picture and we believed she had the requisite quality of the seductress, Lucy (also confirmed by a reviewer who pronounced that 'Jean Kent as a wanton in a come-hither scene is alone worth the price of admission').

There was a strange, slightly surrealistic quality about Graham Greene's conception of the story which was difficult to capture on film; but as far as I can remember, neither Sydney, who wrote the final draft screenplay during April of 1946, nor I, who completed the first draft in a little over a month, considered it a serious problem, possibly because we were intrigued by its quality.

The result was, said one contemporary critic, 'a starry, Technicolor, costume drama with queer bits', or that is how it must have appeared to a public who revelled in as mindless an offering as *The Wicked Lady*, she added. And in a sense, her rather back-handed summation backs up my continuing feeling that the producer-writers and director Bernard Knowles made a more than decent stab at both the content and spirit of the book.

Made on an altogether broader canvas, the film opens with Francis in the custody of the revenue officers being questioned about the night smugglers broke into Elizabeth's cottage. We then go into a series of flashbacks as Francis relates his tale. How he was forced to become a smuggler against his will, in the shadow of his late father and under the protection of his father's successor Carlyon. When Carlyon orders his thrashing after Francis is unjustly convicted of stealing from the gang's stores, the boy runs away and betrays the gang to the authorities. At the trial, he loses his nerve and the gang goes free.

In flashback, we learn that Francis returned to the cottage to find Carlyon already there. Carlyon tells Francis that there was a struggle in which a smuggler was killed and Elizabeth managed to escape. Officers arrive to arrest them. The 'man within' now emerges and Francis tells the authorities that it was he who killed the smuggler and that Carlyon should be freed. When Carlyon is made aware of Francis's selflessness, he confesses to his own misdeeds, knowing that he will be hanged but with the satisfaction that the boy, who is allowed to go free and whom Carlyon had regarded with almost paternal affection, has been made a man.

Stirring stuff beautifully photographed on Sussex locations by
Geoffrey Unsworth! How came, though, asked the critic Angela
Milne,

> this most edgily restricted of novelists to compass the fancy
> dress of a smuggling story in olde-time Sussex? Did he, as the
> film does, tell his story through the mouth of the tortured boy
> who hated and betrayed his fellow sailors and fled from the
> fatherly sea-captain who finally died to save him from the
> gallows? Did he limit explicit symbolism to the motto from Sir
> Thomas Browne, 'There is another man within me and he is
> angry with me', and yet make the conflict between the
> wretched boy and his charming guardian as clear an allegory of
> a divided spirit walking the razor-edge to resolution as the film
> reveals it?[9]

The film, rightly I think, tidies up the book's improbable
resolution – first Elizabeth's, then Francis's, suicide with the same
knife. Call it dramatic licence, but in a sense Carlyon's execution
fulfils the function in the film of the book's double suicide and in
an altogether more meaningful way. As it is, the producers
agonized over their ending: 'We had such doubt and difficulty
over the ending that we devised and shot two different endings.
The final one was not chosen until after the film was viewed by
Michael Redgrave and others in January of 1947.' The final shot of
the film is Carlyon's face, bearing just the hint of a smile, as he
watches, through a barred window, Francis striding off towards
happiness.

There was no happiness, however, on Greene's part about what
he described as a 'highly coloured' film of his book. It was, he
says, 'an extraordinary script which showed torture with branding
irons as part of the eighteenth-century legal system' and the entire
exercise was a 'treachery', which Greene claims hurt him more
than Joseph Mankiewicz's later tampering with *The Quiet
American*, because it affected his 'first-born'. This accusation of
'treachery' bemused the producers:

> We were both naturally upset on hearing Graham Greene's
> comment on seeing the finished film. I do not believe this
> stemmed from the torture scene with Dickie Attenborough, but

from his own annoyance that Ralph Keene had sold the rights to Sydney for £400. In fact I'm amused by his comment on the torture scene. Torture may or may not have been part of our eighteenth-century legal system, but from all other accounts during the last 300–400 years, it was prevalent, even until relatively recently. Flogging, the treadmill and solitary confinement were continually used as punishments and there is little reason to doubt that it was much worse probably during the period of *The Man Within* than at later periods. Greene made no contact with us during the shooting of the picture, neither before nor after it was finished and showed no interest in it at all.

Despite rather good reviews all round, the film, released during a heatwave, 'fared only tolerably well at the box office'. So Greene really had the last laugh and he turned the knife by adding a clause to every future film contract forbidding a resale to Sydney Box. There was, though, one amusing sequel. Greene received a letter from Istanbul in which the correspondent 'praised the film for its daring homosexuality. Had I, he asked, devoted any other novels to this daring subject?'[10] Perhaps this is what that critic had meant about the film's 'queer bits'.

4
Young Scarface

Brighton today is a large, jolly, friendly seaside town in Sussex exactly one hour's journey from London but in the years between the wars behind the Regency terraces and crowded beaches there was another Brighton of dark alleyways and festering slums. From here, the poison of crime and violence, gang warfare began to spread until the challenge was taken up by the police. This is a story of that other Brighton – now happily no more.

The preface to the 1947 film of *Brighton Rock*, which signalled Greene's return to screen-writing after almost a decade and was the first of his adaptations from one of his own published works, rather neatly, if a trifle over-colourfully, helps bridge the gap between the publication of the original novel and the release of the film. The film's ten-year perspective on the events and attitudes portrayed in the book help lift what might have been an outrageous slice of melodrama in some contemporary pre-war adaptation to the realms of a truly intriguing, unfashionably raw, social drama-documentary. If *The Third Man* and *The Fallen Idol* are considered the apogee of Greene's working relationship with the cinema, I would contend that *Brighton Rock* is not far behind in their wake and deserves to be taken far more seriously than its neglected reputation would seem to demand.

Produced in the immediate post-war period when flagwaving opuses and genteel literary adaptations proliferated (and has anything really changed in the forty years since?) the film caused

uproar when it was released. FALSE, NASTY: IS THIS WHAT
YOU WANT TO SEE? barked the headline on the shock-horror
reaction, rather than review, by the *Daily Mirror* film critic Reg
Whitley:

> False, cheap, nasty sensationalism . . . in my view, no woman
> will want to see it. No parents will want their children to see it.
> The razor-slashing scenes are horrific.
>
> Hollywood has banned the production of gangster films
> because they give a false impression of life in America. British
> film studios will have to consider doing the same. For *Brighton
> Rock* will create abroad a similarly untrue picture of life in
> Britain. In all sincerity, I say that we should produce no more
> like it . . . The subtle religious theme that Graham Greene wove
> into the life of a boy leader of a Brighton race gang – and that
> gave his novel some justification for being written – has not
> been put over in the film. Instead there are ninety-two minutes
> of murder, brutality, beating-up. And the characters with
> perhaps one exception, are unpleasant people . . . British films
> are getting a break on foreign screens. *Brighton Rock* probably is
> set for a big showing in the 2000-odd theatres owned by Warner
> Brothers in America. So it is important that overseas should not
> get the impression made by our recent films, that we are a
> nation of toughs who rival in brutality the Chicago gangs in
> their heyday. Mr Censor, please note.[1]

It is only fair to add that, amid all this censorious outpouring,
Mr Whitley does pay back-handed compliments to both the
'skilled craftsmanship of the Boulting Brothers who made the film
and the fine acting of the cast – particularly Richard Attenborough
as the boy killer'. However, he then admonishes: 'I do suggest that
their talents should not be wasted on efforts like *Brighton Rock*.'
   The debate was to continue, for the next day the *Daily Mirror*
published a letter from Greene replying to some of the points
raised by Whitley's criticism.

> I have read the somewhat violent attack by your critic with
> bewilderment. If he had said that the book was 'false, cheap,
> nasty sensationalism', it would have been, to me, a quite
> possible personal point of view, but to praise the author of the

book at the expense of the directors of the film is surely unbalanced.

As it happens, I am also the author of the film play, and I can assure your critic that John Boulting (the director, while his twin brother Roy was producer) worked quite as hard as myself to retain the religious theme. And modifications of that theme are the responsibility of the British Film Censor, who objected to various passages in the dialogue of a specifically religious nature. Apparently one is allowed a certain latitude in using the name of God as an expletive, but any serious quotation from the Bible is not permissible on the English screen.

But in spite of this handicap I should have said that what your critic describes, almost too kindly, as 'the subtle religious theme' was as present in the film as in the book. Mr Whitley remarks that 'Hollywood has banned the production of gangster films because they give a false impression of life in America', but in fact Hollywood has not banned the production of gangster films but only the production of films that hold the gangster up to the sympathy of the audience. Obviously this has not been done in the case of Pinkie Brown, and your critic's disgust is an indication that one purpose of the film – the presentation of a character possessed by evil – has been successfully achieved.[2]

Greene might never have been involved at all in the filming of his novel had the initial arrangement for its adaptation to the screen worked out. The 'property' was owned by producer Anatole de Grunwald together with director Anthony 'Puffin' Asquith and writer Terence Rattigan who had collaborated on a number of earlier films including *French without Tears* and *The Way to the Stars*. That trio, more renowned for gently satirical comedies and stiff-upper-lip drama seemed an unlikely combination to be remotely attracted by such a violent, and frankly sleazy, subject as *Brighton Rock*. And it was clear that they were having problems getting their act together.

The Boultings had long been admirers of the book, and Greene's work in general, and in a round-about way discovered where the rights lay. At a subsequent meeting with de Grunwald, they observed that he was 'very much the Svengali character in the trio with Asquith and Rattigan as the Trilbys'. Rattigan was planning to do a script but 'it was quite clear that someone in the trinity had gone cold on the idea'. So the Boultings took over the rights. The twins had been active in the British film industry from the late thirties, alternately producing and directing films like *Pastor Hall*, before the outbreak of World War Two, and then, during the war years, *Thunder Rock, Journey Together* and *Desert Victory*. In the same year as *Brighton Rock*, they also had an enormous success (with John as producer and Roy director) with their film of Howard Spring's *Fame is the Spur*.

> Rattigan still wanted to do the script but [says John] we had certain reservations about that. Not that Terry wasn't extremely talented and highly sensitive but we just didn't feel it was his sort of area at all. So we had to be a little evasive with him. Anyway we thought it was highly desirable that Graham should do it given that he had a filmic sense and tended to write in very vivid filmic images. He agreed to do it. We were obviously delighted because we had always had this rather old-fashioned idea that the original creator was the best person to write the script even if it meant that he had the burden of collaborating with either Roy or myself as two people who thought they knew what could be done with film.

A long-time lover of Brighton – 'no city before the war . . . had such a hold on my affections. I knew it first as a child of six when I was sent with an aunt to convalesce after some illness – jaundice, I think. It was there I saw my first film, a silent one of course, and the story captured me for ever: *Sophy of Kravonia*, Anthony Hope's tale of a kitchenmaid who became a queen'[3] – Greene began the book in 1937 as a detective story.

But the original suspense yarn turned into a more sombre tale as the characters took over Greene's consciousness. From the very beginning of the book, with Fred Hale's appearance (who did not belong to 'the early summer sun, the cool Whitsun wind off the sea, the holiday crowd')[4] Greene's Brighton in the book is a gloomy background to the dark psyches of the characters. It was as a result of *Brighton Rock* that Greene says he was 'discovered to be – detestable term! – a Catholic writer'.[5] In fact he had become a Catholic nearly ten years earlier and all his books had been written as a Catholic. Nevertheless he admits that, by 1937, 'the time was ripe for me to use Catholic characters'[6] and agonized theology peppers the novel.

Fred Hale knows from the start that Pinkie and his mob are seeking to kill him for throwing in his lot with Colleoni's rival gang. Hale had betrayed Kite, the leader of Pinkie's gang, to Colleoni and Pinkie is seeking revenge for Kite's murder in order to prove himself a worthy successor although he is only seventeen. Just before his death Hale befriends Ida Arnold, an old overweight prostitute with a heart of gold. When she learns he has been killed, she seeks revenge. Hale had been in Brighton as part of a publicity stunt from his paper distributing calling cards worth ten shillings each when handed in. The rest of Hale's cards are distributed by Pinkie's gang to confuse the police over the time of death, but when Pinkie learns that one card has been found by a waitress in Snow's Diner who had seen the real Hale earlier, Pinkie sees her to learn exactly what she knows. If she told the police, they might decide that Hale's supposed suicide was murder.

That both Rose, the childlike waitress, and Pinkie were raised as Catholics in the same slum, Nelson Place, gives them something in common. But he is secretly revolted by the girl, as he is by all women – an attitude rooted in childhood when he shared his parents' bedroom and witnessed sex, which he saw as an act of darkness. He had once thought of being a priest to avoid sex. Only music can manage to stir Pinkie's emotions. Rose and Pinkie talk about religion with Pinkie maintaining: 'these atheists, they don't know nothing. Of course there's hell, flames and damnation.'[7] Ida, the self-appointed avenging angel, keeps intruding on their lives but despite her interventions and the continuing scenario of violence and murder as Pinkie struggles both to protect, and assert, himself, Rose remains fiercely protective of him.

The ever-suspicious Pinkie is persuaded that he must marry Rose so as to be absolutely sure of her continuing loyalty – and because it is inadmissible under the law for a wife to give evidence against her husband. Rose is only too delighted to get married (as her parents were, having been promised fifteen guineas by Pinkie to 'give' her away) and after a squalid little register office ceremony, witnessed by gang-member Dallow and the crooked lawyer Prewitt, she persuades Pinkie to record some eternal words of love for her in one of those outdoor recording booths. 'He didn't like the idea of putting anything on record: it reminded him of finger-prints.' Nevertheless 'speaking in a low voice for fear it might carry beyond the box, he gave his message up to be graven on vulcanite: "God damn you, you little bitch, why can't you go back home for ever and let me be?" '8

Rose is confronted again by Ida who tries to spell out Pinkie's utter ruthlessness which would engulf even Rose if necessary.

People change Rose tells Ida. No, they don't, replies Ida: 'Look at me. I've never changed. It's like those sticks of rock: bite it all the way down, you'll still read Brighton. That's human nature.'9 Pinkie is still convinced he cannot trust Rose and is fearful she will betray him to the police. He persuades her to take part in a suicide pact to which he, secretly, has no intention of keeping. They drive to the cliffs above the town and just as Rose is about to shoot herself, Ida arrives with the police and a somewhat chastened Dallow (he had always liked Rose and considered that she did not deserve the fate Pinkie had planned for her). Rose throws the gun away and a now hysterical Pinkie extracts a bottle of acid from his pocket which is, in turn, smashed into his own face. In agony he races off and disappears over the cliff's edge.

Later, in the confessional, Rose tells a priest that she wished she had killed herself. The wheezy old cleric attempts to comfort her with: 'You can't conceive, my child, nor can I or anyone the . . . appalling . . . strangeness of the mercy of God.'10 If Pinkie loved her then that would show that there was some good in him and that there was hope, both for his soul and her future. And, of course, Rose realizes she has proof of his love in the as-yet unplayed record. And so she goes home 'towards the worst horror of all'.11 Greene says:

> *Brighton Rock* is written in such a way that people could plausibly imagine that Pinkie went to hell, but then I cast doubt on it in the ending. The real theme . . . is embodied in the priest's phrase at the end . . . 'You cannot conceive, my child . . .' etc. I wanted to introduce a doubt of Pinkie's future in the words of the priest, a doubt whether even a man like that could possibly merit eternal punishment. It is appalling the strangeness. Because the mercy of God obviously is operating in some inexplicable fashion even with the gas-ovens of Auschwitz. In

fact, I wanted to throw doubt on hell altogether. I'm a great
believer in purgatory. Purgatory to me makes sense, while hell
doesn't.[12]

The Brighton of the novel and the film is painted as a kind of
purgatory. Greene admits: 'it's true that I have a predilection for
shady places. It enabled me, for instance, to understand Brighton
and its seamy side. As a child, I was very fond of the place. When I
went there to work on novels, I would read up all the news about
the fights between rival gangs for in those days knives and
razor-blades were quickly drawn, particularly in the racing
crowd.'[13]

And yet elsewhere, he says,

> the setting of *Brighton Rock* may in part belong to an imaginary
> geographic region . . . I must plead guilty to manufacturing this
> Brighton of mine as I never manufactured Mexico or Indo-
> China . . . Why did I exclude so much of the Brighton I really
> knew from this imaginary Brighton? I had every intention of
> describing it, but it was as though my characters had taken the
> Brighton I knew into their own consciousness and transformed
> the whole picture.[14]

Into the living and breathing purgatory of Pinkie, Rose and the
rest?

Right from the very start of the film, from the first shot of the
beach at Brighton, there is the sense of location that was unusual
for British films of that day. Apart from a few interiors filmed at
the tiny Welwyn studios, the Boultings shot their movie at a cost
of around £178,000 (a little less than the average budget of most
films at that time) entirely in and around Brighton itself. Filming
was undertaken at the height of the season and so the attendant
problems must have been plentiful. Newspaper reports at the time
tell of the Boultings and their production being ordered to vacate
Brighton racecourse, where 500 holidaymaker 'extras' had been
drafted to aid authenticity.

According to one Alderman Thompson, who refused to allow
filming to continue because of damage done in the grandstand
enclosure, 'The agreement was for three days' filming and they
have had their three days. I have given them a day's grace so they

can remove their equipment.' Greene's Colleoni gang fictionally represented the real-life Sabini gang which had been such a menace in Brighton between the wars and, says John Boulting, 'we had a marvellous little man called Carl Ramon, who used to carry the razor for Sabini, as our technical adviser'.

Certainly the slashings, a particularly unpleasant form of violence when graphically represented, were neatly done doubt-less thanks to the advisory knowledge of Mr Ramon. And it was not entirely unsurprising that the film should be retitled *Young Scarface* for American release even though Pinkie does not actually become facially marked until a good way through the piece.

It is difficult to imagine Richard Attenborough, today soft-spoken, pink-faced, white-haired, plump and knighted as the vicious young punk with frightened eyes and a permanent sneer in the 1947 film. He was then twenty-four, playing a seventeen-year-old (a couple of years later he was to play a thirteen-year-old in the Boultings' *The Guinea Pig*) and had been even closer to the right age as Pinkie in Frank Harvey's stage play of *Brighton Rock*, mounted a couple of years earlier with Hermione Baddeley as Ida and Dulcie Gray as Rose.

Greene had seen the play and hated it so much he asked for his name to be taken off it. He had also not approved of Attenbor-ough's casting as Pinkie. The Boultings never saw the play but after working with him in a film John directed for the RAF Film Unit called *Journey Together* – coincidentally, scripted by Terence Rattigan – allied to his scene-stealing work in Noël Coward's *In Which We Serve* (as the cowardly seaman), they felt he could be an ideal Pinkie. John Boulting:

When we indicated to Graham that we were going to play Attenborough as Pinkie – and it had nothing to do with the fact he had been in the play – Graham did his very best to oppose us. And it was very hard for us to resist his opposition, that Dickie was not right physically and would not be able to convey the complexities of this young lad with an aura of evil. However, it was an issue on which we decided that our knowledge and our judgement of Dickie's potential was something we felt was rather greater than Graham's. And we told him so. It has to be said that he was pretty apprehensive and disappointed.

Attenborough now adds:

But here's the marvellous pay-off! Greene wrote to me after seeing the film, he mentioned his misgivings, but added he didn't think it could have been done any better. I've kept and treasured that letter . . . in those days the character of Pinkie was a macabre novelty in British films. It was hard to understand how somebody like that would feel as he razor-slashed you, or as he told a girl to put a gun in her mouth to shoot herself. That is the kind of enormity I had to convey.[15]

The other key casting was for Rose and Pinkie's Nemesis, Ida. John Boulting:

For Rose, we saw literally hundreds of girls and one day we were talking to Olive Dodds who was in charge of the Rank Film School who told us they had a girl called Carol Marsh under contract. 'She's talented, totally lacking in confidence and no beauty,' Olive said. We met her and she was extremely shy but we tested her. She certainly was very inhibited and we found it difficult to get her to deal with the subtler parts of the characterization. We knew it was going to be a tough job but we felt we could get something from her.

She was, the Boultings agreed, 'the embodiment of ordinariness'.
If Rose is a thankless role then Ida, as conceived in Greene's novel, is an almost impossible one to make flesh and blood: the tart (lady of easy virtue seems almost more apt) with a heart of gold combined with the doggedness of a Miss Marple. For the film, she has become a larger-than-life concert-party pierrette, beery and blowsy, turned amateur detective. Despite Greene's own reservations about Hermione Baddeley – 'she was the music-hall type playing a straight actress, as it were, and she stuck out like a sore thumb' – I'm more inclined to go along with John Boulting who says, 'I thought she was good casting and extremely convincing. We both felt that she was very close to the Ida that Greene had created.'
However, Roy Boulting makes the point that

the depth of Ida's character would be difficult for most people to comprehend. She embodies all of the lower-middle-class virtues; yet Graham seems to imply in the story that Pinkie has a better chance for salvation than Ida because he is operating in the realm of Grace, whereas Ida, who is an atheist, is outside that realm. I think Ida as Graham created her is explicable only in those terms, but it was very difficult to convey the depth of her character in the film as a result.[16]

The American writer and critic R.W.B. Lewis refers to the book as betraying an 'initial confusion between what Greene calls an "entertainment" and what he finally offered as a tragedy; but here the confusion is unexpectedly exploited . . . in the composition of an immensely impressive novel' and his words could as properly refer to the film which tends to run a similar gamut in a fairly smooth transition from the original text. Apart from the ending of the film, which is the only significant change to the original, the main differences are of emphasis, explicitness and theological reference. The last was, to some extent, dictated following the intervention of the then censor Brooke Wilkinson to whom Greene and the Boultings had submitted the script before shooting.

John Boulting says: 'He was an incredible man. The fact that a great number of British films of that day were opiates of a kind derived from the fact that so much power was vested in this rather arrogant and highly bigoted old man who was, I seem to remember, about ninety at the time, slightly deaf and almost blind.' Any references by Pinkie to the Mass had to be cut out, for example, because he was a murderer and it was felt it could offend Roman Catholics. Greene was very bitter about the censor's input – 'the whole film was weakened by his well-meaning care for the belief of others'.

The film's faintly apologetic preface was a sort of compromise to ensure full co-operation for the extensive location filming and the Boultings believed that it was also 'a statement that, in the circumstances, was a fair one to make'. After the first shot on the beach and a glimpse of a newspaper front page showing Hale's face and spelling out details of his stunt, we switch to the thieves' kitchen where Pinkie and his gang are deciding just what to do with Hale.

Pinkie's character is established from the outset. First we see just his hands mindlessly twiddling a sort of cat's cradle before he spits his first line: 'Won't anyone shut that grass's mouth!' (A neat thuggish variation on 'Who will rid me of this turbulent priest?')

The next section of the film is enormously impressive as – aided by Hans May's urgent score and Harry Waxman's freewheeling camerawork – we see Hale tracked, trapped and finally killed amid the bustle of the resort's holiday crowds. Hale's death is referred to but not actually dealt with in the book. In the film, he disappears into the ghost-train tunnel – appropriately called Dante's Inferno – with Pinkie slipping in alongside him in the open carriage. Just before the end of the nightmare ride, Hale plunges over the side and into the sea far below, clearly – for us – pushed by Pinkie but, strictly for later post-mortem purposes, having died of a heart-attack (from fear?) After this the pattern of the novel is fairly faithfully followed.

For the sake of later plotting, and possibly one of the censor's interventions, the wording of Pinkie's recording of 'love' for Rose becomes: 'What you want me to say is "I love you". I hate you, you little slut. Why don't you go back to Nelson Place and leave me be.' The couple's suicide 'pact' switches locale from the clifftop to Brighton Pier and the acid element is not introduced as Pinkie, like some trapped animal, falls from the pier on to the steel girders and to the sea below.

Now, instead of the wheezy old priest and the confessional, Rose is closeted in a bright room with a smartly-garbed nun who confides in the pathetic Rose 'the appalling strangeness of the mercy of God'. Our hearts are in our mouths as a gramophone is produced for Rose to play her record. She, and we, now hear: 'What you want me to say is "I love you" . . . "I love you" . . . "I love you" ' (the record has been scratched earlier when Pinkie tried to smash it) and the needle has – miraculously? – stuck. The camera pans up to a crucifix on the wall and then it is the end-credits.

Terence Rattigan had written a treatment with, according to Greene 'a softened ending' and had not, say the Boultings, 'managed to convey the brooding atmosphere' of the tale. In a sense, this too was a softened ending and yet if it had been as the book it would have been almost unbearable in terms of drama and, believe the Boultings, something of an anti-climax whereas this ending, as devised by Greene, is splendidly ironic. Greene:

The original ending, with the old priest and the young girl
going off to play her record would, I think, have been
disastrous for the film. In this way, anybody who wanted a
happy ending would feel they had had a happy ending.
Anybody who had any sense would know that next time Rose
would probably push the needle over the scratch and get the full
message.

What Greene objected to was the way the Boultings had styled
the ending round his device. 'In my script, I had made it a rather
shabby room in hospital with an old nun. Instead what they had
was a beautiful nun, a beautiful white room, the crucifix on the
wall, probably doves flying outside the window . . . God knows
what else!'
That is a slight exaggeration, but, in any case, John Boulting
accepts the blame:

Yes, it was entirely my fault. The person I cast as the nun was
certainly too conventional and saintlike. There's a cleanliness
about her that's probably wrong.
    She should have been a woman with a slight moustache,
perhaps some pimples on her face. It is said that the pan up to
the crucifix on the wall indicated divine intervention with the
cracked record. That wasn't the intention at all as far as I was
concerned. The point of the cross, certainly my meaning for it,
was that here was a girl who had, in a sense, been crucified too.

If the censor was in some part responsible for some detheologiz-
ing of the piece, it was not entirely without the support, even in
extreme retrospect, of John Boulting:

I think we felt that the Roman Catholic mystical quality did not
always ring true as expressed from time to time by Rose and
Pinkie. It was the only thing I had doubts about within the
book. I accepted the idea of it but they were really too articulate.
I think we reduced the articulation of Pinkie's theological ideas
just enough to convey them without going overboard.

As a slice of film-making, *Brighton Rock* is a fine achievement,
with exciting set-pieces (the Hale chase, gang warfare on the

racecourse) to more intimate scenes (Pinkie's meeting with Colleoni, Ida trying to break down Prewitt) as well as a clutch of marvellous performances supporting the principals. Harcourt Williams says, as Prewitt, 'I've sunk so deep, I've drunk the secrets of the sewer' – and first Alan Wheatley then Wylie Watson, as the respectively doomed Hale and Spicer, stand out particularly. It is also one of the best-photographed films of its period, for apart from a couple of months' locations in a crowded Brighton there were the cramped interiors filmed at Welwyn. John Boulting: 'Film-stock at that time was very slow compared with today. Therefore, in order to get deep focus, you had to pile on the light and then stop down. Harry Waxman did an incredible job.' Greene is, on the whole, quite happy with the film:

> There were some very good scenes. Richard Attenborough was extremely good, as was the man who played Spicer, I thought, but the Boulting Brothers didn't give me enough control. In fact, I didn't have any control. I sat typing and sent in page after page of script as they wanted, more or less, a shooting-script with descriptions of the shots and so on. And of course that was a waste of time because the director has to do that. After that, I've never tried to do shooting-scripts; I've only done screenplays.

John Boulting remembers it a little differently:

> I think Graham probably misunderstood us. What we had wanted from him was a detailed master scene script. What Graham produced was carved up by us, but mostly Roy, into a shooting-script. Certainly he never complained to us that the demands on him were unduly onerous. He seemed to be as anxious to see that his book was translated as closely to the mood and atmosphere, spirit and intention of the original as we were. I was very much in awe of Graham and his work.

The critics divided themselves into those who reviewed the film entirely in isolation (and, generally, favourably) and those who referred back to the novel which resulted in less acclaim for the adaptation. In the latter category, the *Manchester Guardian* concluded: 'Perhaps Graham Greene's writing set his directors an insoluble problem. However that may be, the result is that the film wears religion like an almost meaningless ornament. It is the difference between a monk's crucifix and the little ornamental gold cross worn by a debutante . . .'[17] The *News Chronicle* asked 'What will a person untutored as to the book, and Graham Greene's preoccupation with cosmic evil, make of these characters? They come from nowhere to flit motiveless before us. Pinkie is not explained. The hell that lay around him in his infancy and drives him from horror to horror is unexplained . . .'

The *News Chronicle* reviewer does, however, make some interesting points in the debate about the suitability of transposing certain novels to the screen:

Had I been a film-maker, that relentless and terrible book would have tempted me from the moment of its publication. It is the most filmically written book of Britain's most filmic writer. It is also the clearest exposition of his view of humanity. Because of that, I should have resisted. To make the film truly – and what is the point of doing otherwise – would be to circulate a drab and nihilistic Roman Catholic conception which I hate. To bowdlerize and sweeten the book for censor and box-office purposes is an alternative . . .[18]

Brighton Rock was not an outstanding box-office success. Says John Boulting. 'It performed pretty well in the big cities but outside, it was probably altogether too strong meat for the times. The dominant American film was all saccharine and romance and had, in a sense, conditioned audiences.' Despite their admiration for Greene's work, the Boultings never worked again with the writer. There was, though, a thought-provoking near miss. 'After Graham had seen a first cut of the film, we went for a drink and he said "What do you think about this?" and, on the grounds we might be interested, started to tell us the lines that were to be the basis for *The Third Man*. "Well, Graham," we said, "that could be fascinating." '

5
A Perfect Collaboration

If, after what he had described as his ' 'prentice scripts' for Korda
in the late thirties, Greene was ever going to commit more
substantial work in the film medium, there was a sort of
inevitability that he should one day collaborate with Carol Reed.
Reed, two years younger than Greene, started out as an actor
before becoming Edgar Wallace's representative at British Lion on
the production of Wallace's films. After a spell as dialogue director
to Basil Dean at Ealing, Reed made his own feature debut with
Midshipman Easy in 1935 – the year Greene began reviewing films
for the *Spectator*. Greene's growing respect for this new young
film-maker could be traced through various notices over the
ensuing four and a half years.

> January 1936 – *Midshipman Easy* . . . is the first film of a new
> English director, Mr Carol Reed, who has more sense of the
> cinema than most veteran British directors . . . it is simply and
> dramatically cut, it contains the best fight I can remember on
> the screen, and I can imagine no child too sophisticated to be
> excited and amused.
> July 1936 – Here at last is an English film one can unreservedly
> praise . . . I refer to Mr Carol Reed's *Laburnum Grove* . . .
> maintains the promise of his first picture . . . both films are
> thoroughly workmanlike and unpretentious, with just the hint
> of a personal manner which makes one believe that Mr Reed,
> when he gets the right script, will prove far more than efficient
> . . . Nine directors out of ten would simply have canned (J.B.

Priestley's) play for mass consumption: Mr Reed has made a film out of it . . . [His] camera acts with a kind of quick shrewd independence of the dialogue, and presents its own equally dramatic commentary, so that the picture of suburbia seems to be drawn simultaneously from two angles – which is as near the screen can come as yet to stereoscopy.

January 1940 – Dr Cronin's mining novel (*The Stars Look Down*) has made a very good film – I doubt whether in England we have ever produced a better. Mr Carol Reed, who began some years ago so impressively with *Midshipman Easy* and then became involved in the cheap little second features that were regularly churned out by the smaller English studios, has at last had his chance and magnificently taken it. Since this is the story of a mine disaster his work will inevitably be compared with Pabst's in *Kameradschaft*: he can bear the comparison . . . Once before Mr Reed tried his hand at a documentary story – *Bank Holiday*. It was highly praised and was full of 'characters', but it smelt of the studio. Here one forgets the casting altogether: he handles his players like a master, so that one remembers them only as people.[1]

Now, a couple of years after the Second World War had ended, Greene was about to resume his working relationship with Korda by adapting his short story, 'The Basement Room', in collaboration with Reed, who had gone on to even greater glories in the intervening years with films like *Night Train to Munich*, *The Way Ahead* and *Odd Man Out*. Written in 1935 on a cargo steamer to relieve the tedium of a return voyage from Liberia, 'The Basement Room' was first published a year later before being included in the *Nineteen Stories* collection more than a decade on.

Greene professes some surprise that Reed should have been attracted by the original material: 'It seemed to me that the subject matter was unfilmable – a murder committed by the most sympathetic character and an unhappy ending.' Despite his own earlier estimate of Reed's potential, signalled in the reviews, Greene had also reckoned without what he has described to me as Reed's 'fine film and literary intelligence'. The result of this, their first tandem (to be followed by *The Third Man* and *Our Man in Havana*) was *The Fallen Idol*, a more emotive title than *The Basement Room* but less pretentious than *The Lost Illusion* and *Lost*

Illusions, working titles during the film's production.

The original story tells of seven-year-old Philip Lane, left alone in a great Belgravia house with the butler Baines and his wife while Philip's parents are away on a fortnight's holiday.

Philip hero-worships Baines, who regales the boy with over-colourful African memories. It also becomes clear that Baines and his shrewish wife live together in a state of armed neutrality. Through Philip's eyes we discover that Baines has a pretty 'niece' (in reality, a lover Emmy) whom he catches in mid-assignation in a nearby teashop, after the boy has innocently followed the butler from the house. When Mrs Baines quizzes him later about his having been out alone and spending his pocket-money on sweet cakes, Philip blurts out how it was 'they' who bought the cakes for him and how Baines's 'niece' was 'nice'. Mrs Baines tells Philip to keep their little talk a secret before announcing that she is going off for a couple of days to visit her apparently dying mother. In fact, she wants to slip out of sight so she can observe Baines.

After a day out together the butler and the boy return to find Emmy who joins them for supper. He sees them kissing each other and when they put him to bed we assume that they too will bed down together in the house. In the middle of the night, Philip is awoken out of his sleep by a snarling Mrs Baines demanding to know where the lovers are before she chases off to try and confront them *in flagrante*. Philip sees her and Baines struggling at the top of the stairs before she topples back over the banisters to her death.

A terrified and confused Philip races out of the house into the night, is found wandering the streets and taken to a police station before being returned to the house. Baines, who had moved his wife's body to make it appear like an accident, is implicated in murder as the boy reveals unwittingly what he has seen as well. He is also given a motive as Philip 'protested with a quaver that reminded Baines that after all he was only a child, "It was all Emmy's fault." '[2] The story ends with Philip, as a lonely old man of nearly seventy, recalling Baines as he himself sinks closer to death.

There is an intriguing parallel between the story and its tailpiece and L.P. Hartley's masterpiece *The Go-Between* (published in 1953) which seems clearly to owe something to 'The Basement Room'. Hartley's central character, the youngster Leo, is observed from the character's sterile old age, a youthful victim, like Philip, of secrets, illicit sex and adult deception.

And what might have served as Greene's inspiration for this deceptively simple, and compact, tale of shattered childhood dreams? A clue can be gleaned from an early recollection of the nursery. He recalls Kipling's short story 'Ba Ba Black Sheep', being read aloud to him as a child. The story is possibly the most poignant, certainly the most heart-tugging, account of the corruption of childhood innocence in English literature – it was 'like a warning not to take happiness in childhood for granted',[3] says Greene.

Fundamental changes took place between story and screenplay, confirming possibly Greene's original fears that the subject matter, as it was, was unfilmable. No longer was Mrs Baines's death to be murder, rather a terrible accident, interpreted by the terrified child as murder, thus increasing tension and suspense as the real truth might or might not come out. It dealt instead, says Greene, with 'a small boy who believed that his friend was a murderer and nearly procured his arrest by telling lies in his defence'. The setting became the embassy of a foreign diplomat, based in London, and the child Felipe instead of Philip. 'This was Reed's idea since we both felt that the large Belgravia house was already in these post-war years a period piece, and we did not want to make an historical film. I fought the solution for a while and then wholeheartedly concurred.'[4]

During this development period, Reed and Greene had just one conference with Korda. Greene told me: 'Korda was very good like that. I mean he let us work and never interfered', except on that one occasion when,

Korda had the very bad idea that, instead of being a butler, Baines should be a chauffeur. He said that children loved to be shown the insides of cars and that they made heroes out of chauffeurs. This way, he said, one could begin with the ambassador being driven off to catch a plane and the first scene would be at the airport. I told him, 'Alex, how many films have started with scenes at airports?' And so he just forgot about it. I don't think he was convinced but he let us have our own way.

What, however, is most perfectly matched in the transition

from story to screen is the sense of a child's observation of a complex adult world, which is established from the very first shot of a small, blond boy peering at a Friday night's comings and goings through the banisters of the embassy's tall, central staircase. The camera also confirms an immediate rapport between the boy and Baines (Sir Ralph Richardson) as the butler helps to clear the decks before the departure of staff for the weekend. We also get our first glimpse of Julie (Emmy of the story and now an embassy typist) being secretive with Baines before she too leaves. There is instant menace with what we assume is the shadow of Mrs Baines, followed by a shrill chilling cry of 'Baines!', echoed mockingly by Felipe. The embassy is now deserted except for Baines, the boy, and his beloved grass snake, McGregor – 'the snake was mine (I have always liked snakes), and for a short while it met with Reed's sympathetic opposition',[5] says Greene.

The awful screech of 'Baines!' takes on an altogether more ominous ring when it is used by Felipe as he beards the butler and Julie in the nearby teashop. Baines swings round with a terrible, red-handed look of sheer horror before calming down to entwine the boy in the initial deception. 'You can trust me – I'll never let you down, Baines,' Felipe tells him as they return to the embassy, where a suspicious Mrs Baines wheedles a 'they' out of the boy before she, in her turn, resorts to attempting a conspiratorial alliance with him. When Mrs Baines 'leaves', the atmosphere is instantly one of glorious liberation for both Baines and Felipe.

Baines takes the boy to the zoo where, fortuitously, they meet Julie. Felipe is shown to be resentful, more likely jealous, of the adult relationship; whenever he turns to seek a reaction from Baines, the butler is always some way off with Julie, communicating wordlessly, desperately. There is also a good visual gag by Reed as he has the boy offering food through some bars to a man, as he comes out of the 'Gents'. The trio goes back to the embassy for supper and games, played in and out of the rooms and hallways of a half-darkened great house. In the midst of these games, we also realize that Mrs Baines is a silent, lurking observer.

As in the story, Mrs Baines's nocturnal reappearance at Felipe's bedside is dramatically signalled by one of her hairpins plopping on to his pillow. As he sleepily looks up into her snarling features, she demands to know where the other two are. First she tries to ingratiate herself, then spits, in stronger terms than the story: 'You're not such a child as you pretend to be; you're a nasty wicked boy and it should be beaten out of you.'

Mrs Baines's death is most cunningly filmed – from Felipe's aspect to give the appearance of murder and from ours to detail fully a tragic accident. The boy sees the struggle at the top of the stairs before retreating to the fire-escape. In that time, Baines has left his wife and disappeared, presumably to protect Julie. Mrs Baines climbs off the stairway on to a ledge to peer in a large, hinged window through which she hopes to see the guilty pair. When the window swings open because of her weight against it, she is knocked off balance and pitched from the ledge on to the stairs and, finally, the floor below. Felipe is now outside only in time to see Mrs Baines tumbling down the last few steps. He makes a false connection before frantically running off into the night.

Felipe's gentle apprehending by a policeman, and the following sequence in the police station as the law tries to find out what an uncommunicative young boy is doing out of doors at the dead of night in his pyjamas, is played very lightly indeed. Rose, a sullen policewoman in the story, becomes Rose, a golden-hearted prostitute in the film. The desk sergeant tries to get Rose, as a potential mother figure, to try and make contact with the boy. The cheery whore can only mouth professional platitudes like: 'Hello dearie, where do you live?', 'Shall I take you home?', 'Come along, dearie, you'd like to come home with me dearie!' but eventually does make a breakthrough (unlike the police-woman who signally failed) as Felipe snuggles up to her. When a phone goes to report the accident at the embassy, Felipe's reaction reveals his home. 'Does your father work at the embassy?' asks the sergeant. 'No, he's *the* ambassador,' replies the boy. 'Oh, I know your daddy,' adds Rose in a cryptic, unexplained aside.

Baines's downfall in the original story is just a couple of pages long and with a single, inquisitive constable in attendance. The dénouement in the film is spun out with positively Hitchcockian relish as hordes of police and officials weave their way round the embassy that night and the following morning.

Maybe because we know Baines is innocent of murder and must somehow eventually be exonerated despite the misguided efforts of the confused boy to help/implicate the butler further, the events

are handled with some levity. There are the two charladies, Mrs
Patterson and Mrs Barrow, gleefully speculating if there is any
blood; Baines, in mid-explanation to the police suddenly having
to cope with the delivery of forty gilt chairs from Selfridges; a
plump elderly clock-winder silencing everyone as he officiously
cuts a swathe through the solemn gathering to cope with an
embassy timepiece – 'they behave much better if they're looked
after' (this interruption was Reed's invention).

As the boy draws Baines in yet deeper with his lies – 'I killed
Mrs Baines' Felipe tells the police, alerting them for the first time
to the possibility that this was murder and not merely an accident
– so the butler's heroic (for the boy) mask slips more and more.
When Felipe asks Baines if 'it' was 'self-defence, like in Africa', the
police ask for an explanation. 'I've never been out of the country,
except Ostend,' Baines retorts. The 'idol' clearly has feet of clay.

There is one last twist of a sort. When the police discover Mrs
Baines's footprint in some earth from a spilled flower-pot on the
high window ledge, they believe it is evidence clearing the butler.
Felipe, now determined to tell only the truth, wants to say that it
was he who spilled the pot and that Mrs Baines had trodden in it
the day before. The police just shoo him away. Gene Phillips
writes: 'He is left standing alone, puzzled because no one wants to
hear the truth now that he has finally decided to tell it. He climbs
the stairs to the nursery, having decided to return to his own
world after his bewildering experiences among adults, while
down below Baines is rightly being freed – but on the basis of
evidence that Felipe thinks is worthless.'[6] Felipe's idol may have
fallen but the boy is not going to be permanently damaged as
indicated in the story; the film fades out with the boy's mother and
father returning, to his obvious pleasure.

One would expect marvellous acting from the ensemble
including Sir Ralph Richardson, Sonia Dresdel (as Mrs Baines),
Michele Morgan (as Julie) and Denis O'Dea, Jack Hawkins and
Bernard Lee as the various policemen. What was key had to be the
casting, and resulting performance of Felipe. In *Charmed Lives*,
Michael Korda gives an indication of Carol Reed's facility with
youngsters at a stuffy dinner party hosted by his uncle Alex:

> [Reed] was perhaps the gentlest and kindest person I had ever
> met. He immediately put me at my ease by telling me about a

pet hedgehog he had installed in the garden of his new house . . . Pempy (Reed's wife, Penelope) . . . too had the bright, instinctive ability to put one at ease, and showed no indication to make grandiose plans for my future (Michael was then just thirteen). 'You must find all this terribly boring,' she said, 'and I think you're being wonderfully patient about it, much better than Carol in fact. He would much rather be back with his hedgehog, you see, the poor darling, but he does adore Alex, and wouldn't dream of not coming.' Carol . . . adored children almost as much as he and Pempy loved animals.'[7]

Some sort of reward would come twenty years later with Reed winning his only American Oscar for *Oliver!*

It was Bill O'Brien, a production executive of Korda's London Films who spotted the photograph of a likely-looking candidate for Felipe – a then four-year-old Bobby Henrey pictured in his father Robert's book, *A Village in Piccadilly*. O'Brien promptly wrote to Mrs Henrey asking if Bobby, now eight, could test for the film.

What has been regarded as one of the greatest Svengali acts in the history of cinema is explained in a fascinating article by Francis Levison:

Carol Reed crouched beside the child hour after hour, month after month. He created a separate world for himself and the child, and the vast superstructures of the cinema, the lights, cameras, actors and technicians, were shut out. Reed talked, cajoled, demonstrated, rehearsed, explained. Sometimes he would rise from his knees and squirm, shuffle, gesticulate in exact facsimile of a child. Reed had studied Bobby's gestures, then selected appropriate ones and demonstrated them himself . . . the boy followed, painstakingly perfecting the mimicry. Explains Reed, 'What Bobby really was doing was copying me copying him.' He had Bobby rehearse every least gesture, repeat every brief speech anywhere from twenty to 100 times. Bobby grew accustomed to the game of mime. When asked how he knew how to sob heartbrokenly over the death of a pet snake, Bobby exploded with brief indignation: 'Well, he *showed* me. What's the producer for?'

Reed contends 'a child of eight can't act. I wasn't looking for an exhibitionist. Adults have habitual gestures and defences. A good actor must take something away, lose part of himself before he can create a role. But with the right sort of child, such as Bobby, there is nothing in the way. There is absolutely no resistance. He will do everything you tell him.' Reed deliberately used the child's body to express emotion. 'Adults are controlled, they hold their arms still, but if a boy is upset he twiddles a string, arches his back, twists his legs.' Various devices were used by Reed to achieve natural expressiveness in Bobby. In the opening scenes Bobby leans over a banister, his face supposedly warm with admiration as Baines stood in the lobby below him. Although Bobby knew that he liked Baines, he did not know how to *show* affection and his face remained cold. So Reed hired a magician and his tricks entranced Bobby while the cameras caught on his face the rapt smile that starts off the film.

With a little boy of short memory and no histrionic training, Reed knew he would have to create a heavily-cut film. In the finished version of ninety-four minutes' duration, smooth as it seems to the uninitiated, there is a total of 1,040 separate splices. Although the audience thinks of Bobby as an integral part of the entire drama, actually he plays most of his scenes alone. Sometimes he is seen walking beside Baines. The coats and pants of Baines, however, are Carol Reed's.

Because every scene involved remembering a cue, expression, action as well as words, the longest line Bobby was ever given to say without a cue made up a grand total of fourteen words: 'Funny, Julie working at the embassy and all the time she was your niece.'

Because the film tells a tale of adultery, madness and violent death, everyone was concerned with how much of it the eight-year-old boy was to know, how it would affect him. The studio word went out that the 'secret' of the plot had to be kept from Bobby. Actually in the early sequences on location, Reed merely told Bobby to run, wave, laugh. Gradually just before each scene, Reed unfolded more of the story to the boy. Halfway through Bobby was given the script to read. Bobby did not witness the filming of the adult drama, but he did see all the rushes.[8]

After *The Fallen Idol*, Bobby Henrey was reported to have signed a £30,000 contract with Korda to make four more films before 1952. He retired in 1950, after *The Wonder Kid*, at the grand old age of eleven.

From its opening credit sequence rolled over a plucking zither to that final, bleak long shot of figures on the road stretching away from the cemetery, *The Third Man* still conjures a persistent *frisson* of pleasure. Like all great films, it remains timeless in its appeal and despite Greene's great body of work over six decades, *The Third Man* probably remains his most popular quoted work. Which is so ironic for what had begun merely as a hastily scribbled paragraph on the back of an envelope, developed some twenty years later into a treatment and finally honed to its eventual perfection by sheer collaboration. It was, of course, Greene's first, and only, fully worked original screenplay. 'It was never written to be read but only to be seen,' Greene reminds us.

In *The Man Who Could Work Miracles*, Karol Kulik writes:

> The project derived from a suggestion by Alex Kòrda. Ever since the end of the war Korda had been gathering ideas for a film about the aftermath of war in a European city. At first he envisaged it as a comedy set in Vienna and starring Cary Grant. Then R.C. Sherriff was hired to adapt Paul Tabori's novel *Epitaph for Europe* with the prospects that Ian Dalrymple might produce and Spencer Tracy might play in the film. Finally Korda tried his idea on (Carol) Reed and Greene over dinner.[9]

To begin with, Greene offered Korda the germ of an idea contained on an envelope flap: 'I had paid my last farewell to Harry a week ago, when his coffin was lowered into the frozen February ground, so that it was with incredulity that I saw him pass by, without a sign of recognition, among a host of strangers in the Strand.'[10] An opening paragraph penned in the past and with, up to that moment, nowhere to go.

What Korda really wanted was a film about the four-power occupation of Vienna. In 1948 Vienna was still divided into American, Russian, French and British zones, while the Inner

City was administered by each power in turn for a month and patrolled day and night by groups of four soldiers drawn from the four powers. It was this complex situation which Korda wanted put on film, but he was prepared all the same to let me pursue the tracks of Harry. So to Vienna I went.[11]

That was in the winter of 1948 and for about a fortnight in the city, Greene found nothing but frustration. Inspiration obstinately refused to come, when about three days before he was due to leave he lunched with a young British intelligence officer who told him not only about the city's complex underground sewer system but also of a penicillin racket that operated in Vienna. That, combined with the researches he had made into the workings of the four-power occupation, visits to the Josefstadt Theatre, the home of an old servant of his mother's in the Russian zone and drinking in the Oriental night-club (which he arranged, for effect, to have raided the night he took the novelist Elizabeth Bowen who was lecturing in Vienna as a guest of the British Council) were the necessary sparks – 'I had my film'.

Greene wrote the treatment in Italy before returning to Vienna in the spring with Carol Reed to work it up into a screenplay. That three-month gap had seen some considerable changes in the city, much to Greene's initial embarrassment; ruins had been cleared away, decent food was being served in restaurants and 'over and over again, I found myself saying to Carol Reed, "But I assure you Vienna was like that – three months ago." '.

Greene's preliminary treatment, eventually published as a novella in its own right a year or so after the film's release, is now worth a closer examination if only to signpost the switches that would come about in its gestation.

The text is a first-person narrative by a British military policeman, Colonel Calloway. Rollo Martins, a British writer of American westerns under the pen-name Buck Dexter, has arrived in Vienna at the invitation of his old school chum Harry Lime only to hear that Lime has been run over in an accident and is being buried that day. Naturally upset by the sudden death of his friend Martins gets talking to Calloway who reveals that Lime was 'about the worst racketeer who ever made a dirty living in this city'.[12] Martins is incredulous, completely dismissive of Calloway's charges and determined to prove him wrong.

At his hotel, Martins meets a British Council official Crabbin who, having mistaken him for an altogether more esoteric novelist of the same surname, has fixed him up with lecture engagements as well as a room for a week. This is just the lifeline that Martins, desperately short of cash, needs to continue his own investigations into Lime's death. Crabbin also tells him about a girlfriend of Harry's, Anna Schmidt, an actress at the Josefstadt Theatre (whom Martins had glimpsed earlier at the funeral). Martins is contacted by Kurtz, a friend of Lime's who was with him when he died. When they meet the next day, Kurtz explains the circumstances of Lime's death which was also witnessed by another friend, an American called Cooler. Martins tells Kurtz he wants to clear Lime's name and thereby discredit the police.

At the theatre Anna tells him that Harry's own doctor was also very swiftly at the scene of the accident, which took place on the road across from Harry's own apartment building. The doctor, Winkler, gives Martins his own very guarded account of the accident. At Lime's apartment, the porter Herr Koch tells his own version of the aftermath of the accident which he had observed from the window; how three men had carried the body to the house. Two men and the driver of the car, Martins spells out? No, the driver stayed where he was. So, a mysterious third man! Martins confronts Calloway with the new 'evidence' and his theory that Lime was murdered. Martins meets Cooler who vehemently discounts the possibility that Lime was involved in any racket. Martins tells Cooler about Koch's account which had never been given at the inquest.

When Anna and Martins go to see Koch again, there is a throng outside the building – Koch has been found murdered. A child tells of how a 'foreigner' had been seen earlier at the apartment block. Anna and Martins split up with Martins returning to the hotel, where he is whisked off in a military-style truck. Martins thinks he is being arrested. In fact, he is being taken to one of Crabbin's literary gatherings, which becomes a shambles as confusion about Martins's literary *alter ego* is further compounded. When he spots a military policeman, he panics and races off to hide and is only reluctantly persuaded out. With Calloway again, Martins is finally made aware of Lime's criminality – his organization of the penicillin racket, in particular the watering down of penicillin (to make it go further) which has led to the death of men and children. When Martins tells Anna the truth about Lime, she is singularly unmoved – 'I loved a man . . . I told you – a man doesn't alter because you find out more about him. He's still the same man.'

Calloway then details an attempted kidnap of Anna by the Russians, on the basis that she was carrying false papers (pertaining to Austrian citizenship when she was, in truth, Hungarian). Martins tells Calloway he thinks he has seen Lime, albeit fleetingly, alive and well, and that he must have disappeared into a kiosk down to the city's sewers. Via Kurtz, Martins sets up a meeting with Lime at the Great Wheel to get Harry's version of the events. His old friend is outwardly friendly but chilling. He confirms that it was he who put the Russians on to Anna – 'the price of living in this zone is service', that it is Harbin (a double-agent in the racket) in his (Lime's) grave. He also spells out his contempt for mankind generally in justifying his money-making business. He makes some veiled threats towards Martins yet fliply suggests that his old friend might like to be cut in on the racket.

As Lime hurries away from the rendezvous, Martins calls after him: 'Don't trust me Harry' but Lime is too far away for the words to carry. Calloway draws up a plan to use Martins as a now-willing decoy to bring Lime into the open so he can be arrested. The idea is he will be lured to a café near an opening of the sewers, so he can take Martins, ostensibly still wanted by the police and without friends, back with him 'for old times' sake'. The plan initially misfires. When Lime arrives, none of Calloway's men is in position and Martins is on the phone which makes Lime suspicious. He bolts back down into the sewer, pursued by Calloway's men and Martins who, himself, finally shoots a trapped Lime. After Lime's second funeral, Martins and Anna leave, wordlessly, arm in arm.

In Vienna, Greene and Reed worked on the script – 'that is to say, I would do a section which I would hand to him while he was lying in bed and then we'd discuss it later'. His treatment, Greene explains, was:

Never intended to be more than the raw material for a picture . . . for me it is impossible to write a film play without first writing a story. A film depends on more than plot; it depends on a certain measure of characterization, on mood and atmosphere, and these seem impossible to capture for the first time in the dull shorthand of a conventional treatment . . . the reader will notice many differences between the story and the film and he should not imagine these changes were forced on an unwilling author: as likely as not they were suggested by the author. The film in fact is better than the story because it is in this case the finished state of the story.[13]

Some of these differences came about directly out of the close collaboration with Reed; some arose from the involvement in the project of the American producer, David O. Selznick.

Selznick, who for twenty years had produced a string of hit films including *Gone with the Wind*, *Rebecca*, and *Duel in the Sun*, stopped making films in 1948 because he was, in his own words, 'tired'. Also as the sole stockowner in his company he was getting increasingly concerned about his debt to the bank which stood at about $12,000,000 and was rising. He believed that by better exploitation of his backlog of films around the world, he could take the sting out of the debt. It would also be combining business with pleasure as he needed a break from the Hollywood grind. In fact, it was going to take a full five years before Selznick could repay those loans in full and a further four years – until 1957 – when he would bounce back as a solo producer again with his remake of *A Farewell to Arms*.

During those years I learned much about foreign distribution, about foreign production and about the tastes of foreign audiences; and although I had always tried to make pictures for a world market, at last I fully realized the necessity for a world viewpoint in the making of Hollywood films. I learned too something of foreign production methods, and came to have an even greater respect for the talents of motion-picture-makers abroad. Consistent with this and as part of the plans for the liquidation of my company and its debts, we devised what has since come to be known as co-production; and since it was neither easy nor my desire to invest money in films in those times, we invested certain foreign rights of my pictures in acquiring Western hemisphere rights in these co-productions.[14]

Korda struck a deal with Selznick by which Selznick, in exchange for the film's American distribution rights, would provide some financing – 'I think it took care of Joseph Cotten and Orson Welles's valets,' opined Carol Reed – and arrange the stars. It was also part of the deal that the director had to consult with Selznick about the script at least sixty days before shooting began. So Reed and Greene struck out west to California. Greene's account of those meetings is hilarious.

'I don't like the title,' Selznick told them bluntly at their first encounter. 'Listen, boys, who the hell is going to a film called *The Third Man*?' Greene replied that he thought it was a simple title, easily remembered. 'You can do better than that, Graham. You are a writer. A good writer. I'm no writer, but you are. Now, what we want – it's not right, mind you, of course it's not right, I'm not saying it's right, but then I'm no writer and you are, what we want is something like *Night in Vienna*, a title which will bring them in.'

And so it went on with Selznick expounding his views and prejudices about the script and story at an increasingly more bizarre series of conferences. For example: 'There's something I don't understand in this script, Graham. Why the hell does Harry Lime . . .?' and went on to describe some 'extraordinary action' on Lime's part. Greene told him that Lime did not do what Selznick had described. 'Christ, boys, I'm thinking of a different script.'[15]

Greene told me: 'Luckily, the contract didn't say if we had to accept what Selznick suggested. It was a very gruelling experience. There was a secretary making notes the whole time and, because Selznick seemed so plausible I was continually thinking, "well, my God, perhaps he's right". Carol would see that I was weakening and swiftly jump in with, "Graham and I will discuss that between us afterwards". The result of those meetings was about forty pages of notes. Later, Korda told Carol to stuff them in a drawer and pay no attention to them.' They could not however, fob him off completely and, were, inevitably, blitzed with a barrage of famous Selznick memos. Typical was one sent via his foreign co-ordinator, Betty Goldsmith:

I have read complete September 20 script of 'Third Man' very carefully and have made detailed notes on it. However, not yet

compared script with prior draft, also with my notes . . .
However, in advance of referring to this comparison, I can tell
you the following:
(1) It is basically a very good script and in Reed's hands should
make a very good picture.
(2) It is, as Korda said, a great improvement over the prior
draft: for this in modesty, I can take bows, because most of
these improvements are due to their following a large percen-
tage of my changes . . .
(3) Despite the improvements, it is not satisfactory from the
standpoint of the price of the picture or its acceptability to
American audiences . . .
(4) I am convinced that Reed has no familiarity whatsoever
with our rights in the matter; and therefore has seen fit to take
only those changes which suit him and Greene from the
standpoints of English story-tellers, making the picture for
English audiences. I therefore urgently repeat my prior sugges-
tion that you make . . . Reed personally familiar and in detail,
with our rights under the contract, without further delay . . .
(5) It is absolutely essential that there be an American writer on
the job at once . . . who can make the dialogue acceptable from
an American standpoint, even if it is not as good as it should be.
Presently the dialogue is in many cases so ludicrous, from a
standpoint of American characters, that the picture would be
kidded to death by our gallery audiences . . .

I'm certainly not going to insist upon lots of little detailed
things with a man of Reed's understanding and ability; but on
the other hand, I certainly am going to insist upon certain basic
things on which I spent many, many long hours wrangling in
order to get Reed's and Greene's agreement; thus, for instance,
the script is written as though England were the sole occupying
power of Vienna, with some Russians vaguely in the distance;
with an occasional Frenchman wandering around; and with,
most important from the standpoint of this criticism, the only
American being an occasional soldier who apparently is merely
part of the British occupying force, plus the heavy (Lime), plus
the hero (who is Canadian in some scenes and American in
others), plus another American heavy named Tyler. And, just
to make matters worse, the American hero, apparently, is
completely subject to the orders and instructions of the British

authorities, and behaves as though there were no American whatsoever among the occupying powers, nor any American authority, and indeed as far as this figure is concerned, there is none. It would be little short of disgraceful on our part as Americans if we tolerated this nonsensical handling of the four-power occupation of Vienna . . . I went through this at the greatest length and in the greatest detail with Reed and with Greene, and come hell or high water, I simply will not stand for it in its present form . . .

I am sure that Korda told them I knew my business, and that they could count on getting intelligent and helpful suggestions from me; but to follow what they saw only fit to follow . . . I spent countless hours going through with Reed and Greene, and getting agreement on, the treatment of the whole background of Vienna today, to give the picture size, and more importantly . . . to give it understandability, from the standpoint of American audiences. We laid out in the greatest detail scenes of the changing of authority from one occupying power to another, with the four powers in turn, changing in the chair; and in order that this might not be extraneous material, we went to the greatest pains to make this material background of the personal story, and to tie it in with the personal story. We frankly made the Russians the heavies, in pursuit of the girl. All of this has been eliminated, even what was in the original script. We must insist upon its return, for patriotic reasons, for purposes of the picture's importance and size . . . and for purposes of understanding of what on earth is going on in Vienna that these things can be happening? As it is there is not one person in a thousand among our audiences who would even be able to follow the background of the picture, the knowledge of which is absolutely essential to the film's acceptability and even a limited popular success.[16]

This overbearing, sanctimonious, repetitive and tiresomely chauvinistic missive from a once all-powerful Hollywood mogul seems to have been given short shrift by the British contingent. No American writers were assigned, the American presence in Vienna was not emphasized and as for Selznick's insistent, 'patriotic' desire for Russian 'heavies', there was even less of a Russian influence in the film than there had been in Greene's original treatment.

In their essay 'Looking for the Third Man', Judy Adamson and Philip Stratford develop the point:

> This can best be seen in the episode where the Russians try to kidnap Anna, which, Greene tells us 'was eliminated at a fairly late stage because it was not satisfactorily tied into the screenplay'. Another reason Greene gives for the omission of this 'perfectly plausible' incident was that it threatened to turn the film into a propagandist picture. Greene: 'We had no desire to move people's political emotions, we wanted to entertain them, to frighten them a little, to make them laugh.' On the surface this may seem a plausible explanation. It certainly is a non-political one. But is Greene not a little disingenuous when he would have us believe that it was possible to set a film in post-war Vienna, a British and American co-production at that, and keep politics out. We might speculate that he and Reed softened the Russian image in the film as a direct counter-reaction to Selznick's stormy Cold War attitude.[17]

It is worth mentioning here that Reed and Greene's single-mindedness did get some sort of come uppance at a later stage with the American publication in book form of Greene's story. Adamson and Stratford tell us how it was both 'heavily and purposefully reworked' from the original. 'Not only were many of Greene's acid observations on American mores expurgated but, more surprisingly, most of his nasty references to the Russians were also eliminated . . . the rewrite not only emasculated the story politically but did some injury to it artistically.'[18] So the Russians were 'toned down' (a kind of poetic justice in view of the finished script, I suppose) and the Americans 'prettied up'. Adamson and Stratford's clear concern is that this 'corrupt American *Third Man*' should have had such an 'unexpectedly wide currency' for, as they point out, both the French and Russian translations were derived from the American version.

As the script evolved and the casting became clearer, so the changes between treatment and final film became more understandable. In the story both Martins and Lime were British subjects. Reed was, though, desperately keen to have the American actor Orson Welles to play Lime.

I told Orson there was a wonderful part in the film for him. He asked to read it, but I said: 'Look, the script's not ready yet, but I'm sure you'll like it even though you don't come on until halfway through.' 'I'd much rather come in two-thirds of the way through,' he replied. By this time Selznick wanted me to do *Tess of the D'Urbevilles* which we both thought pretty bad, so I asked him to have some work done to it and meanwhile to let me go ahead with *The Third Man* since it was something we could knock off quick. I said I wanted Orson Welles and Joseph Cotten (as Martins), who I knew was under contract to Selznick, as was Valli (who would play Anna). 'Cotten and Valli, you can have,' he said, 'but you can't have Orson.' I asked why knowing very well that Orson wasn't under contract to him and that he preferred me to use someone who was.[19]

That 'someone', Selznick's preference for the role of the suave, slippery, amoral penicillin racketeer, was none other than Noël Coward. On the face of it a quite extraordinary notion and yet, with hindsight, perhaps not so bizarre as all that. One can imagine Coward dealing rather well with Greene's sly aphorisms uttered atop the Great Wheel – 'in these days, old man, nobody thinks in terms of human beings. Governments don't, why should we? They talk of the people and the proletariat. I talk about the suckers and the mugs . . .' However it is a shade fruitless to speculate about how Coward would have dealt with probably the film's most famous invention, the cuckoo-clock speech uttered by Lime:

When you make up your mind (Lime tells Martins) send me a message – I'll meet you any place, any time, and when we do meet, old man, it's you I want to see, not the police . . . And don't be so gloomy . . . After all, it's not that awful – you know what the fellow said: In Italy for thirty years under the Borgias they had warfare, terror, murder, bloodshed – and they produced Michelangelo, Leonardo da Vinci and the Renaissance. In Switzerland, they had brotherly love, five hundred years of democracy and peace, and what did that produce? The cuckoo-clock. So long, Holly.[20]

It was, of course, of Welles's own conjuring.
Coward, who ten years later would make a marvellous creation

of Hawthorne, the spy recruiter in the final Reed–Greene collaboration, *Our Man in Havana*, was, thought Reed, 'a disastrous' idea for Lime. 'When I started to film, Selznick was still going on about Noël. Korda didn't care, however, so in the end I got Orson.' With Cotten as Martins, that character became American too, (having been Canadian in an earlier draft) with a change of Christian name. Greene had chosen Rollo, 'an absurd name' to contrast with the 'sturdy Dutch' of Martins but Cotten complained to him that Rollo would be considered 'sissy' in America. Greene substituted Holly, derived from 'that figure of fun, the nineteenth-century American poet Thomas Holley Chivers'. After that, said Cotten, 'I stopped complaining for fear he'd change it to Pansy.'

With Lime as the principal American villain, and perhaps in slight deference to Selznick's frenzied wishes, Greene/Reed changed another US heavy (Tyler, Cooler of the treatment) to Popescu, a Rumanian. Anna underwent a veritable evolution – from an Hungarian with false Austrian papers, to Estonian and finally Czechoslovakian, still with false papers. Mr Kurtz became Baron Kurtz; Dr Winkler, Dr Winkel; Calloway was reduced to Major from Colonel and was no longer the narrator and western writer 'Buck Dexter' was no longer confused with Benjamin Dexter (based on E.M. Forster) – 'the confusion of identities would have been impossible, even if Carol Reed had not rightly objected to a rather far-fetched situation involving a great deal of explanation that increased the length of a film already far too long'.[21]

A particularly intriguing change that was mooted and then scrapped was to turn the British Council official, Crabbin, into two characters, Captain Carter and Captain Tombs, as vehicles for the comedy duo, Basil Radford and Naunton Wayne. They made at least eight films together, most memorably as the imperturbable cricket-obsessed Englishmen abroad in Hitchcock's *The Lady Vanishes* and then two years later, in Reed's own *Night Train to Munich*. But with a large cast already, Crabbin finally came full circle and was portrayed brilliantly by Wilfrid Hyde White.

Selznick's obvious concern about a wide audience's 'understandability' of the complicated Vienna politics must have been appeased by the decision – possibly Korda's, more likely Reed's –

to tack an opening narration on to the film. This was added three months after the completion of principal photography and in the final stages of editing. In rather jaunty tones, belonging to Reed himself, the four-power occupation is explained as simply as possible and the character of Holly Martins introduced – 'There he was, happy as a lark . . . and without a cent.'

Now Selznick, when it came to organizing the American release version of the film, believed that the unexplained, unidentified narrator would be too confusing for the audience and so the voice of Joseph Cotten was substituted for Reed's and the final words of the narration were suitably changed: 'Anyway, I was dead broke when I got to Vienna. A close pal of mine had gotten me a job doing some publicity work for some kind of charity he was running. Anyway down I came to old Vienna, happy as a lark and without a dime.' It was not an appropriate change, argues the critic Lynette Carpenter: 'Although Reed might have used Cotten, who was under contract to Selznick, had Cotten still been available, he and Greene turned necessity to their advantage in composing a speech that would set the proper tone for the film. As a result, the speech seems out of character for Holly Martins; it is too glib, too ironic even for an older Martins.'[22]

The single, most dramatic change wrought between treatment and 'finished state of the story' was, of course, the ending. It was the cause of 'one of the few major disputes' between Reed and Greene, who concedes that Reed was:

> proved triumphantly right . . . I held the view that an entertainment of this kind was too light an affair to carry the weight of an unhappy ending. Reed, on his side, felt that my ending – indeterminate as it was, with no words spoken, Holly joining the girl in silence and walking away with her from the cemetery where her lover Harry was buried – would strike the audience who had just seen Harry's death and burial as unpleasantly cynical. I was only half-convinced: I was afraid few people would wait in their seats during the girl's long walk from the graveside towards Holly, and the others would leave the cinema under the impression that the ending was still going to be as conventional as my suggested ending of boy joining girl. I had not given enough credit to the mastery of Reed's direction.[23]

Ralph Morgan *(centre)* and Heather Angel *(foreground)* in *Orient Express* (NATIONAL FILM ARCHIVE)

Rene Ray and John Mills in *The Green Cockatoo* (NATIONAL FILM ARCHIVE)

Laurence Olivier and Vivien Leigh shoot a scene for *21 Days* at the Kursaal in Southend. Note the man holding screen over the microphone to prevent the roar of the wind (LONDON FILMS/KOBAL COLLECTION)

Mervyn Johns *(centre)* confronts helmeted Basil Sydney in *Went The Day Well?* (KOBAL COLLECTION)

Veronica Lake and Alan Ladd in *This Gun For Hire* (KOBAL COLLECTION)

Ray Milland and Marjorie Reynolds in *Ministry Of Fear* (KOBAL COLLECTION)

Charles Boyer and Lauren Bacall in *The Confidential Agent* (KOBAL COLLECTION)

Richard Attenborough and Michael Redgrave are put to torture in *The Man Within* (KOBAL COLLECTION)

Richard Attenborough and Carol Marsh in *Brighton Rock* (KOBAL COLLECTION)

Henry Fonda and Ward Bond in *The Fugitive* (KOBAL COLLECTION)

Bobby Henrey looks on at Sonia Dresdel in *The Fallen Idol* (KOBAL COLLECTION)

Michele Morgan and Ralph Richardson caught out in *The Fallen Idol* (KOBAL COLLECTION)

Ralph Richardson struggles with Sonia Dresdel in *The Fallen Idol* (KOBAL COLLECTION)

Orson Welles as Harry Lime trapped in the Vienna sewers in *The Third Man* (LONDON FILMS)

Alida Valli and Joseph Cotten in *The Third Man*
(KOBAL COLLECTION)

Joseph Cotten *(left)* and Orson Welles in *The Third Man* (KOBAL COLLECTION)

According to Reed:

> At one time it was thought that every picture must end with an
> embrace so that the audience could go out happy. A picture
> should end as it has to. I don't think anything in life ends 'right'.
> Graham wanted Joseph Cotten to overtake Valli in the car, then
> the film would finish with the couple walking down the road. I
> insisted that she pass him by. Selznick, although nice and
> appreciative about the picture when he saw it, said, 'Jesus,
> couldn't we make a shot where the girl gets together with the
> fella? It was in the original script.' I told him we'd chucked it
> out. The whole point with the Valli character in that film is that
> she'd experienced a fatal love.

With the new beginning and end, the film ran pretty much the
course of the original story with some verbal embellishments and
a host of marvellous directorial nuances. Getting rid of the
first-person process helped the narrative flow. In the treatment,
Calloway was not only reporting his encounters with Martins but
also reconstructing scenes from Martins's own accounts. Just
when there is the danger of cliché creeping in, the writer and
director puncture it. Martins tells Calloway that he has discovered
there is a 'third man' and there is a likelihood that Lime has been
murdered, saying: 'I'm going to get to the bottom of it.' Calloway
retorts pompously: 'Death's at the bottom of everything, Martins
leave death to the professionals.' The sting is swiftly taken out of
such an obvious cop-comment with Martins firing back: 'Mind if I
use that line in my next western?'

The first main addition is a purely cinematic moment – a long
shot on a bridge of the accident witnesses/conspirators together
with an unidentified figure – visual confirmation of a 'third man',
followed swiftly by a close-up of the apartment-block porter
(named Koch in the treatment) turning round at his window to
find himself face to face with what we assume to be his murderer.
The shot is in fact held a little too long for my liking, with the
inevitable change of expression from passivity to stark terror. It is
perhaps the film's only false cinematic moment.

Reed also draws more tension from Martins and Anna
discovering the porter's death. They are recognized in the throng
by a plump little child who had seen Martins earlier with the

porter at the apartment and they, fearing they will be linked with
the porter's death, take off followed by the shrill child and a posse
of neighbours. No sooner have we had time to draw breath from
this sequence than Martins is kidnapped and taken on a hair-
raising drive – he thinks to his death – before being deposited at his
lecture date.

As in the treatment, the lecture gives Greene a chance to indulge
in some light relief, sniping at literary pretentiousness. The scene,
however, ends differently in the film. One of the chief heavies,
Popescu, arrives flanked by henchmen and they give chase to
Martins as he makes his escape. Then back with Calloway, he is
finally enlightened as to Lime's racket but even such a grim
catalogue of misery is leavened with some humour. Calloway asks
for a slide show to be set up for visual evidence of Lime's dealings
and the first slide is a water buffalo.

One of the film's great moments is our first glimpse of Lime,
his face lit up just for a moment as he lurks in a doorway near
Anna's apartment, a cat perching on his shoes. Said Reed:

> I was worried about finding Harry in that doorway: I didn't
> want Cotten just to pass by and see him because then the
> audiences wouldn't know who the man in the doorway was.
> Before this, Cotten brings Valli flowers. I placed a cat on her
> bed whom Cotten tries to get to play with the string around the
> gift. But the cat just turns and jumps off the bed and goes out
> through the window. While Cotten has been trying to get the
> cat to play, I had him say: 'Bad-tempered cat.' Then I worked in
> a line for Valli: 'He only liked Harry.' We next look out of the
> window, see a shadowy figure come down the street and go
> into a doorway. As far as we know it might be anyone. By
> going over to him and playing with his lace, the cat establishes it
> is Harry.

Cotten leaves Anna's flat and believes he is being followed:
'Come out, come out, whoever you are?' he cries. The noise
causes someone at a window high above him to pull back the
curtain letting that shaft of light fall across the square on to the
semi-mocking features of Welles as Lime. Reed added: 'We used
so many cats; one in Vienna, running down the street; another in
the studio on the bed, another to play with the lace. What was

difficult was to get the cat to walk up to it.' The trick, said Reed, was to use sardines!

Getting Welles to Vienna also seems to have been something of a trick. In Michael Korda's *Charmed Lives*, Reed is reported to have said to Alex Korda: 'He *wants* to [play the part], Alex, but on the other hand he's bloody-minded about it. He's stuck there in Italy with a film company, doing *Othello* or *Macbeth* (in fact, *Macbeth*) I forget which and half the time they're out of money and the actors have to beg to eat and none of them can get away because there isn't enough money to buy tickets with. Every once in a while he descends on Rome to scare up a little more capital, but when you talk to him about a part, he simply vanishes.'[24]

Recalling Welles's involvement some years later, Reed said:

He was difficult only about the starting-date, telling me how busy he was with this and that. So I said, 'Look, we're going on location for five weeks. Any week – give us two days' notice – we'll be ready for you, and give me one week out of seven in the studio.' He kept to it. He came straight off the train in Vienna one morning, and we did his first shot by nine o'clock. 'Jeez,' he said, 'this is the way to make pictures.' He walked across the Prater, said two lines to Cotten and then I said, 'Go back to the hotel, have breakfast; we're going into the sewers and we'll send for you.'

'Great! Wonderful!' Comes down into the sewers then and says, 'Carol, I can't play this part!'

'What's the matter?'

'I can't do it; I can't work in a sewer. I come from California! My throat! I'm so cold!'

'Look, Orson, in the time it's taking us to talk about this, you can do the shot. All you do is stand there, look off, see some police after you, turn and run away.'

'Carol, look, get someone else to play this. I cannot work under such conditions.'

'Orson, Orson, we're lit for you. Just stand there.'

'All right, but do it quick!' Then he looks off, turns away and runs off into the sewers. All of a sudden I hear a voice shouting, 'Don't cut the cameras! Don't cut the cameras! I'm coming back.' He runs back through the whole river, stands underneath a cascade over his head (all this out of camera range, mind you!)

and does all sorts of things so that he came away absolutely dripping.

'How was that?'

'Wonderful, marvellous.'

'Okay, I'll be back at the hotel. Call me when you need me.'

With Orson everything has to be a drama. But there were no arguments of any sort at all.[25]

Welles, who appeared without make-up for the first and only time in a film role, reportedly detested the character of Lime: 'I hate Harry Lime, he has no passion, he is cold; he is Lucifer, the fallen angel.'[26]

Greene, agreeing that Welles 'gave a wonderful bravura performance and the lines he wrote in about the cuckoo-clock were very good', puts to rest oft-held claims (including one by Welles himself) that Welles wrote all his own dialogue. A glance at the published treatment confirms this. What might have been interpreted as Welles-style aphorisms, in view of the instant mythology of the cuckoo-clock speech, are plainly all Greene. If there was ever the danger that Lime could for one moment have been considered a rather misunderstood villain, after the blackly comic Big Wheel encounter with Martins, his evil is underscored, though not overplayed, in a telling scene at a children's hospital where, without any dialogue, we realize the extent of his crime.

And so, into the sewers for the final chase and shoot-out. An eight-minute sequence – 'too long, I thought', Greene told me – which gave Krasker's mobile, black-and-white photography full rein. As with the treatment, there is a discreetness about the final *coup de grâce*: Lime's hand coming up through the grate, grasping for elusive freedom (in fact, Reed's own hand shot on location before Welles arrived – the preceding shot was done with the actor in the studio because in Vienna there was no staircase leading directly up to a drain) and then slithering back down. He accepts death with a nod of recognition and resignation. Harry's second funeral and bleak aftermath follow with the famous final long shot held for fully a minute.

No discussion about the content and impact of this film, which achieved the best of all possible worlds – a *succès d'estime* and a box-office success – can be complete without mention of Anton Karas's zither music. Carol Reed found this unlikely superstar late on while on location in Vienna. Apparently the composer Richard Addinsell (best known for the Warsaw Concerto from *Dangerous Moonlight*) had been lined up and had even, according to an insider, 'written some great dreary suite'. Reed said:

> I used to store props in a studio outside the city. Whilst the boys were unloading, I'd go to a store to get carafes of wine for them. Nearby there was a tiny beer and sausage restaurant with a courtyard in which this fellow played a zither for coins. I'd never heard a zither before, thought it rather attractive and wondered whether we could use a single instrument throughout the film, especially since the zither is so typical of Vienna. I got Karas to come back to my hotel one night, where he played for about twenty minutes. I then brought a recording of that back to the studio to see if the music fought against the dialogue – as some did – but a good deal of it worked well. Karas then came to London to live. I had a moviola with a dupe of the film so that we could match his playing against portions of the action. One night, he asked me to come back and listen to a new tune he'd done, what came to be called 'The Third Man Theme'. 'Why haven't you played that before?' I said. 'I haven't played it for fifteen years,' he answered, 'because when you play in a café, nobody stops to listen . . . this tune takes a lot out of your fingers. I prefer playing, "Wien, Wien", the sort of thing one can play all night while eating sausages at the same time.' It turned out he'd composed the tune himself but had nearly forgotten it. What's driven other zither players mad (they can never figure out how it's done) is that he played the tune, then with an earphone rerecorded it, adding thirds. In the ordinary way, no zither player could do it.[27]

One can gauge the sort of reaction to the music from an ecstatic Selznick memo of 25 November 1949 to his colleagues in the States:

> Cannot commence to tell you sensation caused by Karas's zither music for 'The Third Man'. It is the rage of England and has already sold more record copies than any other record in entire history of record business in England. It is widest-played dance music in England. It is biggest single success of film, and ads

here use 'Hear Harry Lime Theme' etc. in type dwarfing all other billing. It is one of those unpredictable, tremendous sensations that I cannot expect any of you to understand who have not been here. Entirely unrelated newspaper articles and editorials, even on politics, continually refer to it. Inevitably, this success will be repeated America if we are prepared for it. We should be able to make a fortune out of this music.[28]

The chorus of praise that greeted the film when it opened in England and, later, America was not repeated when it bowed in its 'native' Vienna. The communist evening paper *Der Abend* splashed with 'A Cultural Disgrace – Is Vienna a Robbers' Den? – A Dirty Slander on Vienna and the Viennese'. Greene was attacked as an 'author notorious for his utter trash and who, in collaboration with Carol Reed, went wild at the expense of this defenceless city'. The *Neues Oesterreich* took a similarly mindless approach, criticizing the film-makers for not giving credit to the real heroes of the film – the stand-ins who did all the dirty work, particularly in the sewers. One Otto Schusser, a Viennese butcher doubling for Welles, and three unnamed stand-ins for Joseph Cotten were cited as performing above and beyond etc. with due acclaim.

The Third Man won a host of awards, best British Film of the Year and the Cannes Grand Prix among them, but, surprisingly garnered just one American Oscar – for cinematography. The main Academy Award winners of 1949 were *All the King's Men* (film and actor), *The Heiress* (actress), and *A Letter to Three Wives* (direction). It may have had something to do with the fact that a year earlier, in 1948, was Olivier's British *Hamlet* triumph.

Aside from craft awards, it would have been difficult to indicate acting categories in the film for it is essentially an ensemble piece, a clever, perfectly matched/contrasted jigsaw of performances. The only star I have not mentioned so far is Trevor Howard as Calloway, a performance particularly loved by Greene. In fact, one critic has suggested that Howard's is 'still perhaps the most completely realized portrait' in the film: 'It is built up, detail by detail, nothing superfluous, nothing exaggerated, until a whole man is put before us . . .' As for Howard himself, rarely keen to talk about his work, his only comment about the film is: 'I never see a film until it's absolutely complete. I remember that my old friend Bernard Lee (who plays Sgt Paine) and I once went to see a rough cut of *The Third Man* and came out in tears thinking how terrible it was. So one can never judge.'

Of the consecutive collaborations, Greene still prefers *The Fallen Idol*, 'more of a writer's film, certainly Carol's high-point, I think'.

And he revealed that at a cultural forum held in Paris early in 1983 he had met the American director Francis Ford Coppola who told him that he was in possession of a four-hour, uncut version of *The Third Man*: 'Now that I long to see,' said Greene.

I alluded at the beginning of this chapter to the film's durability. This quality is best summed up by Ivan Butler:

> . . . it is the overall picture that haunts the mind: a city, a world, a concept of life itself in defeat. Even the zither music, cheapened by over-exposure and by attachment to a dismal television series (with Michael Rennie as a resurrected Lime, completely transformed into a sort of latter-day Robin Hood), renews its magical aptness when seen again accompanying the film for which it was composed. The story of black-marketeering, corruption, shabby compromise, bitterness and death, relentlessly holding though it is, seems itself a background to the battered city, with its bare, gimcrack offices erected in the midst of ruined Baroque palaces. With every viewing the power and stature of this great moving picture increases.[29]

An intriguing footnote to the film comes in a *Daily Mail* report from Berlin, some nine months after the film's release in Britain:

> All day long earnest, bespectacled young men keep going to the Hotel Krausler, in the little town of Goslar. Most of them carry manuscripts, and all of them ask for 'Meester Greene'. And when the phone rings it is usually for Meester Greene . . . Greene . . . is staying at this border town between the Soviet Zone and Western Germany, and German's propaganda tiddlers have found it out. He is there for ten days, gathering material for another 'Third Man' film, based on the army of the homeless who daily cross over from the Soviet Zone. But so far work has been held up by this constant stream of Germans

trying to foist on to him every sort of 'anti' story – anti-Russian, anti-British, anti-Western Allies, anti-socialist. 'Anyway,' Greene told me tonight, 'the film which Carol Reed and I will shoot in the enchanting Harz Mountains will be entirely non-political. We shall tell only in terms of human experience and suffering the story of Germany's 8,000,000 refugees.'

Ideas for a 'Third Man' successor, shot in Germany, developed out of Carol Reed's visit two months ago to Berlin. In two or three weeks' time he will join Greene in Goslar to work out this multilingual film, in which German and British actors are to play leading roles. Graham Greene will talk to British and German officials, visit refugee camps, and probably make a trip through the Russian Zone to Berlin – 'but only if local aspiring scriptwriters will let me get on with the work!'[30]

Suffice it to say, nothing ever became of this proposed movie, which, one suspects, had perhaps something to do with the fact that the ground had been at least partially covered a year or so earlier in Fred Zinnemann's fine film *The Search*. Berlin did, however, lure Reed – without Greene – a couple of years later for an only semi-successful thriller *The Man Between*.

PART THREE

The Fifties

6
Saintly Sinners

(Introductory note: I have transposed *The Power and the Glory* by
three years into a different decade to discuss it alongside *The Heart
of the Matter* and *The End of the Affair* with which it is usually
considered to represent an unofficial trilogy in Greene's writing.)

'It was a war – they admitted it – for the soul of the Indian, a war
in which they could use the army consisting mainly of Indians
attracted by a dollar a day.'[1] So Greene encapsulated the scale, and
the irony, of the brutal anti-clerical purges which swept Mexico in
the twenties and thirties and on which he was commissioned to
report in *The Lawless Roads*, published in 1939. Out of his
experiences in Mexico in 1937–38, there was never, initially, any
intention to publish more than one book. It was as if *The Power
and the Glory* crept up on him almost imperceptibly. He says now
that it was easy to detect, in *The Lawless Roads*, many of the
characters that would later emerge in the novel – 'so it is that the
material of a novel accumulates, without the author's knowledge,
not always easily, not always without fatigue or pain or even
fear'.[2]

Mexico clearly had a profound effect on him, not least in
relation to his faith. He recognized the 'first inroads' during that
visit: 'It's all bound up with my loyalty to the underdog – and so it
has been ever since. In Mexico the underdogs were the
Catholics.'[3] If the setting of the novel was specific, its thesis was

equally precise: the whisky priest, coward and lecher that he was, still continued to pass life on – 'I could distinguish even then between the man and his office.'[4]

John Ford's adaptation of *The Power and the Glory* as *The Fugitive* in 1947 chose, among its many other liberties with the novel, to ignore the above distinction, thus rendering it a travesty of Greene's intentions (albeit, separately, a spectacular movie the merits of which I will discuss later). Richard Winnington, under the headline 'Who Cares About the Book?', wrote:

> in his original work Greene makes the clearest definition of his credo: evil exists, therefore good (and God) must exist. Greene's protagonist of power and glory, a seedy 'whisky' priest is the last cleric in a fascist Mexican state that has instituted a pogrom against the Church. He is on the run, baptizing and administering to the Indians who shelter him. He deliberately sacrifices his chance of escape to give the sacrament to a dying American gangster. He is not aware of heroism, only of his cowardice. In him good and evil dwell; in him if you like, salvation. I may be simple, but it does seem to me that in the integration of the priest's contemptible human failings and his unheroic human goodness at the end lies the entire core of the book's meaning.[5]

As a counter to the failed priest, Greene had, as his other protagonist, the lieutenant, 'the idealistic police officer who stifled life from the best possible motives'.[6] Gene Phillips writes:

> Greene emphasizes in the novel how the priest and lieutenant counter each other by cutting back and forth between them throughout the story in true cinematic fashion. The priest, although he is sacrificing himself for his scattered flock, is a drunkard and the father of an illegitimate child; the lieutenant, although he is ruthless in carrying out his orders to exterminate Catholicism from the province, is a celibate and is dedicated to building an earthly paradise for his people. Both men are aware of their own sense of vocation.[7]

The film contained no such dichotomy; the issues were as miraculously black and white as Gabriel Figueroa's photography.

Henry Fonda was the gentle Christ on his inevitable way to the Cross, Pedro Armendariz the brutal, jackbooted oppressor who had even acquired in translation the paternity of the priest's bastard. But to charge Ford with mindless cannibalism of Greene's original would be to misunderstand the great director's inherent streak of sentimental Irish Catholicism. 'For Ford,' explains one of his biographers, Andrew Sinclair, 'the Catholic Church guarded the soul as the American navy guarded the shores. To him the cardinal and the admiral were the two paramount figures of authority, the priest and the sailor the two bond-servants of duty.' He had a 'firm belief that his Catholic faith would carry him through every trial and danger'.[8] It was also as if Ford felt the need, from time to time, to revisit an Irish sense of martyrdom in his films in order to reinforce his own faith. *The Informer, Mary of Scotland* and *The Plough and the Stars* all had this element and it was to Dudley Nichols, his collaborator on those films (as well as on nearly a dozen others from *Men without Women* in 1930) that he turned with this project.

Nichols said:

We had talked about it for years, but no studio would back it. Now Ford was independent . . . and he wanted to do it. I said I was sure it wouldn't make any profit, but I was eager to script it. We soon realized it was impossible to script the Greene novel . . . on account of censorship. His novel was of a guilty priest, and we could have no such guilty priest.[9]

A point reinforced by Ford: 'You couldn't do the original on film because the priest was living with a woman. Even today, you can say "shit" and "fuck" on the screen, but you can't have a priest living with a woman.'[10]

Nichols again:

It was a wonderful tale, I thought, and after I'd worked at its impossible problems for a while, I suggested writing an allegory of the Passion Play, in modern terms, laid in Mexico, using as much of Greene's story as we dared. Ford liked the idea. I did a long draft but was dissatisfied – on the point of throwing it over. Yet Ford showed enthusiasm, and he came to my office at RKO for about a week or ten days and from what I had written and from the novel, and from our own ideas, we redictated the script.[11]

The intention was clear from the first shot of Henry Fonda approaching a village on muleback with a commentary over, saying: 'The following photoplay is timeless. The story is a true one. It is also a very old story that was first told in the Bible. It is timeless and topical and it is still being played in many parts of the world.' At the very outset, Greene's very human being had been transformed into a symbol. Ford's version of the individual versus the state and Christianity versus totalitarianism would be a succession of such dazzling symbols and imagery. When Fonda is shot, he is sublimely heroic, rejecting even a glass of brandy because 'I want to live my death'. It was not Greene but in its own way it was, by Hollywood standards, just as bold. With sublime disregard for a system which, in the main, served as a conveyor-belt of pap for the masses, Ford embarked on an opulent art movie all played out in the shadow of menacing mountains and sunlight and candlelight that kept forming crosses. Though, unlike the novel, not specifically set in Mexico but in some unnamed state south of the border, the film turned out to be an extremely specific love-affair with the iconography that has seduced film-makers right down the years – from Eisenstein to Peckinpah.

Dilys Powell noted:

There are moments in the film when one feels that Mexico itself has taken command: not Graham Greene's squalid Mexico, not Lawrence's Mexico of sun and emptiness, but the Mexico of ink-black and white which Eisenstein and his cameraman Tisse saw when they planned their revolutionary film . . . the most significant contributors to *The Fugitive* are the Mexican scene, the Mexican sunlight and Ford's Mexican collaborators.[12]

With all this visual virtuosity, there had to be other losers than the source material and it is true to say that the characterizations remain, for the most part, trite: Dolores del Rio as a beatific Mary Magdalene, J. Carroll Naish, the oleaginous Judas and, above all, Henry Fonda, sleepwalking in a state of sanctity. Overall, Andrew Sarris concludes, 'Ford's monumental treatment of the material tended to be pious rather than religious . . . [his] achievement is more painterly than poetic, more for the eye than for the mind and the heart.'[13]

Ford had no regrets, despite the fact that the film turned out to be a bad start financially for his new independent company, Argosy:

> It came out the way I wanted it to – that's why it's one of my favourite pictures – to me it was perfect. It wasn't popular. The critics got at it, and evidently it had no appeal to the public, but I was very proud of my work. There are some things in it that I've seen repeated a million times in other pictures and on television – so at least it had that effect.[14]

After *The Fugitive* (Green's book, incidentally, had been retitled *The Labyrinthine Ways* for the United States) Ford proceeded to make five westerns in a row – doing, it seems, what the public liked him to do best.

Greene has never been able to bring himself to see the film – 'everything I heard about it was so awful; I really think I'd hate to see it now'. He was, however, persuaded to London's Curzon cinema when a theatrical version of CBS Television's 1961 remake was shown. With its original title restored, the film, starring Laurence Olivier as the priest and George C. Scott as the lieutenant, had apparently caused Sunday-night shockwaves in the States because it showed the priest as both drunkard and fornicator. It nevertheless contrived to erase the book's (and Ford's) final scene of a new priest arriving in the community, so eliminating the crucial theme of the Church's permanency. 'I wasn't very happy with it,' recalls Greene. 'All one can say about it was that Olivier was very bad and George C. Scott was very good.'

As Trevor Howard sits at his desk in an African bungalow at Shepperton Studios he prepares for suicide, intoning to a Madonna statuette, 'It's *you* I've got to hurt.' While loading each cartridge into his service revolver, sentences he has spoken earlier are played back. The director calls out: 'Trevor, please fill that revolver in phase with the playbacks, rhythmically, as if you were saying the rosary . . .' A secular interjection at a moment of high spiritual drama during the filming of *The Heart of the Matter* in 1953. It is a key moment, though, for it signals the start of a major parting of the ways between the cinema adaptation and the original novel, published five years earlier to great acclaim from public and critics alike.

At the end of the book deputy police commissioner Scobie, wracked by an obsessive pity for his wife and unable to bear the suffering of anyone in need of his sympathy, takes poison – 'This was the worst crime a Catholic could commit, it must be a perfect one.'[15] In the film, Scobie was instead at the wheel of his car poised to blow his brains out when a street disturbance drew him from the vehicle, he intervened and was murdered. Many critics thought the change must have been made as a result of censorship interference. In fact the censor had nothing to do with it; the decision belonged to the film-makers (the director, George More O'Ferrall was a Catholic) who apparently felt that Catholics would object to a Catholic taking his own life.

'It ruined the whole point,' said Greene, 'which was self-elected damnation on the part of Scobie.' If the 'heart of the matter' was, as some Catholic critics had hazarded, 'whether God might not even forgive the ultimate mortal sins of despair and suicide, given certain dispositions' it surely meant that the act of self-destruction was integral to the central thesis, even in a translation of the original. Greene had nothing to do with the adaptation (despite the fact it came from the Korda stable) which was undertaken by the producer Ian Dalrymple and Lesley Storm. But when he was shown a rough cut of the film afterwards, he pleaded with the producers to alter the ending so as to show the clear intention of suicide.

> I thought up a way and suggested it to them; it would only have needed an extra scene with Scobie and Trevor Howard was quite prepared to do the work for nothing: the idea would have been to show Scobie writing a suicide note with his gun at hand. At that moment he would be called away to some police action and be killed, still with the suicide intention in his mind. Anyway, they wouldn't make the alteration.[16]

This does seem curiously nit-picking in view of the chosen cinematic compromise, which would appear to have entailed all these elements save the cliché suicide note.

The critics, while generally liking the film, were extremely mixed in attitude as to its altered climax – from 'ingenious', '[an] end . . . not out of harmony with Greene's open question' to 'failure in courage . . . murder: does it really matter? I think it does.' It may be that what Greene feared was the *Daily Worker* reviewer's kind of interpretation 'when he decides on suicide he fails at that too and the failure that drove him into mortal sin as a Catholic saves him from the unforgivable sin of suicide by getting him honourably murdered (i.e. in the line of duty)'. Certainly my understanding of the film's end is that Scobie's suicidal *mens rea* is quite clear even if the *actus reus* is, fortuitously, at the hands of others.

Greene regards the film as 'a miss, though not a bad miss. Anyway I don't like the book, so perhaps I'm prejudiced. With the war and so on I had got a little rusty and the book wasn't good – certainly not as good as I would have liked it to have been. It was exaggerated too – particularly its religious element.' Set in Sierra Leone in wartime (Greene had been posted there, via Lagos, to run a one-man SIS office in Freetown during 1942–3) the novel, actually written three years after, 'I had closed my small office and burnt my file and code books' contains many echoes of his steamy West African sojourn.

Greene had written *Ministry of Fear* during that period and for Scobie's story he wanted to enlarge upon a theme which he felt he had merely touched on in the earlier work: 'the disastrous effect on human beings of pity as distinct from compassion . . . The character of Scobie was intended to show that pity can be the expression of an almost monstrous pride.'[17] The novel begins with a masterly piece of scene and character setting. We are with government agent Wilson and the cable censor Harris, on a hotel balcony. Together, the men observe the policeman Scobie in the Babel-like streets below. We learn that Scobie is, in an otherwise fairly racist climate, sympathetic towards Africans, and that he is married to the sort of woman who, remarks Harris acidly, would probably make him want to sleep with 'niggers' too.

Vivid as the opening was, it put Greene in a considerable quandary. He felt that two very different novels began on the same balcony with the same character, and he had to make a fundamental choice.

One was the novel I wrote: the other was to have been an 'entertainment'. I had long been haunted by the possibility of a crime story in which the criminal was known to the reader, but the detective was carefully hidden, disguised by false clues which would lead the reader astray until the climax. The story was to be told from the point of view of the criminal, and the detective would necessarily be some kind of undercover agent. MI5 was the obvious organization to use, and the character Wilson is the unsatisfactory relic of the entertainment, for when I left Wilson on the balcony and joined Scobie I plumped for the novel.[18]

Beneath its Catholic agonizing is a marvellous, colourful and fast-moving yarn – the sort of plot that might have been used, suggested Evelyn Waugh, by the likes of Simenon or Somerset Maugham. Scobie, popular though he is among the locals, is passed over for promotion which is the last straw for his wife Louise who, with her artistic pretensions, is already at her wits' end in the claustrophobic community. The couple are also haunted by memories of a dead daughter. To placate Louise he promises to send her away for a vacation to South Africa, though he can ill afford the fare.

We learn of Scobie's humanity when during a routine search of a ship for smuggled goods he discovers some secreted documents. When they turn out to be private correspondence, he burns the evidence rather than turn it over to the authorities which would have resulted in much trouble for the ship's captain. Later, he has to go up-country to investigate the death of a young assistant district commissioner who, it transpires, has committed suicide. Unable to get a loan for Louise's trip from his bank, he borrows money from a dubious Syrian trader, Yusef, who is suspected of diamond smuggling.

While Louise is away the survivors of a torpedo attack are brought in to the town. They include a young widow, Helen Rolt, with whom Scobie has an affair. When evidence of the affair falls into Yusef's hands, he uses it to blackmail Scobie into helping actively with his smuggling, an association which also leads indirectly to the death of Scobie's servant Ali. To appease Louise, now returned and suspicious that her husband has been unfaithful (she is at the same time being unsuccessfully wooed by Wilson whom we also realize is a police spy) Scobie undertakes a sacrilegious communion after being refused absolution by Father Rank following his confession of adultery. Hemmed in on all sides, Scobie kills himself, dying with the ambiguous 'Dear God, I love . . .' on his lips.

Evelyn Waugh saw the novel's affinity to film as: 'everywhere apparent':

> It is as though, out of the indefinite length of film, sequences have been cut which, assembled, comprise an experience which is the reader's alone, without any correspondence to the experience of the protagonists. The writer has become director and producer . . . it is the camera's eye which moves from the hotel balcony to the street below, picks out the policeman, follows him to his office, moves about the room from the handcuffs on the wall to the broken rosary in the drawer, recording significant detail.[19]

Waugh goes on to suggest that 'the art of story-telling has little to do with the choice of plot. One can imagine the dreariest kind of film accurately constructed to these specifications.'[20] He imagines, for instance, Lauren Bacall as the shipwrecked Helen, 'her pretty head lolling on the stretcher'.

There is no Lauren Bacall and certainly the film is very far from dreary, thanks to an adaptation which, though faithful (apart from the end) is not slavish, and to acting of the very highest quality from Trevor Howard, Elizabeth Allan as the neurotic Louise and Maria Schell as Helen (Miss Schell, an Austrian, became an Austrian married to an Englishman for the purposes of the film, doubtless to explain her accent). Apart from being hauntingly attractive, I also found Schell's Helen suitably child–woman–like. Gene Phillips was not so convinced:

> Miss Schell is obviously older (twenty-six, at the time of filming). The moviegoer fails to understand therefore that Scobie is initially attracted to Helen because he sees her as a surrogate of his own dead daughter, and feels very protective toward her. It is consequently easy to miss the point that it is Scobie's excessive sense of pity, and not his sexual desire, which, at the outset at least, is drawing him to Helen.[21]

The decision to shoot locations in Sierra Leone was also a good one for it helped capture the sweaty atmosphere and seething humanity perfectly. Scobie's trip out to the ship in harbour is the first long scene of the film and as the camera tracks him all the way the sense of place is swiftly established, unlike so many other supposed locations when the choice of shots seems merely to act as a kind of tourist travelogue. The later reconstruction of Africa on sets at Shepperton inevitably appears a little flat in comparison.

How, though, to translate the religious 'struggle'? Freda Bruce-Lockhart believes it is:

> admirably faced and stated but . . . stated less in the cold, clear images of the rest of the film, than in the rigid dialogue of set scenes. Perhaps the glimpse of Scobie unwillingly following Louise into the dark mouth of the church door where we know he will make his sacrilegious communion is an adequate substitute for that great scene of suffering in the book. This seemed to me the only really weak change or omission in the film.[22]

Yet while one can sympathize with Helen when she spits at Scobie that his Catholicism 'doesn't stop you from sleeping with me – it only stops you marrying me', it is less easy, certainly for a non–Catholic audience, to grasp the full agony of the policeman whose sacrilegious communion is somehow worse than murder.

Fortunately Howard's performance transcends any problems of dogma. Penelope Houston was right when she wrote: 'Howard brilliantly conveys Scobie's weakness, his despairing compassion and overpowering sense of responsibility'[23] while, at the same time, carefully avoiding self-pity.

Guy Elmes once asked Greene who was 'this man' he was writing about in every book and story.

'Greene told me "it's a terrible thing to say, but it's *Trevor Howard*!" You see, he'd like to be like Trevor Howard. To Greene, he is the near gent combined with man-of-action.'

Perhaps Greene also recognized in Howard that same fear of ennui which has haunted him since childhood (and which had partly led him to contemplate suicide himself during his Sierra Leone posting). Talking about his work once, Howard said: 'We're all Miss Piggies, puppets, the greasy mechanics of the business who get seen by the public. But it can still be fun and I like the hard work. The one thing that terrifies me is *boredom*.'

In fact, Howard has appeared in only three of the Greene adaptations – his work in *Heart of the Matter* flanked by *The Third Man* and *The Stranger's Hand*. It is not difficult to imagine with hindsight what a fine Bendrix in *The End of the Affair* or Brown in *The Comedians* he would have made (bearing in mind he was always Greene's first choice for both Bertram in *Loser Takes All* and Charley Fortnum in *The Honorary Consul*. For producer Dalrymple, Howard was (and still is) 'Unique in his ability to present the man of action in the round – to suggest even the most confident and straightforward of characters are victims of stress and bewilderment.'

Peter Finch, another actor with a somewhat similar hell-raising reputation, failed to make much of an impression as Father Rank, though not for any lack of preparation. A conversation with a drunken priest in a Chelsea pub apparently gave Finch the key to the characterization. The priest told him:

'It's the Pope and his bloody infallibility and this demand for implicit obedience I find I can't stomach.' The perpetual celibacy was also getting him down. 'No problem then,' replied Finchie, 'opt out and be a good Protestant.' 'Christ,' replied the indignant cleric . . . 'I may have lost my faith, but I haven't lost my self-respect.'

'In an instant,' Peter said, 'Father Rank clicked into place.'[24]

Director More O'Ferrall said that a great deal of work was put into the scenes between Scobie and Rank:

Before we shot the film I said to Greene that I thought the priest would have attempted to produce a reason that would enable him to give Scobie absolution, to which Greene replied: 'Then you have been bloody lucky.' We both laughed at this, so I felt free to go ahead, and with the help of a Jesuit theologian made the scene a little longer. When Greene saw the rough cut of the film, he said that because of this (and presumably the ending) the credit must read 'based on a story by . . .' instead of 'Graham Greene's *The Heart of the Matter*'.[25]

O'Ferrall reshot the scene after the film was finished exactly as the author wished, except for a few words which were no part of the argument. Months later the Irish film censor 'who in those days thought it part of his job to make a cut in any film of Greene's' cut out those very words which were not, in fact, written by him.

Audiences in Hong Kong, Singapore and Malaya were not quite so fortunate for there the film was banned outright. The official Malayan censor, one Mrs Cynthia Koek, said that the film depicted a deputy commissioner of police in a British colonial territory in an 'unfavourable manner' so it would not be suitable for audiences in her colony.

This drew a suitably acid reaction from Greene at the time. It was, he said, 'surely Mad Hatter policy to ban a serious British film while admitting "American trash"'. It should be said that prickly reactions to the film were not entirely confined to the colonies. When Korda offered the proceeds of the London première of the film to the voluntary St John and St Elizabeth Roman Catholic Hospital, the governors turned him down with the ambiguous reply that the subject of the book was considered 'too difficult'.

A prequel to all this was the extraordinary case of Greene's own stage adaptation of the novel. Rodgers and Hammerstein wanted Greene to go to New York to work on the transition but when he applied to the Bank of England for a £10 daily allowance during his American stay it turned him down saying it could not gamble on an *unknown quantity* to the extent of £350' (my italics). £4 a day was all they were prepared to gamble. So Greene took his own gamble, cancelled the trip and the contract and wrote the play in London in association with Basil Dean. Rodgers and Hammerstein liked it and bought it. With seven Britons in the cast, including Ian Hunter, Rosalie Crutchley and Alison Leggatt, it opened early in 1950 in Boston. Reaction was poor and the play never made the planned transfer to New York.

A sequel was the film's bizarre distribution in Italy under the title *The Mau Mau Story*! Responsible for this was Guy Elmes, who, after helping to adapt *The Stranger's Hand*, had stayed on in Italy as one of Korda's representatives. Elmes says:

They just couldn't sell the film in Italy so I entirely rewrote the story, dubbed the film and called it by its new title. Scandalous wasn't it – and Greene hated me for it. Mau Mau was very topical just then. It was Africa, albeit the wrong side of it, and you had Trevor Howard walking around as a policeman. What was he looking for? The Mau Mau, not God. I took all of Graham's God out of it. You had the drums beating and the music and it did very good business. Nothing really mattered when you were trying to earn a buck!

In August 1954, the *Daily Sketch* reported Greene, 'that sad-faced chronicler of sin and sex', visiting the Shepperton set of *The End of the Affair*. Had he, they asked him, had any part in adapting his novel for the screen? No, he replied, a shade tersely it seems, adding, 'scripting your own stories can be unwelcome and fatiguing. You do the work twice; it's just a rehash.' The paper's dogged Greene-watcher then eavesdropped as the author encountered one of the film's stars, Deborah Kerr. 'Do you recognize your lines?' Miss Kerr asked Greene. 'I recognize the people,' he replied cryptically.

Things went from bad to worse that day. Greene was watching an intimate scene between Miss Kerr and the American actor, Van Johnson, playing her lover, Maurice Bendrix. Greene told me: 'They were trying to do those shots where you get the same scene from each person's point of view; you had Johnson embracing Deborah Kerr with the camera on him and then the camera moved to be on her in the same close embrace. Anyway, while the camera was on her, he put chewing-gum in his mouth!'

No wonder Greene thought Johnson was 'unsuitable' for the role but in a sense he was slightly responsible for the casting. The previous winter he had been on his annual trip to Vietnam to report the war when he was asked, by the film's producers, if he would return home via Hollywood. They wanted Gregory Peck to play Bendrix. 'I was very much against him but we went to see Peck who told us that he would only do the film if I wrote the script.' That, as far as Greene was concerned, was out of the question, 'so I stymied Gregory Peck. But then to find that Van Johnson took his place was a disaster.'

You can infer from these Hollywood references that Greene's fiercely parochial drama was being mounted as an Anglo-

American effort, one of those hybrids that have so often, both
before and since, contrived to fall straight into the mid-Atlantic,
without hope of rescue. That Edward Dmytryk's film manages to
avoid the usual transatlantic pitfalls perhaps says more about the
inherent quality of the original material than the wisdom of
casting a light-weight American actor for box-office clout. In the
event, Johnson was just about adequate. The film, and Greene
certainly would not agree, is much more than that. It is a serious
and very worthy attempt to find visual correlatives, underscored
by the strong dialogue from Greene's powerful novel, of, in his
own words, 'obsessive love and obsessive hate', jealousy and
religious experience.

Baldly, the novel deals with the wartime affair between a
middle-aged novelist, Bendrix, and Sarah Miles, wife of a senior
civil servant, which comes to an end during an air-raid. Bendrix is
knocked out and when he comes to, he finds Sarah on her knees
praying. She leaves the house and he does not see her again.
Eighteen months later, he runs into Sarah's husband, Henry, who
tells Bendrix that he is desperately concerned about his wife's
increasing and unexplained absences from home. He wants to hire
the services of a private detective and Bendrix says that he will
make the arrangement – more for his own benefit, since Bendrix is
himself consumed with jealousy about Sarah's possible activities.

When Bendrix manages to get hold of Sarah's private journal he
discovers that, during that earlier air-raid, she had made a bargain
with God believing Bendrix to be dead. She would give him up if
He restored her lover to life. It is clear from her words that she still
loves Bendrix and she visits a rationalist preacher, Smythe, to try
and help her break her bargain. In fact Smythe's intervention
merely contrives to feed her faith.

Moved by her account, Bendrix desperately tries to make
contact with her and they meet, chastely, for the last time when it
is clear that Sarah is desperately unwell. She dies, and after her
death we learn that not only was she baptized a Catholic (without
her knowledge) when she was a child but that her apparent
intervention has resulted in two small miracles – the ridding of the
private detective's son's appendicitis and the preacher's unsightly
birthmark. Bendrix moves in with Henry; his jealousy and hatred
of Sarah's lover is, nevertheless, unabated by the fact that his rival
was not human but divine.

The way these events unfold is no strict chronological recitation. For the most part narrated in the first person by Bendrix – apart from extracts from Sarah's journal – it begins with the novelist's chance meeting with Henry, those eighteen months after the affair had ended. As Sarah's new 'affair' is uncovered, so the past is revealed too in Bendrix's own words and the journal jottings.

Dmytryk's film was originally shot in flashback fashion, much in the way that the novel is written, with more of Bendrix's comments on the soundtrack. However the American distribution company, Columbia, was concerned that a story told out of strict sequence would be confusing so the film was eventually re-edited to arrange, for the most part, the scenes in proper chronological order. According to Dmytryk, Greene saw the film in its original, pre-release form and 'liked it very much. He was disappointed when the film was re-edited, and I personally prefer the picture in its original form myself.'

Lenore Coffee's script was really very true to Greene's own dialogue, and in its attempt to visualize some of the thoughts of the characters. This can be seen for example by reproducing the section of Coffee's script that deals with what is perhaps the book and film's key moment, Sarah's pact with God in exchange for Bendrix's life:

129. INTERIOR: BENDRIX'S SITTING-ROOM
SARAH comes in stunned and shocked by the belief that BENDRIX is dead. Suddenly, overcome with despair, she drops down on her knees in a corner of the room. A shaft of light from the kitchen falls on her.
SARAH'S VOICE
I knelt down on the floor. I must have been mad to do such a thing. I never even had to do it as a child; I wasn't brought up to believe in prayer. I hadn't any idea what to say – only that Maurice was dead and I knew that I had to cry out for help to someone.

The following dialogue is between SARAH as she tries to pray and the whispered voice of her driving conscience.
SARAH (slowly and painfully)
Dear God – make me believe. I can't believe. *Make* me.
HER WHISPERED VOICE

WHY 'DEAR'? HOW CAN ANYTHING YOU DON'T
BELIEVE IN BE 'DEAR'?
> SARAH

I will believe. Only let Maurice be alive and I will believe.
> HER WHISPERED VOICE

THAT ISN'T ENOUGH. IT DOESN'T HURT TO BE-
LIEVE.
> SARAH

Very well. I love him and I'll do anything – if you will let him
be alive.
> HER WHISPERED VOICE

THAT STILL ISN'T ENOUGH. YOU KNOW IT ISN'T.
AND WHAT DO YOU MEAN BY 'ANYTHING'?
> SARAH

I'll never quarrel with him again or make him unhappy.
> HER WHISPERED VOICE

YOU KNOW THAT'S IMPOSSIBLE. THE VERY
NATURE OF YOUR LIVES TOGETHER MAKES IT
IMPOSSIBLE.
> SARAH

I'll be sweet and kind and patient to Henry –
> HER WHISPERED VOICE

YOU ALREADY ARE. AND IT DOESN'T COST YOU
ANYTHING. YOU LIKE TO BE KIND.

As SARAH fights with her conscience she digs her nails into
the palms of her hands and the perspiration begins to stand out
on her face and forehead. It is a real battle of the soul. She takes a
deep shuddering breath and says, the words spaced out slowly –
> SARAH

I'll – give – Maurice – up – for-ever – (Then in a rush of words) If
you'll only let him be alive!
> HER WHISPERED VOICE

FOR EVER?
> SARAH (with panic in her voice)

People can love each other without being together, can't they?
> HER WHISPERED VOICE

PEOPLE WHO BELIEVE IN HIM
> SARAH

I *do* believe! I *will* believe! Make me. I can't do anything of
myself. Make him be alive – and I will believe. *I promise!*

HER WHISPERED VOICE
ARE YOU SURE YOU WANT TO PROMISE?
REMEMBER YOU SAW HIM LYING DEAD UNDER
THAT DOOR. YOU SAW HIS DEAD HAND. YOU
TOUCHED IT.

SARAH

If there is a God, can't He heal the sick and raise the dead? (her nails digging deeper into her palms) All I can feel now is pain – and I accept pain. Give me nothing else and I will bear it. (opens her hands and we see the bloody marks) Oh God, they say You are merciful. But how can there be a merciful God and this despair? Show me that You are! *Prove* it to me! And I'll believe! If You are really God, You can do anything!

As SARAH'S voice dies away there is the sound of the 'ALL CLEAR'. And it is still sounding when SARAH hears BENDRIX'S voice calling – 'Sarah – Sarah' – She crouches against the wall and turns a terrified face to BENDRIX as he walks into the open door.[26]

Robert Muller says:

What makes the film so poignant is that the struggle between the sacred and profane love is not played out in the mind of some Catholic peasant girl, bred in an atmosphere of prayer and incense, but in the mind of a modern English woman, in whose life religion has hitherto played little part. This is no parable, but a story, bizarre though it may seem at first, which could happen to anybody. Or so the film compels us to believe.[27]

It could, one feels, almost be a sequel to *Brief Encounter*. It occupies the same sort of middle-class territory. Laura Jesson may be less sensual than Sarah Miles, and Alec Harvey less selfish and possessive than Bendrix, but who knows what might have happened had not guilt and his career plans cut short their passionate moment.

There are some slight departures from the novel in the film. We find the priest, Father Crompton, asking Sarah why she should feel herself bound by a promise to a God in whom she does not believe. In another encounter, Father Crompton intones: 'When we seek God, it means we have already found Him.' She replies: 'I don't want Him! And what does He want with me? What could I give Him but a shabby second best?' To which the priest replies: 'I'm afraid He's used to that' – 'pseudo-Greene' noted one clerical commentator, 'but not unorthodox'. The British version of the film also varied from the American in one respect: it deleted the novel/film's powerful scene when Bendrix loses his temper with the priest, abusing him and Sarah's memory. It seems as though the British Board of Film Censors objected to the spectacle of a minister of religion being subjected to dialectical attack.

The final scene also wanders both from Greene and orthodoxy. Bendrix finds a letter in which Sarah tells how she attained belief by falling into it 'like I fell into love'. Her voice is heard, speaking the words as Bendrix reads them: 'So you see, you're part of it all, Maurice, as you are part of me, and we both are part of God', which our clerical commentator admonishes as 'really nothing but a sentimental pantheism which Greene would have known better than to perpetrate'.

For the most part, the critics centred on Van Johnson's inadequacy and what they regarded as a dullness about the whole enterprise. The *Manchester Guardian* however tried to put its finger on the specific problems of translating this work to film:

> This was a hard film to make – hard to make, that is, in such satisfying cinematic style as to smother damaging comparisons of the film with the novel. There were scenes in the book – which, to put it discreetly, were far too intimate for translation to the screen; there was, above all, that perennial problem of adaptation from novel to film – the special quality of the author's writing . . . in spite of all that may be said about this novelist's 'moving camera manner' – the fact remains that when, as most patently in this novel, Mr Greene's words are exploring difficult spiritual realms of human motive and behaviour the moving camera becomes a lumbering interpreter.[28]

It is an extremely well-put, indeed plausible, argument. Yet with all the possible pitfalls, some clearly insurmountable, the film nevertheless remains a valiant attempt to people a religious subject with more lively *dramatis personae* than some of the angst-ridden ciphers of Greene's pages.

7
Behind the Camera

At first glance *The Stranger's Hand* seems like a catchpenny attempt to recapture the past glories of *The Fallen Idol* and *The Third Man* in one curious amalgam. Certainly its genesis could not have been more bizarre. Neither from novel nor from short story, it was, in fact, derived from a Greene entry in one of those rather inventive *New Statesman* competitions. In this case a title and an opening paragraph 'in the style of Graham Greene'. Greene himself entered and, ironically, only came second. Later he decided to sketch out the idea a bit and his friend, the Italian director Mario Soldati, suggested he turn it into a film. Greene jotted his ideas on a couple of pieces of paper before the serious business of turning it into a screenplay for genuine consideration was begun.

That job fell to Guy Elmes who was both a friend of Soldati and of John Stafford, who came in to produce the film (Elmes and Stafford had worked together before a couple of years earlier on *The Planter's Wife*). Elmes, a colourful character who now lives quietly in Berkshire, was in the early fifties based in Italy mostly helping to arrange Italian–American co-productions 'not so much writing as pulling scripts round to suit the Italian market as well as the Americans who were financing'. Elmes also worked as a newspaperman in Rome and Capri and was a self-styled 'bit of a social tit'.

Elmes recalls:

This funny little piece of paper came to me and the idea was I had to tack a story on to it. It started off typically Greene 'a little boy walking between the cracks in the pavement in Venice . . .'

and somehow I did produce a story out of it. The next thing I knew I was flying to Venice to look for very precise locations and then I realized I could do even more with the story once I had seen the city and so there I sat for another month doing yet another rewrite.

The story centres around an eight-year-old boy, Roger Court, who arrives in Venice alone to meet his father, a British intelligence officer (Major Court) whom he has not seen for three years. Court has, in fact, been kidnapped by communist agents shortly before his son's arrival.

When his father fails to turn up, the worried boy is befriended by Roberta, the hotel receptionist and a Yugoslav refugee, and her American sailor boyfriend Joe Hamstringer. Police are called in but have little success. At first Roberta and Joe are not convinced that Roger's father is being held a prisoner in Venice but eventually agree to help him in his search. With their aid, but mostly by his own obstinate efforts, Roger tracks down his father's kidnappers who are keeping the major on board a ship before transporting him back behind the Iron Curtain. The officer is rescued from shipboard by Venice's high-speed canal-borne fire-brigade.

The casting had echoes of things past with Trevor Howard as Major Court and Alida Valli as Roberta – both had registered so strongly in *The Third Man*. Richard Basehart plays Joe and Richard O'Sullivan, who since has gone on to become one of Britain's best light entertainment actors, was a precociously talented child actor making his debut as Roger.

Undoubtedly the most intriguing character in the whole piece is a shabby local doctor, Dr Vivaldi, played by Eduardo Ciannelli. Vivaldi has thrown in his lot with the kidnappers but makes friends with the boy before realizing just who he is and remains amicable even after he knows. He makes two rings of string, one for him and one for Roger, telling the boy that if ever he feels lonely he knows he always has a friend.

And it is the doctor who eventually saves Roger's father by jumping between one of the communist agents and Major Court just as the officer is about to be shot. Dr Vivaldi is killed instead. When Roger asks his father later if anyone died during the storming of the ship, the reply is 'Nobody, just a stranger' and the final shot of the film is one of that 'stranger's' hand, still wearing a ring of string. Guy Elmes was rewriting away when:

Graham, Trevor Howard and all of them, just descended on Venice. We were terrible Grappa drinkers – you can imagine. Graham liked the hard stuff, Trevor adored it and I got pretty fond of it. Then we also had an absolutely dotty director in Mario. Graham read my script and just giggled. We then realized later, after we'd started shooting, certain things did not quite work and he and I used to sit together in the Piazza in Venice and he would toy with a pencil and perhaps come up with a line. Other than that, I can't remember his interfering. [Elmes received a joint screenplay credit with Georgio Bassani.] In those days I couldn't speak Italian and we wanted to keep the film rights for the Italian market too so Bassani was brought in and he gave me nice things like *ciao*. I think it may have been the first picture that kept using the word *ciao*.

I had in my mind this kind of allegorical notion about the falling away of the West, seen against the sinking of Venice. Unfortunately we didn't have enough money to do the picture properly. Mario became very hysterical and tried to do things on the cheap, and not very effectively. There was the whole business, for instance, of Eduardo Ciannelli in a boat looking back at Venice. We did that on a raft with just a porthole and every time steamers went by, everything would collapse – camera, dolly, everything. I also wanted Mario and his cameraman Serafin to try and get a *Third Man* look – to have Venice looking very wet and shiny. Unfortunately it was done in such a half-hearted way and there were so many takes that it was always dry again by the time the shot came.

That slightly shambolic approach appears to have been a feature of the film-making which, according to both Greene and Elmes, suffered from the limitations of being an 'Anglo-Italian' co-production.

Elmes says:

We really wanted an almost all-Italian crew – we had become absolutely fed up with British crews – but because the film had to qualify for Quota in England, we brought out a British unit,

with their wives, and, effectively, gave them a free holiday for
the whole picture. That's where the money went. Then when
the Italians, without charging any overtime, would willingly
work on until dark, you'd get the British union coming forward
and saying *they'd* worked so many hours' overtime. We would
work on a Sunday while the British crew just went bathing with
their wives.

The 'Anglo-Italian' experience was terrible, agrees Greene:

The English technicians were put up at hotels on the Grand
Canal and they'd complain that they couldn't get eggs and
bacon for breakfast. Then there was the question of 'the
tea-break'. On one occasion, we were shooting on a kind of raft
and the Italian electricians were clambering about putting up
lights between people's legs and the assistant director had to
clap his hands and declare a four-thirty tea-break. Of course, the
Italians had never heard of a tea-break. But if it wasn't taken,
the English technicians, who were mostly sailing boats at sea or
having ices in the piazza, would have to be paid overtime to
make up for the missed tea-break. As far as I can remember, the
only people functioning on the English side during the
production were the producer, the assistant and the clapper boy.
The rest were just having a Grand Canal holiday.

And if that was not bad enough, there was more than a hint of
the home-movie about the enterprise. 'Too many friends got jobs
in it,' says Elmes, 'for example, the air hostesses were some of the
crew's wives dressed up.' Greene, who had an official co-producer
credit, even got into the act. 'It was my first appearance on the
screen, or rather, my hand's. It appeared in the film undoing the
rope of the fire-boat.'
    Greene also enjoyed his first experience of the editing process. 'I
actually did a bit of the cutting on the end of the English version of
the film using one of those moviola machines and it was most
interesting.'
    The timing of the film could not have been less fortuitous.
Greene:

In that respect we were very unlucky. By the time the film was

Trevor Howard and Elizabeth Allan in *The Heart Of The Matter* (KOBAL COLLECTION)

Trevor Howard and Maria Schell in *The Heart Of The Matter* (KOBAL COLLECTION)

Alida Valli comforts Richard O'Sullivan in *The Stranger's Hand* (KOBAL COLLECTION)

Van Johnson *(left)* Deborah Kerr and Peter Cushing in *The End Of The Affair* (KOBAL COLLECTION)

Stephen Murray listens to Deborah Kerr in
The End Of The Affair (KOBAL COLLECTION)

Rossano Brazzi and Glynis Johns in a cut
sequence from *Loser Takes All* (KOBAL COLLECTION)

Graham Greene *(left)* visits Deborah Kerr and Van Johnson on the Shepperton set of *The End Of The
Affair* (COLUMBIA PICTURES)

Rod Steiger at the climax of *Across The Bridge* (KOBAL COLLECTION)

Rod Steiger undergoes a change of identity in *Across The Bridge*
(KOBAL COLLECTION)

Robert Ivers as a cut-price Alan Ladd in *Short Cut To Hell* (NATIONAL FILM ARCHIVE)

Grahame Greene with Jean Seberg on the set of *Saint Joan* (NATIONAL FILM ARCHIVE)

Jean Seberg as Saint Joan at the climax of the film (KOBAL COLLECTION)

Michael Redgrave *(left)* and Audie Murphy in *The Quiet American* (KOBAL COLLECTION)

Noel Coward and Alec Guinness in *Our Man In Havana* (COLUMBIA PICTURES)

Graham Greene *(centre)* with Carol Reed and Alec Guinness on the set of *Our Man In Havana* (NATIONAL FILM ARCHIVE)

Peter Ustinov, a disguised Alec Guinness, and Richard Burton in *The Comedians* (KOBAL COLLECTION)

A passionate encounter between Elizabeth Taylor and Richard Burton in *The Comedians*
(KOBAL COLLECTION)

finished and ready to be shown, Tito had become a kind of white-headed boy of the West; he had split with Russia. Now, of course, the film was about a Yugoslavian kidnapping of a British officer – in that sense, Tito would have been the villain of the piece – which didn't do the film any good.

I don't think it was a bad little film. We got a very good notice from Dilys Powell who complained that it hadn't come on in the West End – it was showing only at the Dominion, on the corner of Tottenham Court Road – and Dilys said it was a much better film than many others that were on in the West End proper.

As I have pointed out before, *The Stranger's Hand* is a curious amalgam of *The Fallen Idol* and *The Third Man*: it contains strong elements of both but never really reaches the heights of either film. It was filmed, as had been *The Fallen Idol,* from the child's point of view and, in many ways, Richard O'Sullivan gives just as remarkable a performance as Bobby Henrey did in *Idol.* His is bewilderment and loneliness in a large crowd – and the atmosphere of Venice is shrewdly caught – whereas Bobby Henrey operated in the essentially claustrophobic climate of a large house and its immediate environs. However the ironies of Greene's unique scene-setting and words are probably the film's most serious omission. *The Fallen Idol* is all subtlety. Subtlety is certainly not the strong point of *The Stranger's Hand.*

The mood of escape was still there, but this time it took me no further than to Monte Carlo, to live luxuriously for a few weeks in the Hotel de Paris . . . to work long hours at the casino tables . . . and to write what I hoped would prove an amusing, agreeable novella – something which neither my friends nor my enemies would expect. It was to be called *Loser Takes All.* A reputation is like a death mask, I wanted to smash that mask.[1]

A slight and frothy tale, it deals with a young middle-aged accountant Bertram who works for a rather shadowy tycoon Dreuther. About to marry his second wife, the pretty, and much younger, Cary, Bertram helps Dreuther out of a hitch over some figures, and the tycoon offers to pay for his honeymoon in Monte

Carlo and will himself sail to the principality to be a witness at the ceremony. Killing time in Monte until Dreuther arrives, Bertram starts gambling, unsuccessfully, at the casino.

With still no sign of Dreuther, the couple marry and by now Bertram has devised a system for winning at gambling and is able to put the system into practice thanks to a loan from the hotelier. He wins millions but is now so engrossed in his system and making money that he alienates Cary who begins to see more and more of the handsome, but penniless, gambler Philippe.

Bertram is now rich enough to be able to buy one of his employer's companies when Dreuther finally turns up and explains to Bertram how he can win Cary back. He hands over all his money to Philippe to pay for half an hour with Cary. And Philippe, secretly as avaricious as the next person, is only too happy to take the cash as it will cover the cost of his own system.

When Bertram returns Cary after the allotted time, Philippe asks not to be disturbed because he is now winning. Bertram promises to Cary that he is giving up his system and gambling for ever. Back on the yacht, Dreuther promotes him to chief accountant.

Loser Takes All was the first and, probably, the last time that Greene used a real-life person as one of his principal character models. 'Dreuther is undeniably Alexander Korda, and the story remains important to me because it is soaked in memories of Alex, a man whom I loved.'[2] Korda also contrived to provide the plot, for it was while Greene and a friend were waiting for Korda to pick them up in his yacht from Athens that they started to become extravagant, 'well, Alex like Dreuther did eventually turn up in time to pay our "honeymoon" bill, and the story of *Loser Takes All* had been born over the retsina wine of the anxious picnic lunch'.[3]

The story may have had sentimental connotations but it was nevertheless merely a 'frivolity', according to Greene. The film, adapted by Greene himself and released in 1956 a year after the novella's publication, was 'a disaster', he says. While the film story followed along the general lines of the original, the eventual casting threw the initial concept into some confusion by having Rossano Brazzi as Bertram (now called Bertrand), a thirty-three-year-old Glynis Johns as Cary and Robert Morley, quite unlike Korda, as Dreuther.

The director, Ken Annakin, explains the intriguing anatomy of this film:

Originally it was going to be made at Elstree by Associated British, run by Robert Clark, who was probably looking forward to taking a friendly knock at Alex Korda. Anyway, everything went wrong there. They couldn't get the cast they wanted and they also wanted to change the script a great deal; and Graham was very adamant that he wanted it as he had intended it. Producing the film was Graham's great friend John Stafford and the only deal he was able to make was with British Lion who were in rather a shaky position as British distributors at that time. In fact it was only a short time after this they went broke. I worked with Graham on the final version of the script in Monte Carlo where we stayed at the Hotel de Paris. He was a very favoured client and we had two wonderful suites over-looking the casino. He didn't like to work with us both sitting in the same room so we would first discuss scenes, their shape and what it was we wanted. He'd write from about eight until eleven o'clock every morning then we'd have drinks and a very good lunch before going out in the afternoon to explore all round the countryside, to places like St Paul. And we visited people like Onassis and Clouzot (the French director of *Les Diaboliques* and *Les Salaires de Peur*). We used to go and gamble a little most nights and Graham would show me the types he based his gamblers on.

One evening we ran into Alex Korda himself about whom, of course, the story was written. Graham had done a great deal for Korda but it seemed to be a love–hate relationship. He believed that Alex always messed people's lives about; he made people work *where* he wanted and *how* he wanted and Graham had claimed to have suffered a great deal under this sort of dictatorship and it was as a result of this he wrote *Loser Takes All*. Strangely enough, at one time, he hoped that Korda himself might back it.

It was fascinating being in Monte Carlo with Graham. I learned a great deal about the approach of a great writer to his work. Graham was a perfectionist. His mentor, the man he admired most, was Henry James – the great stylist – and that's why words and phrases also mattered to him a great deal. It was

quite a struggle to get the script right and also the locations
Graham wanted. I remember we went crazy with delight
watching some old people playing *boules* and so we had to have
Rossano and Glynis playing *boules* in the film. Now it came to
the casting. Graham wanted Trevor Howard to play the
clerk-accountant. David Lean had just had a great success with
Summertime starring Katharine Hepburn and Rossano Brazzi
and Sir Arthur Jarrett, the head of British Lion, said he would
only think of going into the film with Brazzi 'because he's hot at
the moment'. As for Trevor, said Sir Arthur, 'you couldn't give
him away. No one wants him.' Trevor, of course, would have
been perfect as the clerk working many floors below the Korda
figure, and the picture would have been a very different one. As
it was, Brazzi is an excellent actor but he had a strong,
sentimental quality – an Italian quality – not the dryness Greene
wanted; and when you hire Brazzi, you hire the man as he is.
There was obviously no way he could portray a downtrodden
English clerk.

For Cary, there was a wonderful American girl we wanted
called Maggie McNamara who had been in Otto Preminger's
film *The Moon is Blue* with William Holden. She came over to
England but after a couple of days decided she didn't like it and
wanted to go home. So various people were approached and we
eventually ended up with Glynis and she's an excellent actress
but she wasn't dead right either for the part. She had a certain
flamboyance and a certain sexiness, more sexiness than the part
really called for. And when we started shooting in Monte
Carlo, I was shattered to find she had put on quite a lot of
weight. She'd been having a bad time, was rather down, not
bubbly and alive. We looked at her and even thought we might
have to recast.

However, Brazzi told us not to worry and that he would look
after her and he immediately started a love-affair with her that
carried her through the picture and that gave her a certain light
in the eye. But this did all mean that we were making the
picture with the cast that neither Graham nor I had originally
envisaged.

Then there was the casting of Dreuther, or the Grand Old Man,
as he is referred to in the novella.

Greene recalls: 'We wanted Alec Guinness to play Dreuther but Korda, who realized it was based on him, was unco-operative and refused to release Alec from some engagement he had, and so we had Robert Morley instead. And Robert Morley plays only Robert Morley . . .' French director René Clement was also briefly involved with the project. Greene:

I discussed it with him in Monte Carlo. He was there with his wife and while I was working on the script, his wife was going off to the casino. And there was a French producer too who was going to put up the money and his wife was also going off to the casino every night. And I thought: 'My God, if they make the film in the end, what expenses they'll claim.' Anyway the producer eventually withdrew probably because of the amount of money his wife was spending. And René Clement dropped out as well. But I do think he would have made a good film.

Greene appears not to have much good to say about Annakin's direction of the material. 'Even though one likes a screenplay, one is still in the director's hands. It's not that he necessarily adds, or takes away, words but he can add actions and movements which one has not intended and that can be fatal and which are completely out of the spirit of the thing.' This cryptic put-down could be a bitter reference to what Annakin, for his part, claims was the only time Greene visited the set:

He saw a scene where Brazzi was pushing the old man around the casino in a wheelchair and Brazzi changed a line. I didn't think it was perfect but very often my way of working with an actor is to let him do a line as he wants and then bring him back to do the line as I want. Because Brazzi changed two or three words, Graham got absolutely furious, made a big scene and never came back to visit us again.

The critics were not kind to the film. *The Times* said:

Books have a way of changing their characters on the journey from print to the screen, but something altogether out of the ordinary seems to have happened to *Loser Takes All*. As a novel, it appeared harmless, and as a film, it is still, in the ultimate sense, harmless, but it has somehow acquired a disquieting, all-pervading vulgarity. *Loser Takes All* has suffered a sea-change – and it is a change for the worse.

The *Daily Mail*'s Fred Majdalany wrote: 'Had I not seen it in writing, I would find it hard to believe that such feeble dialogue could be Graham Greene's.' The film had become, in Greene's words 'instead of a light comedy, a rather heavy piece'.
Ken Annakin says:

I'm sorry that Graham regards the film as a total disaster. It wasn't a great success but I regard it with a certain fondness still. I made, I think, quite an acceptable, amusing picture. I have a feeling that the film would have failed whatever cast we had had. The story was of a girl going against her man because he becomes rich and, for a period, is obsessed with making money. She sees in him the same elements as the all-powerful Sir Alex figure, the man who doesn't think about the little people and who pushes people about just as she's been pushed about into having her wedding and honeymoon outside England and away from her family. So she turns away from Brazzi and has an affair with a young, penniless man.

The point is, I think, that everyone loves to see people making money. Graham saw this as a challenge and, in a sense, it was a marvellously Faustian thing to have people's values turned topsy-turvy. I don't, though, think that an audience anywhere was prepared to accept the idea that it is better to turn away and have young love rather than make money. I never saw this facet until after I'd made the film.

Bernard Shaw must have been gazing into some crystal ball as he penned his preface for *Saint Joan*. In the 'well-meant proposals for the improvement of the play', he wrote:

The experienced knights of the blue pencil having saved an hour and a half by disembowelling the play, would at once proceed to waste two hours in building elaborate scenery, having real water in the river Loire and a real bridge across it . . . the coronation would eclipse all previous theatrical displays, showing, first, the procession through the street of Rheims, and then the service in the cathedral, with special music written for both. Joan would be burnt on the stage . . . on the principle that it does not matter in the least why a woman is burnt, and people can pay to see it done.[4]

Shaw died six years before Otto Preminger's disastrous film of *Saint Joan* which might have been blueprinted from the author's own admonitions of more than three decades earlier.

Greene, in his second and last assignment as pure 'writer-for-hire' (the first had been *First and the Last* in 1937) was given just six weeks by Preminger to be a 'knight of the blue pencil' and today remains perfectly satisfied that he kept a sense of responsibility to the author as he went about reducing a three-and-a-half-hour play to a film of less than two hours. 'Anyway, Shaw isn't a sacred name to me. I didn't mind adapting his work.' The adaptation took very much second place to the Great Hunt for a New Star. Preminger said at the time 'we are strictly adhering to the Shaw dialogue, but we are telling the story in a little different continuity, in order to adjust it and adapt it to the picture medium'.[5]

Sybil Thorndike was forty-one when she created the teenaged role back in the twenties in what many regard as the definitive performance, but Preminger felt that for a film, with the ever-discerning camera, it was necessary to have an actress much nearer the correct age. So he declared an open audition, for 'an actress who actually was young but had enough understanding of the play's intellectual concept to interpret the part'.[6] Some 18,000 were auditioned and history relates that it was a seventeen-year-old chemist's daughter from Marshalltown, Iowa who landed the 'Role of the Century' – Jean Seberg, who had had a few roles in her local stock company but was completely inexperienced professionally. In the event Seberg was far from the worst thing in a film that tried to make such concessions to a potential American audience as casting the screen's favourite giggling killer, Richard Widmark, as the sensitive Dauphin. I rather like *Time*'s comment on Seberg's performance: 'Shaw's Joan is a chunk of hard brown bread, dipped in the red wine of battle and devoured by ravenous angels. Actress Seberg is the sort of honeybun that drugstore desperados like to nibble with their milkshakes.'[7]

The main structural device contrived by Greene and Preminger was to switch the play's epilogue from back to front and use it as a platform for flashbacks to Joan's temporal life. Greene told me: 'I'm sure I was right having Shaw's epilogue as a sort of prologue, starting with the king in bed and the ghost coming to him. On film, the way you had to finish was the execution.'

Other 'improvements', pointed out *Observer* critic Peter Dyer, included, 'a game of hopscotch in the Archbishop's garden; a fashionable rout of blindman's buff; a final fitting of a maid for the torture rack; a Billy Bunter page-boy curious to discover how the torture gadgets really work, and a number of new jokes for the Earl of Warwick. There is also a great deal of music, vocal, instrumental and celestial.' In the play, Joan's execution is offstage. Here it was patently on. Nine-tenths of the Inquisitor's speech was slashed – to the immense relief of *New Statesman*'s William Whitebait.

However the overall result, concluded *Time*, was the feat of 'turning Shaw into pshaw'. Preminger said later:

I alone am to blame because . . . I misunderstood something fundamental about Shaw's play. It is not a dramatization of the legend of Joan of Arc which is filled with emotion and religious passion. It is a deep but cool intellectual examination of the role religion plays in the history of man. Am I sorry to have made the film? No.[8]

Greene is unrepentent too:

Anyway I got a few laughs that were not in Bernard Shaw; at least I can claim that. Poor Jean Seberg wasn't up to the film. When Preminger told me that he was trying to find an unknown actress, I thought it was just a publicity stunt and that we'd end up with a well-known actress. But not a bit of it. She became an actress later, though, with *Au Bout du Souffle*. And I came to regret that when Carol Reed and I were planning *Our Man in Havana*. We went out to New York to see the Columbia man about casting and he suggested Jean Seberg for Guinness's daughter. *Au Bout du Souffle* hadn't come out then, so I rejected her, saying 'but she can't act'. Instead we ended up with the most appalling girl.

8
Aspects of Americana

Director Ken Annakin and writer Guy Elmes had first collaborated in 1952 on a steamy, studio-bound melodrama, *The Planter's Wife* with Claudette Colbert and Jack Hawkins. They had both since made separate ventures into Greeneland – Elmes with *The Stranger's Hand* and Annakin with *Loser Takes All*. Always an admirer of Greene's and, after *Stranger's Hand*, a friend too, Elmes had been taking a careful look at the short stories to see what he and Annakin, now also a close friend, could develop into some future project.

Annakin recalls: 'He and I both loved the story of *Across the Bridge* and of course Graham wrote only half of the story we wanted to tell. We wanted to show how this buนิ၊ ฉนเฑนน came to be in the state he was and which Graham had observed and wrote about only around the bridge between the United States and Mexico.

Published first as one of the *Nineteen Stories* collection of 1947, the ten-page tale (which had been actually written in 1938) reappeared in the amended *Twenty-one Stories* volume of 1954. It is easy to understand why the film-makers were excited, for like so much of Greene's work, notably his short stories, *Across the Bridge* is pregnant with filmic possibilities.

Through a narrator we observe Joseph Calloway, an English financier on the run after swindling his shareholders, as he kicks his heels in a dingy little Mexican border town. 'I don't know how,' says the narrator, 'to treat this story – it was a tragedy for Mr Calloway, it was poetic retribution, I suppose, in the eyes of the shareholders whom he'd ruined with his bogus transactions, and to . . . me, at this stage, it was a comedy – except when he kicked the dog.'[1] Calloway's dog is in fact the disgraced businessman's only friend – although it is a love–hate relationship – and, ultimately, his downfall.

While Calloway is attempting to find ways of permanently staying in Mexico, the two British detectives on his trail realize that as extradition is likely to prove a long and onerous business, they will have to try some other way of getting their man.

They manage to kidnap the dog and take it back across the US border thinking, rightly, that Calloway will be desperate, in spite of the danger, to retrieve his four-footed friend. In the tragi-comic finale – which we now view from the American side of the bridge – the dog has leapt from his captor's car and is joyfully attempting to rejoin his approaching master. On the bridge, the police car swerves to avoid the dog, and instead knocks down and kills Calloway. His only mourner is the dog.

The dog motif was one that particularly fascinated Guy Elmes: 'I wanted to call it *The Power of the Dog*, from Kipling's poem:

> There is sorrow enough in the natural way
> From men and women to fill our day;
> But when we are certain of sorrow in store,
> Why do we always arrange for more?
> Brothers and Sisters, I bid you beware
> Of giving your heart to a dog to tear.[2]

The point was, here you had a hard and wicked criminal and yet he gave his heart to a dog. In fact I couldn't make anyone understand that and they thought that with a title like that it would be all about hypnotizing dogs, or something.' Elmes managed to flesh out a full-length script from Greene's germ using the idea that the financier has had to take on a new personality to get to Mexico but unwittingly has assumed the identity of someone who is in even worse trouble than he. Annakin liked the notion, but at that stage they could not find a backer and it had to be shelved.

Guy Elmes:

A couple of years later, we were called into Rank's because they wanted to do a picture with Ken and he submitted some other script we had written together and they said 'no'. We then had the horror of one of the people at Rank saying to us, 'my wife has read a book and liked it very much. It's all about South Africa. You two can do that.' We went away and read it – it was called *Nor the Moon by Night* – and it was dreadful. We said we'd do it only if they let us do *Across the Bridge* and, somewhat to our surprise, they said 'yes'. I remember it was by then a rather dusty old script. I popped it into a taxi which took it to Pinewood and the deal was done the next evening.

John Stafford was brought in to produce the third and last of his Greene adaptations. Ken Annakin:

I remember we had a ball working on the script at my home. When we delivered it to John we thought he'd rave about it; but, in fact, he raved rather negatively. He said that we'd written a fabulous story 'but Graham will hate it' apparently because the characters we'd fashioned were far more ours than Graham's, even though they fitted into the story. He made us simplify the story and go back to simpler characters. The result was a final draft (with some dialogue 'polishing' by another writer, Denis Freeman) that John showed to Graham and Graham approved.

Quite why Greene had to be appeased is not clear; *Across the Bridge* was like many other films made from his original material; the rights had been sold and someone else was doing the adaptation. The most likely explanation was that since John Stafford was a particularly close friend of the author, he probably felt that a tacit approval from source was preferable, if not strictly necessary.

Considering the slimness of the original, its translation into a 103-minute film is a masterpiece of expansion and invention until the almost common dénouement at the fateful bridge. Calloway, however, is no more. Instead, he has become Carl Schaffner, a New York-based millionaire, British by passport though not by birth.

Hearing that Scotland Yard have started investigations of the ledgers at his London office, which will reveal deficiencies of

£3,000,000, Schaffner decides to get away to Mexico where he has a fortune in pesos stored away against such an emergency. On the trip he meets a Mexican, Paul Scarff, throws him off the speeding train and takes over his identity. Scarff's ticket was not booked through to Mexico so Schaffner has to get out at a border town where, to his surprise, he is handed a dog, Dolores, which belonged to Scarff. Hoping to cross the Mexican border as Scarff, the financier hires a car but on the way he finds evidence that Scarff is a political assassin and that a large reward is offered for his capture.

Realizing that his plan has misfired, Schaffner goes to the place where Scarff was thrown but it is deserted as Scarff has been taken, badly injured, to a nearby motel. Schaffner manages to trace him and retrieve his own passport. Schaffner tricks a truck driver into believing him to be Scarff, anticipating (rightly) that he will take him over the border to retrieve the reward. To clear himself in Mexico, he himself tells the police chief where the real Paul Scarff is and claims the reward himself. But the policeman withholds Schaffner's passport hoping to blackmail him for some of the money he knows Schaffner to have and without his passport Schaffner cannot get his cache of pesos.

It also transpires that Scarff was a hero to the Mexican peasants of the border town and so Schaffner, because he betrayed him, is hated, finds himself without food, accommodation or a friendly word. He is forced to live out in the open with only Dolores as his friend. One day the dog strays across the bridge, is spotted by the watchful Scotland Yard men on Schaffner's trail and is tethered to the bridge, just on the US side . . .

Guy Elmes: 'I remember saying, "we must get Rod Steiger to play Schaffner" and everyone replying "who's Rod Steiger?"' From almost the opening shot of the film, as a black, square back posed atop a skyscraper turns round to disclose himself as thick-set, Germanic, wearing rimless glasses and speaking with a faint foreign accent, Rod Steiger dominates the proceedings as the financier. Steiger, one of the graduates from the then extremely fashionable method school of acting, had made some nine films before *Across the Bridge*, including *On the Waterfront* (as the memorable Charlie, Brando's older brother), *The Big Knife* (as a vicious film-studio chief) and *Oklahoma!* (as the loathsome Jud). Ken Annakin said:

Steiger and I had to work very hard on the part before we could adapt his technique to the rest of the acting. He gave us a fortnight of his time, without pay, so that we could thrash the whole thing out quietly in his London flat before shooting began. I have never known an actor put so much thought and preparation into a performance. At times he overdid it, and we had some tense moments on the floor. For the first week of filming things were touch and go between us. There was one especially trying day when he found nothing right with the script or the other performances. He decided that British scriptwriters knew nothing about dialogue and seemed to think all British actors were savages. I let him go on airing his method jargon but the next day I put my foot down. It came home to him then that the British did know something about acting after all.[3]

The critics seemed to be more interested in the notion of method coming to a British film than in the film itself. Leonard Mosley wrote:

Rod Steiger is a Hollywood star who does not mind how many of his faces are left lying on the cutting-room floor so long as ten per cent of what goes into the camera comes up on the screen . . . he mouths, he weeps, he grovels, splutters, shudders, grunts and moans his way through the script. Then with the help of a strong-minded director, he cuts out the surplus nonsense and shapes from the rest a true picture of the character he is attempting to portray.[4]

Paul Dehn:

St Sebastian never gazed skyward with so monumental a look of martyrdom as Dolores (the dog) in her final anguish. Landseer never found a sitter whose nose was more moist with devotion. Had the film been a silent one, she might have queened it over all comers; but though she can snarl and yelp and whimper as evocatively as any exponent of the method, she cannot speak – and here Mr Steiger has the measure of her.[5]

Although around eighty per cent is of the film-maker's

invention, *Across the Bridge* does catch many Greeneland under-
tones, not least the use of a thriller plot allied to a study of grubby
desperation. And although there are certain technical differences in
the finale, the short story's element of tragi-comedy is kept almost
wholly intact. As with the story, the pathetic financier eventually,
if somewhat fortuitously, manages to elicit our sympathy.

Ken Annakin considers it his best work but explains why he
believes the film was not commercially successful:

> I felt the film had a style, a sharpness and a poignancy but it was
> too near the harshness of real life to be popular. It would be easy
> to say that Rod Steiger was not a big enough star name to bring
> people into the cinema. But on the other hand, it wouldn't have
> been *Across the Bridge* without Rod . . . it was a downbeat story,
> harsh and pulled no punches. I suppose we might have done
> better with a woman integrated into the story, but it wasn't that
> type of story.[6]

There were also problems in showing the film in the States
because, it seems, the Mexicans were upset as they felt the movie
showed them to be venal.

The final word is with Steiger himself:

> Everyone is so afraid of failure. Actors have the myth that it is
> ruinous to do a scene with a dog or a baby. When I told my
> Hollywood friends that I was making a picture called *Across the
> Bridge*, they all said, 'You're through, finished. You're doing a
> picture with a dog.' I told them, 'I don't understand what
> you're saying. Where the dog is important we'll photograph the
> dog. Where I'm important, we'll photograph me.' That's what
> we did, and the dog and I both came out alive.[7]

Perhaps the best thing about Paramount's *Short Cut to Hell*, the
1957 low-budget remake of *This Gun for Hire*, was the studio's
handout to accompany release. The film, it proclaimed, 'has the
ingredients most sought after by the movie-going public: love,
action, suspense and entertainment'. It also had the legendary
James Cagney as its debutant director: 'the property so entranced
him that he decided to abandon acting for the time being for the

opportunity to direct it. It was a happy decision both for Jimmy and Paramount, because he experienced the thrill of a new dimension in show business, and the studio received the benefit of his years of experience as a screen actor.'

It is difficult to know quite what 'entranced' Cagney about this particular 'property' particularly when, later in the same handout, he is quoted as saying:

> I am directing *Short Cut to Hell* for one reason only. That's because my young friend, former publicist, A.C. Lyles, asked me to. I doubt if I'll direct another film. After all I'm an actor and that's the way I like it. Unlike a lot of actors, I have no desire to direct permanently. I find it's fun and a challenge, and I like challenges. But as far as I'm concerned, this'll be it.

Which it was. Sad to relate that, unlike his fellow actor Charles Laughton's one and only venture behind the camera which resulted in the masterpiece *Night of the Hunter*, Cagney's one-off was pretty undistinguished – even though he was to wear his 'lucky' *Yankee Doodle Dandy* (for which he won an Oscar) shoes throughout shooting.

While Greene is allowed a 'from a novel' credit, the screenplay by Ted Berkman and Raphael Blau is virtually lifted intact from Burnett and Maltz's 1942 effort, with just the names and a few plot points changed. Raven is now Kyle, Anne/Ellen becomes Glory and Davis/Gates turns into Bahrwell. There are no international implications this time round. Kyle is hired to kill because of the imminent disclosure of faulty building specifications. His 'redemption' is suitably mundane. Riddled with police bullets, he hands over to Glory's cop boyfriend Big Business's taped confession.

Kyle/Raven is not far removed from a number of the tough-guy roles perpetrated by Cagney in some of his best Warner Brothers movies but, remarks Patrick McGilligan, a Cagney biographer, the beginning of the film where Kyle 'viciously manhandles a young girl, bouncing her sadistically out of his apartment' has 'the only hint of any kind of Cagney touch'. The rest of the film, says McGilligan is 'humdrum, downright trite and just plain routine. Cagney's contribution is difficult to unravel but it is certain that his one fling at direction was an unqualified disaster.'

Apart from those splendid publicity notes which also reveal such delights that Cagney had to direct in sign language because of the deafening noise inside one of the factory locations, and that Rhubarb, Kyle's cat, had appeared in a movie some six years earlier with Ray Milland and Jan Sterling, *Short Cut to Hell* did employ a gimmick that I can recall being used only one other time, on Cecil B. de Mille's *The Ten Commandments* – a director's prologue.

Seated in a director's chair, with his name grandiosely emblazoned on the back, Cagney turns to face the camera. He explains that the film is his first directing endeavour and that he is 'thrilled' to introduce two 'exciting young actors – Robert Ivers (as Kyle) and Georgann Johnson (as Glory)'. That said, he turns his back and the film begins. Greene never got round to seeing this third-hand version of his work.

'A complete treachery' is how Greene dismisses, even now with pain, Joseph Mankiewicz's film of *The Quiet American*. He must have had early wind of the kind of liberties Mankiewicz – as screen-writer, producer and director of the project – would take, via a *Times* report of 9 January 1957 from the paper's Saigon correspondent under the sub-heading: FILM 'TRAVESTY' OF THE NOVEL:

> Mr Joseph L. Mankiewicz, the Hollywood producer, has arrived here to make arrangements for filming Mr Graham Greene's novel, *The Quiet American*. He and his staff will stay in Vietnam for eight weeks to take views of Saigon and the surrounding countryside which form the setting of Mr Greene's story . . . Owing to its somewhat cavalier treatment of Vietnamese nationalists, the book has not been popular in official circles here, where it has been discreetly banned. Many people were therefore interested to hear that the story would be filmed in Saigon. Any qualms the Vietnamese might have had have been set at rest as it transpires that the general theme of the film will bear little relation to that of the book. Hollywood's version will be a safe one – that of the triumphant emergence of the democratic forces in the young and independent state of Vietnam backed by the United States, accompanied by the

downfall of the British and French imperialists. The Vietnamese
heroine, after the death of the American whom she loved, acts
as a good nationalist by rejecting the cynical opium-smoking
Englishman in favour of a politically irreproachable Vietnamese
husband. Though some commentators here are mildly shocked
that Mr Greene should permit this travesty of his work, others
are saying 'it serves him right for writing such an anti-American
book'. There is quite a controversy about it.

About three weeks after that report, Greene entered the fray by
writing *The Times* a short note, addressed from the suitably
literary confines of the Algonquin Hotel in New York. His
remarks were pragmatic, even occasionally flippant, rather than
conveying that earlier retrospective feeling of great betrayal:

> It is certainly true that if a story is sold to Hollywood the author
> retains no control over the adaptation. But perhaps a
> Machiavellian policy is justified – one can trust Hollywood to
> overbid its hand. If such changes as your correspondent
> describes have been made in the film of *The Quiet American* they
> will make only the more obvious the discrepancy between what
> the State Department would like the world to believe and what
> in fact happened in Vietnam. In that case, I can imagine some
> happy evenings of laughter not only in Paris but in the cinemas
> of Saigon.[8]

If *The Times* correspondent was being partially wise *before* the
event, it is worth noting the remarks of the *Financial Times* critic
after viewing the finished film a little over a year later:

> Mr Greene wrote a novel which, though often overpleading and
> at times offensive, was very clear indeed in its intentions. The
> aim was to contrast the comparatively harmless ways of a
> cynical, disengaged British journalist with the unwitting havoc
> spread by a well-meaning American anxious to do good to
> foreigners. Explicitly, but none the less brazenly, Mr Man-
> kiewicz has simply turned the issue inside out: the American
> dies a martyr, the Englishman is exposed as a murderous dupe.[9]

To put it another way, the story was switched from being

anti-American – or an attack on American political ingenuousness, at its mildest – to being specifically anti-communist. All of which makes a little suspect a companion letter to Greene's in those same *Times* columns from Michael Redgrave, who was to play Fowler, the British journalist. Hoisting himself well and truly on his own petard, Redgrave writes:

> Projected films of well-known novels always arouse a host of people who are prepared to wager that 'they won't get it right', a bet which on more than one occasion may be claimed to have been won. But your correspondent . . . is surely speculating unwarrantably. Either he has not read the script and is basing his report on local gossip, as his use of the phrase 'it transpires' seems to indicate, or his interpretation of it differs in several important details from mine . . . as the only English member of the cast I would like to assure the many admirers of the novel, and a great many more people as well, that in no way is the 'downfall of the French and British imperialists' injected into the film translation of Mr Greene's novel.[10]

Greene's reaction to Hollywood tampering was rightly pragmatic. It had happened before with adaptations; it would happen again. In the particular case of *The Quiet American*, he had handed over the rights to his daughter so she could sell them to buy a ranch in Canada. He had no control over the subsequent purchaser and surely expected none. His own longer-term bitterness probably stems from what he felt was the corruption of two main tenets – his own innate anti-Americanism and of a particular view of a country with which, he admits, he had fallen in love after spending four winters there between 1951 and 1955 – 'In Indo-China I drained a magic potion, a loving-cup which I have shared since with many retired *colons* and officers of the Foreign Legion whose eyes light up at the mention of Saigon and Hanoi.'[11]

His brief flirtation with communism at Oxford – 'a youthful prank' – had subsequent repercussions long after the joke had worn off. He fell victim to the notorious McCarran Act of 1952, was deported from Puerto Rico in 1954 and was deemed a 'prohibited immigrant' to the States for a number of years – all of which cannot have helped to improve his feelings for a country for which he had held a long-time 'revulsion'. He explained:

You can find traces of anti-Americanism in film reviews I wrote in the thirties . . . but my animosity doesn't derive from the cinema. It goes back to my first visit to the United States, between 1937 and 1938. That winter I travelled about a great deal before going to Mexico to look into the religious persecution there. I have always felt very ill at ease in the States . . . the terrifying weight of this consumer society oppresses me.[12]

The dream of 'communism with a human face' is one still nurtured by Greene; a naïve dream, he has to admit – 'one concludes that communism is unlikely ever to escape from Stalinism or dictatorship'.[13]

It is worth noting here a comment made by George Orwell on Greene in 1949: 'Of course Greene is a Catholic and on some issues has to take sides politically with the Church, but in outlook he is just a mild left with faint Communist Party leanings. I have even thought that he might become our first Catholic fellow-traveller.'

Before embarking on the book, Greene wrote to Evelyn Waugh telling him: 'It will be a relief not to have to write about *God* for a change.' A mock-horrified Waugh replied with, 'Oh, I wouldn't drop God if I were you. Not at this stage anyway. It would be like P.G. Wodehouse dropping Jeeves halfway through the Wooster series.'

Apart from the story being, says Greene, 'turned upside down' at the end, Mankiewicz generally sticks pretty closely to the novel. The film begins with a spectacularly photographed (by Robert Krasker, who had lit *The Third Man*) Chinese New Year procession in Saigon. A paper-dragon's head becomes detached from the main throng and drifts away, eventually alighting near the body of the 'quiet American' Pyle (Audie Murphy) face down in a ditch near the river. We cut to Fowler who is being asked by the Saigon Sûreté chief Vigot (Claude Dauphin) to identify the body and so begins a long flashback which comprises most of the film.

Pyle, working for an economic aid mission, believes that problems could be solved in Indo-China by the intervention of a 'third force' which is why he seems to be closely involved with the supporters of the rebel General The. He also falls in love with Fowler's girlfriend, the dance-hall hostess Phuong. Fowler, for his part, finds Pyle both exasperating and desperately naïve as well as becoming bitterly jealous about his involvement with Phuong.

When Pyle saves Fowler's life after they are both caught in a communist ambush, the journalist's resentment is heightened by an inevitable sense of obligation. And when Fowler gets a letter back from his wife in England refusing the divorce he seeks so he can marry Phuong, he lies to her; she then leaves him after learning of his deception. Fowler is approached by the communists who tell him that Pyle is importing plastics being used for the manufacture of bombs by The's terrorists. Following a street bomb-outrage, Fowler confronts Pyle with complicity in the civilian killings which the American denies, though he does admit contact with The, independent of any US government involvement. He also declares he wants to marry Phuong. Fowler betrays Pyle to the communists, knowing he is sending him to his death. David Robinson writes:

> Up to the point where Fowler is persuaded to betray Pyle to General The's opponents, who quietly murder him and dump his body in the river mud, Mankiewicz follows the story with almost pedestrian fidelity. The moral conflicts, it is true, are largely suppressed, and there are small changes of detail which only later become significant. There is now no indication that Fowler is an opium addict; the police chief Vigot no longer reads Pascal . . . the two or three horrific little incidents which in the novel confirm Fowler in his loathing of war have been clearly excised, Fowler's resentment of the material opulence and sterilized organization of the American way of life is reduced to one incident in which he asks the American for a cigarette and boorishly refuses the counter-offer of a whole packet – 'I asked for one cigarette, not economic aid.' But the film completely departs from the book, however, only after Pyle's death. Mankiewicz makes Vigot, until now a minor figure, come to Fowler and reveal that it was all a communist plot. Pyle was innocent all the time; he, Fowler, has been duped into acting as an accessory to his murder. Setting aside the inconsistency of this revelation with Pyle's insistence, earlier in the film, that the American government so disapproves of his actions that it is having him sent back to the States, and the improbability of the communists hatching so involved a plot to

effect the murder of an innocent and quiet American, this new dénouement quite nullifies the problem Greene seemed to intend. So there is no longer any doubt of Fowler's moral position in the affair.[14]

At the end of the novel and the film, Fowler receives a telegram from his wife finally agreeing to start divorce proceedings. In the book, Phuong is delighted at the prospect of becoming the second 'Mrs Fowlair'. Fowler concludes that everything had gone right for him since Pyle had died 'but how I wished there existed someone to whom I could say I was sorry'. Robinson continues:

> In the film, to ensure everything goes wrong with him, the character of Phuong, the stoical Indo-Chinese girl who leaves Fowler for Pyle and quite easily and naturally returns to him on the night Pyle dies, has been forced into a more recognizably moral Western mould. Ferociously resentful, she returns to her former life as a dance hostess rather than ever speak to Fowler again. The significance of the last words of the novel, which are also the last words of the film, is ironically changed.[15]

Mankiewicz was attracted to Greene's original material by the character of Fowler: 'I've often wanted to do a picture about one of those ice-blooded intellectuals whose intellectualism is really just a mask for completely irrational passion. Fowler, I felt, was such a character.'

On the eve of the film's release in the States, the producer-director of such durable masterpieces as *All About Eve*, *Letter to Three Wives* and *The Barefoot Contessa*, was clearly concerned as to how the public would take to *The Quiet American*: 'How many of them ever heard of Michael Redgrave? And what will Audie Murphy fans think when they find their hero dead in the mud in the very first shot?'

Viewed in isolation, it has to be said that Mankiewicz's film is rather a fine one. It is exciting, intelligent and well acted. Audie Murphy's brand of earnest all-Americanness is rather well suited to portraying Pyle even if his lack of acting experience makes him come off second best particularly in his scenes with Redgrave, who is admirable as the cynical and disillusioned Fowler.

Curiously enough the best scene in the film is pure Mankiewicz

– when Vigot, well played by Claude Dauphin, confronts Fowler with his own moral bankruptcy after Pyle's death. David Robinson expounds an intriguing rationale of Mankiewicz's 'distortions . . . to have treated the novel in this audacious manner must elicit a kind of admiration. It seems a much more clever way to impose an ideology to redirect the writings of its critics rather than to suppress them directly, as is the custom of Catholics and communists, for example.'[16] Greene is more specific: 'The only reason they were allowed to make the film there was because they turned it into propaganda for the Heroic South. After all, the book had been forbidden in South Vietnam.'

Interestingly, a year or so after the film's release, an altogether more faithful version of *The Quiet American* in play version was being performed to packed houses on the Moscow stage. It was reported that a French film company was negotiating for the film rights to the play and had asked Greene to undertake his own script, which, the report went on, Greene said he would be delighted to do.

Greene told me there never was any possibility he would do such a thing – he had seen the play himself in Russia, 'it was terrible, very old-fashioned and badly acted'. He did add that now, more than a quarter of a century on, he had been alerted to the possibility of a new film version, had seen a 'reasonably good script' but had absolutely no interest in a remake, even if it meant an honest revision of past distortions. Greene: 'I'd rather just forget about it, forget everything except the book because I get nothing out of it.' He has also said: 'One could almost believe that [Mankiewicz's] film was made deliberately to attack the book and its author. But the book was based on a closer knowledge of the Indo-China war than the American director possessed and I am vain enough to believe that the book will survive a few years longer than Mr Mankiewicz's incoherent picture.'[17]

In view of the tragic subsequent events that have overtaken Vietnam, there is something especially fascinating now about revisiting both the novel and the film. And one has to admire Greene's percipience in detecting the role the Americans would play in Vietnam post mid-fifties. He is more modest:

It was very easy for someone who had spent four winters in Indo-China to grasp the situation in which the Americans were going to be enmeshed. One could put a finger on a number of operations set in hand by the CIA (the CIA was behind the bomb attack in the Saigon square which I mentioned in the novel, for example). But that did not represent war and I can't say that I predicted it; I was content to suggest the American undercurrents in the French war.

It's not a question of foresight but of ground reconnaissance; every good journalist should be able to recognize the signs of the times.[18]

PART FOUR

The Sixties

9
Caribbean Cocktails

A month or so before *Our Man in Havana* was published (in 1958), Alfred Hitchcock was reported as being a chief bidder for the film rights. The asking price? £50,000. The possibility of a Hitch–Greene association was a piquant prospect, in view of the sort of lashing that Hitchcock the director received from the pen of Greene the reviewer in the thirties:

> an inadequate sense of reality . . . His films consist of a series of small 'amusing' melodramatic situations: the murderer's buttons dropped on the baccarat board; the strangled organist's hands prolonging the notes in an empty church . . . very perfunctorily he builds up to these tricky situations (paying no attention on the way to inconsistencies, loose ends, psychological absurdities) and then drops them they mean nothing. they lead to nothing.[1]

Greene admitted to me that he liked some of Hitchcock's later work (after he went to Hollywood) such as *Notorious*. But as far as *Our Man in Havana* was concerned, some of Hitch's older habits had died hard. Says Greene: 'Hitchcock tried, and claimed he was, buying the rights but I refused to sell them to him. I felt the book just wouldn't survive his touch.'

In ruling Hitchcock out for this subject he may, subconsciously, have been recalling his remarks voicing concern about the film-maker's auteurism in a review of *Secret Agent*:

How unfortunate it is that Mr Hitchcock, a clever director, is allowed to produce and even to write his own films. Though as a producer he has no sense of continuity and as a writer he has no sense of life . . . as for Mr (Somerset) Maugham's *Ashenden*, on which this film is said to be based, nothing is left of that witty and realistic fiction.[2]

Greene recalls that the idea of writing a Secret Service comedy came to him following a request soon after the Second World War from his friend Alberto Cavalcanti to write a film for him. His experiences in, first, West Africa, and then as part of Kim Philby's sub-section of the Secret Service dealing with counter-espionage in the Iberian Peninsula, had been a spectacular source of good, satiric material. Yet the seed had been planted more than ten years before that. Reviewing Pierre Billon's *Deuxième Bureau* in January 1936, he wrote, prophetically: 'what an amusing film of the Secret Service could be made if the intention was satiric and not romantic, the treatment realistic and not violent'.[3]

In tracing German Abwehr activity in Portugal, he had come across many cases of officers sending home completely fictitious reports based on 'information' received from imaginary agents. A lucrative ruse too, with the officers claiming all kinds of expenses on behalf of their supposedly valuable contacts.

For Cavalcanti, who had directed *Went the Day Well?*, he wrote a single-page outline. The setting was Tallinn, capital of Estonia, in 1938, where an English agent, with a grossly extravagant wife, is led into bamboozling the Secret Service. As war approached, so his enemies and the local police begin to take him more seriously.

Before they started work together, Cavalcanti told Greene he thought it would be necessary to get clearance for such a tale from the censor – 'and he was told that no certificate could be issued to a film that made fun of the Secret Service. At least that was the story he told me. Perhaps he invented an excuse because he was not enamoured of the subject.'[4] So the subject and a film went into abeyance.

During the fifties, Greene visited Cuba and its capital Havana a number of times, finding the atmosphere agreeably *louche*:

Suddenly it struck me that here in this extraordinary city, where every vice was permissible and every trade possible, lay the true background for my comedy. I realized I had been planning the wrong situation and placing it at the wrong period. The shadows in 1938 of the war to come had been too dark for comedy; the reader could feel no sympathy for a man who was cheating his country in Hitler's day for the sake of an extravagant wife. But in fantastic Havana, among the absurdities of the Cold War . . . there was a situation allowably comic, all the more if I changed the wife into a daughter.[5]

Jim Wormold, manager of a vacuum-cleaner agency in Havana, is single-handedly bringing up a pretty daughter – his wife has left him – of increasingly extravagant late-teenage tastes. When he is propositioned by the British Secret Service's Caribbean network head, Hawthorne, to become 'Our Man in Havana' with the promise of $150 a month, plus expenses 'tax free' he sees it as a way out of his financial burdens. Hawthorne gives him a brief instruction in how to send messages by book code, some invisible ink and a code number before leaving him to his own devices.

Wormold has no idea how to recruit his own local spy ring nor what he would do with it if he had one but his newfound affluence soon encourages him to invent what he cannot find, including plans for some gigantically mysterious installations in the mountains that look suspiciously like vacuum cleaners. London is delighted and decides to send a secretary, Beatrice, and a radio operator, Rudy, to help him out. Wormold's elaborate deception soon begins to turn in on itself, trapping innocent people. The 'other side' is now out to get him and he is also threatened with deportation by the notorious Captain Segura, dubbed 'The Red Vulture'. When Wormold's best friend Dr Hasselbacher – who has been dragged into the charade-turned-real to act for the 'other side' – is murdered and he is nearly poisoned at a businessmen's luncheon, he decides to fight back, though when it comes actually to dispatching the 'other side's' agent Carter, it ends up being in self-defence rather than cold-bloodedly.

The truth is now out and father and daughter are deported – to Segura's slight chagrin since he had designs on Milly – back to London where far from receiving a fearful reckoning from the authorities, Wormold is offered a fresh assignment as a lecturer and a decoration, 'in your case . . . we can hardly suggest anything higher than an OBE'. We also assume that Wormold will make a life with Beatrice.

In his earlier visits to the island, Greene says that he had never stayed long enough to learn much about the harsh Batista regime with its imprisonment and torture, but as he planned the story, so some of the realities became more apparent and it became clear that civil war and ultimate revolution were in the offing (which would bring forth Fidel Castro). The book was published in the last days of the Batista regime which also remained intact during the first recces by Greene and his new collaborator, who was for the third and last time, Carol Reed.

By the time the cast and crew descended on Havana six months later, the Castro revolt had succeeded, which posed some mundane, if fundamental, problems such as how to keep Castro's bearded followers out of crowd scenes; how to make extras wear the hated blue uniform of the Batista police and how to get the Ministry of the Interior's seal of approval on the 30,000-word script.

Greene admits that the book had done him little good with the new powers in Cuba:

> In poking fun at the British Secret Service, I had minimized the terror of Batista's rule. I had not wanted too black a background for a light-hearted comedy, but those who had suffered during the years of dictatorship could hardly be expected to appreciate that my real subject was the absurdity of the British agent and not the justice of a revolution, nor did my aesthetic reasons for changing a savage Captain Ventura (head of Batista's police) into a cynical Captain Segura appeal to them.[6]

According to B.J. Bedard:

> the sensitivity of the new revolutionary government caused Reed a number of problems. Thirty-nine changes were required in the script, and a censor was assigned to the location shooting. Reed may have helped to minimize the problems by using a Cuban assistant director, employing Cuban stand-by technicians and an extremely large number of extras (with beards suitably trimmed). The puritanism of the new government made it difficult to re-create fully the bawdiness of such Havana establishments as the Shanghai Theatre (long known for its nude shows). The garish Tropicana was available for Milly's

birthday as the casinos had not all been closed. The new government was also sensitive to the Cuban image and even insisted that a bootblack have clean trousers.[7]

Early on, during location scenes, Reed said:

What they want is to make sure that our story, which is set in the old regime, shows just what a police state it was then. We are doing that anyway with odd little scenes outside police stations and references to torture of political prisoners. But most of the plot is comedy and we cannot make it too heavy. The authorities here don't want to make it appear that anything that happens under Batista could possibly happen again now. So when they saw Noël Coward (as Hawthorne) being pursued down a street by three musicians twanging guitars in his face, they thought this might give a wrong impression. We just go on filming; there's no question of our having to stop because of trouble.[8]

Then there was the arrival of the American actor Ernie Kovacs, who was to play Segura, wearing a heavy beard. It was considered too much a symbol of the Castro regime to be worn by a character resembling the hated Captain Ventura; so Kovacs was shorn of all but a slim moustache.

As with *The Fallen Idol* and *The Third Man*, Reed and Greene worked very closely during the adaptation. Greene says:

There was always a moment during the writing – usually about midway through the script – when one despaired and said 'for God's sake, let's chuck this up!' followed by some hard words. Always coming from me, I'm afraid. On *Our Man in Havana*, we took a suite at the Metropole in Brighton. I had a bedroom, there was a sitting-room where a secretary worked and beyond that another bedroom where Carol slept. I would get up fairly early, do a quota of pages, hand them to the secretary who would type them before passing them on to Carol in bed. Carol and I would meet at lunchtime and discuss progress before going back to work again the same way in the afternoon. In the evenings we amused ourselves. We had that kind of closeness.

Following a caption that 'this film is set in Cuba before the recent revolution', Reed launches his film with a spectacular piece of scene-setting. The camera, angled down on a long-haired Latin-American girl swimming in a shimmering pool, tilts slowly upwards to reveal that the pool is set on a skyscraper rooftop from where one can see the whole layout of Havana. The camera then swoops down to street level and settles on a street corner where a local boy and girl are eyeing each other provocatively. They are frozen and the credits roll with Hermanos Deniz's Cuban Rhythm Band moving into its insistent stride. Unfrozen, the couple set off together across the street as round the corner strides an immaculately suited Noël Coward, hemmed in by humanity. Now we are into the tale, which with a few changes of emphasis, some more explanatory dialogue and merely a handful of incidental scenes omitted, otherwise follows the book very faithfully.

In the film we are from the very start made much more aware of a sinister police presence as a car with Segura in the back is shown shadowing Hawthorne (Coward), the Caribbean network chief. When a man springs forward to protest some injustice through the car window, he is quickly pulled away and savagely dealt with. As Hawthorne and Wormold make their initial contact in the shop, we cut to the street bar where Hasselbacher, first reluctant to show his papers at the police's request, moves hurriedly and fearfully when the policeman utters: 'I am Captain Segura.' No more need be said.

The point is underlined when Wormold tells Hasselbacher: 'I don't want Milly to grow up in an atmosphere like this with men like Captain Segura', and emphasized yet further when Milly, explaining away her friendship with Segura, tells her father: 'I know he tortures prisoners but he never touches me.' These more explicit reminders of the Batista regime do not however hurt the transition of the book's splendid comedy which works particularly well on screen in famous scenes like Wormold's recruitment by Hawthorne in the lavatory of Sloppy Joe's street bar. A bemused Wormold is told to go to the loo and he, Hawthorne, will follow: 'Don't let me down. You're an Englishman.'

The film's only principal additions, which are in themselves by way of being developments of an existing plot point, are scenes in the country club where Wormold is actually shown trying to recruit his own ring of agents. It all goes embarrassingly wrong in

On muleback, Maggie Smith, Louis Gossett Jnr and Alec McCowen in *Travels With My Aunt* (KOBAL COLLECTION)

Maggie Smith and Corinne Marchand in *Travels With My Aunt* (KOBAL COLLECTION)

Michael York and Hildegarde Neil in *England Made Me* (KOBAL COLLECTION)

Peter Finch, Hildegarde Neil and Michael York in *England Made Me* (KOBAL COLLECTION)

Otto Preminger *(centre)* on the set of *The Human Factor* with Derek Jacobi and Nicol Williamson *(right)*. (WHEEL PRODUCTIONS)

Nicol Williamson and Iman in *The Human Factor* (KOBAL COLLECTION)

Elpidia Carrillo and Richard Gere in *The Honorary Consul* (KOBAL COLLECTION)

Michael Caine, Bob Hoskins and Elpidia Carrillo in *The Honorary Consul* (KOBAL COLLECTION)

Rupert Everett and Jenny Seagrove in *A Shocking Accident* (FLAMINGO PICTURES)

Graham Greene *(left)* as an insurance representative in a scene from *Day For Night* (WARNER BROS)

James Mason as *Dr Fischer Of Geneva*
(BBC/CONSOLIDATED)

Alexander Korda with Graham Greene (right)
aboard Korda's yacht *Elsewhere* (MICHAEL KORDA)

Greta Scacchi and Alan Bates in *Dr Fischer Of Geneva* (BBC/CONSOLIDATED)

Graham Greene pictured at his apartment in Antibes (GRAHAM WOOD/DAILY MAIL)

Graham Greene pictured at his apartment in Antibes (GRAHAM WOOD/DAILY MAIL)

Paul Scofield in *When Greek Meets Greek*, one of the
Shades of Greene series (THAMES TELEVISION)

Michael Gough and Liz Gebhardt in *The Case For The Defence*, one of the *Shades Of Greene* series
(THAMES TELEVISION)

the case of Engineer Cifuentes when Wormold attempts a Hawthorne-style recruiting in the club lavatory. His cryptic approach is badly misinterpreted. When Wormold sends his list of recruits back to London we see a visual re-enactment of wholly successful enlistments, including that of Cifuentes, which are merely part of his fertile imagination.

Inevitably the switch to a rather darker mood as Wormold's fantasies begin to rebound badly is slightly uneasy but is nevertheless, I feel, nicely achieved. The businessmen's banquet where Wormold is due to be poisoned and only, in the nick of time, discovers his adversary, is nail-bitingly effective and darkly droll as eventually 'the dog it was that died'. With Hasselbacher now dead too, Carter, the enemy with the tell-tale stammer, is marked down for retribution by Wormold. He lures Segura into a game of checkers using his collection of alcoholic miniatures instead of the normal pieces. When a piece is taken, it must be drunk. The idea is that Wormold will get Segura drunk so that he can steal the police chief's gun with which he will dispatch Carter. When Segura does lapse into an alcoholic sleep, the film itself totally changes direction, albeit temporarily, into stark melodrama as Wormold and Carter play a cat-and-mouse game round the bars and streets of Havana.

Reed changed his lighting to suit the switch of mood, using first a wide-angle lens to convey the effect of walls closing in and then using sharp, hard lights in the night exteriors, 'making the streets slick and slimy, getting that little black and white feeling.

With Carter dead, the mood is immediately lightened and after Wormold's deportation – 'I don't feel safe with you around,' Segura tells him – there is the splendidly stiff-upper-lip confrontation back in London with his spymasters. At least Wormold's elaborately conceived plans of giant installations never left this office, they all muse thankfully. We cut to a corner of Parliament Square where Wormold, Beatrice and Milly walk past a street vendor selling 'Made in Japan' motorized toy models oddly reminiscent of those very same contraptions featured in the hush-hush plans. A neat, if slightly facetious, final curtain.

As far as casting was concerned, Alec Guinness must have, theoretically, seemed perfect for Wormold – a personification of the small man getting into matters way over his head with a perpetual mask of innocence. As far as the critics were concerned, something was distinctly amiss in the normally critic-proof Guinness performance – 'There is the problem of Sir Alec Guinness who has often been called the faceless actor. This time he is almost disembodied as well. He presents an aura of brilliance, but the aura surrounds nothing at all.'[9] And: 'Guinness, for whom the part of Wormold seems made on purpose, seems almost to parody one's image of him: as good as ever and as limited, as ironically funny, as sad, and, in the last count, as inscrutable.'[10]

The criticism of Guinness tended to stem from a more fundamental criticism of the piece as a whole – that is, what many felt was the story's uncomfortable switch between the early comedy and later melodrama with Guinness having to straddle those moods. Perhaps it was too light a presentation to suffer such a grim turn. This is not helped by Ernie Kovacs's performance. His Segura matches more the shadowy figure of the book than a more blatantly evil figure which appears to have been carved from the film's outset. Kovacs's Segura, though nicely acted, is frankly a bit of a pussycat.

Guinness himself thought the film disappointing: 'I liked the book enormously but I hated what Carol Reed did. For example, the introduction of that totally phoney Latin-American couple, always munching apples and eyeing each other. It was a boring linking process.' In fact, the couple reappear alone or separately with others at various points during the film though it would take an eagle-eye to spot them. It seems that Reed had an idea for some sort of counterpoint in the principals' story, but it got left behind in the editing. All that is left is a pointless red herring.

Guinness continues: 'I also had a totally different concept of my own character – I saw him much more as a rather untidy *New Statesman* and *Nation* type. Reed really rather hamstrung me; it's awfully difficult playing a long leading part where all the really interesting characters come on one at a time and they were always in big close-up while I was receded.' Guinness's consolation was working with Greene:

whose professionalism was, as always, absolutely marvellous. Often if I'm learning lines I write them out on little cards and then look at the cards from time to time to help me memorize them. One morning in Havana I wasn't working and walking down the street with my cards when I bumped into Graham.

Now he'd written a speech for me where every other word seemed to start with an *s* or *th*, very sibilant anyway. I told him that I thought it would sound funny in quite the wrong way. We went straight into a bar, sat down, had a drink and he rewrote the speech there and then. He was tremendously helpful that way.

Greene, for his part, felt that the film turned out to be a bit pedestrian.

Poor Alec Guinness got the blame but his performance was ruined by Jo Morrow, the girl who played his daughter. I remember we were all in the bar in Havana – Alec and Noël had arrived in from Jamaica – and Carol brought in the girl to introduce her to everyone. We went on to dinner without her and sat at a table outside a seafront restaurant. There was a long, long silence then Noël said: 'Carol, what on earth induced you to hire that girl?' Carol replied that she had been shy 'meeting all you famous people'. 'That little tart shy!' said Noël. And all Alec did was rub his hand up and down on the edge of the table, saying nothing with a look of despair on his face. Later on during the shooting I found myself talking to her and she told me that she was engaged to be married: 'Of course,' she said, 'I don't know what he will feel about being known as Mr Jo Morrow.' She was quite determined she was going to be a star.

Greene is a little too hard on a newcomer who was more wooden than actually inept and attractive enough to draw very favourable comments from many reviewers. Her nationality, though, needed some explanation in the dialogue. As Wormold tells Hasselbacher: 'They [the convent] have even given her an American accent. Sometimes when I'm with her, I feel like a foreigner.'

Coward's Hawthorne is justly remembered as the film's most showy role and 'the Master' creamed it for all its worth. In his diary of 1 January 1960, he wrote:

The year begins for me in a blaze of slightly tawdry triumph. I have had rave notices for my performance in *Our Man in Havana*. One paper carried a screaming headline and stated that

I had 'stolen the picture' from Alec Guinness. It then went on to insult the rest of the cast and abuse Carol Reed. Delighted as I am to have made such a spectacular success in what is after all a minor part, my pleasure is tempered with irritation at being used as a flail against my fellow artists. This is not noble modesty on my part. I *am* very good, the picture *is* slow in parts and Alec *is* dull at moments. But I would rather have made a nice, honest, deserved success which was not at the expense of other people.[11]

It could have been Coward's kind of flamboyance that sparked Australian composer Malcolm Williamson to score an opera based on the novel for production at Sadler's Wells. Greene was approached to write the libretto but turned it down as a 'job not quite in my line' and so another veteran film man, Sidney Gilliatt, did the adaptation. Wormold became Bramble and when the opera opened in July 1963, one critic described it thus: 'Treatment falls between that of a musical and, as the sombreness takes charge, of opera.' It was also said to be 'a travesty of the novel'. At which point Greene leapt to the defence to say publicly and generously: 'As author of the film-script, may I say I infinitely preferred Mr Gilliatt's libretto.'

As for Alfred Hitchcock, who had been so summarily repelled in his bid for the film rights, he did eventually make his own Cuba movie ten years later – a Cold War espionage thriller called *Topaz* based on Leon Uris's best-seller, and it was indeed feeble by Hitch's own high standards. As for Miss Jo Morrow, the stardom Greene believed she so nakedly craved was to remain elusive.

The Comedians is Greene's most political novel, charting, quite unequivocally, the hell-on-earth that was Papa Doc Duvalier's, (and probably, for that matter, is still his son, Baby Doc's) Haiti. Positively Conradian, we follow the descent of a handful of hearts in darkness into a kind of living hell. And yet Greene leavens this dark tale with a persistent undercurrent of equally black humour.

Such unrelieved gloom needs the sprig of irony just as Armageddon requires Dr Strangelove. The economy of language, the *hint* of barbarity is just what is missing from the film of *The Comedians*, which positively raced out of the Hollywood trap a little over a year after the publication of his shattering book.

Adapted by Greene himself, and directed by another Briton Peter Glenville (who made *The Term of Trial* and *Becket* but is probably best known as a stage director; he directed Greene's *The Living Room* in the theatre), the film had everything an MGM big budget could offer – star cast (including Burton at $750,000 and Taylor at $500,000), exotic settings and lavish production values. For that reason this is perhaps the most disappointing of all Greeneland excursions on film (including the dreary *Human Factor*); certainly inferior to any that had previously involved the author's close collaboration.

It is perhaps no surprise that *The Comedians* marks Greene's last (for ever?) venture in screenplay writing. I suggested that the production had all the necessary logistics to facilitate ease of a careful celluloid translation but of course it is naïve to suggest that those elements can in any way *guarantee* success. Underpin, yes; guarantee, no. Here, they merely contrived to overload the production into a great, unwieldy thing. And yet despite this, there is just enough, in individual scenes and certain images, to suggest that a great film could have emerged. That is probably the real disappointment.

The film rights were bought before the novel was finished and Greene says he was tempted to turn down the offer of adapting it into a screenplay simply because, having just completed the book, he was 'too close' to it. Nevertheless, he went ahead.

Almost the first forty pages of the novel are set on board a cargo ship, bound for Haiti as we encounter our comedians – rather *comediens*, in the French actor sense as opposed merely to funny men (though the irony is obvious) – lining up for the ensuing drama. Brown, the narrator, returning to the hotel he owns after an abortive attempt to sell it; the mysterious, but cheerful, 'Major' Jones with his tales of World War Two heroics, and an elderly, ingenuous American couple, the Smiths (he is an unremembered past presidential candidate) aiming to bring vegetarianism to the 'natives': Brown, Jones, Smith, the names are all suitably mundane. The prospect of the approaching horrors is subtly drawn in veiled references and ominous asides.

There is no such subtlety at the outset of the 150-minute film for after an effective credit sequence scored with angelic, young voices intoning that Papa Doc is president for life, the film goes straight into a series of grisly photographs of the regime's victims scored out with red pencil crosses. This is the headquarters of the uniformed Captain Concasseur, flanked by slouching, dark-glassed plain-clothes thugs – the dreaded Tontons Macoute.

The film misses out entirely the on-board sequence of the book and an initial chance to build necessary tension; instead the ship has docked and the human cargo is making its way to the quayside. Major Jones, optimistically wielding a letter of intro-duction from a now disgraced and jailed ex-minister, is whisked off to a cell by the suspicious Captain Concasseur and tortured by a Tonton; Brown is met by the dapper Petit Pierre, a local journalist and gossip columnist, and fills him in on his colourful travelling companions before racing to a rather fortuitous tryst with his mistress, Martha, the wife of a South American envoy, Dr Pineda.

Back, finally, at his hotel, Brown discovers the bloodied body of the 'missing' Minister for Social Welfare, Dr Philipot, lying at the bottom of the empty swimming-pool. As the Smiths turn up, Brown is considering how he is going to dispose of a much unneeded corpse which also, it just so happens, is of the man who was going to provide the official entrée for the Smiths and their health schemes in Haiti.

The next part of the novel is an elongated flashback to Brown's origins, just how he came to inherit his mother's hotel in Haiti and the roots of his affair with Martha Pineda. Greene explains:

> One of the problems that I encountered was what to do about the flashbacks in the novel covering Brown's past life. I realized that I would have to leave out Brown's past life for all practical purposes since there wasn't time to develop it in the film. His mother, his days at Jesuit college, etc., all had to be virtually passed over. But, beginning in the present without the past, Brown would not have had any character. So, bit by bit, I brought out different sides of his character and developed them in the dialogue in order to make up for the missing flashbacks. My biggest problem when adapting one of my novels for the screen is that one cannot tell a story from the single point of view of one character in a film as one can in a novel. You cannot look through the eyes of one character in a film. The book of *The Comedians* was told from Brown's point of view. It is true

that Brown remains on the screen more than any of the others in the film and his comments on the others are often in his dialogue. But we still do not see others completely from his point of view as we do in the novel. For example, Martha's husband is despised by Brown in the book, but on the screen he is seen by others as a noble character.[12]

So we have, for instance, Jones's arrest and treatment in jail presented directly to the camera whereas it is merely suggested, via Brown, in the novel. In the film the disillusionment of the Smiths takes place in three set-pieces; first, the official visit to the crumbling ruins of what was intended to be the model city of Duvalierville; second the bizarre funeral of Dr Philipot with his coffin being kidnapped by Tontons, and last, and most shattering of all for the guileless couple, their innocent presence at a mass public execution. The first two are in the book but in reverse running order, the third is the film's invention. The Smiths exit by jet plane, a little older but certainly no wiser. We had met the dreadful Captain Concasseur at the very outset of the film; in the book, he is introduced by name more than halfway through, telling Brown things like: 'My personal view of every white man is very low. I admit I am offended by the colour, which reminds me of turd ['toad's belly' is substituted for 'turd' in the film]. But we accept some of you – if you are useful to the state.'[13]

And now reappearing as mysteriously as he disappeared is the genial Jones who, it transpires, has been attempting to finalize an arms deal with the authorities. He is suddenly 'useful to the state'. The deal goes sour and Jones is now on the run. Brown, who though openly critical of the regime has somehow managed to keep himself clear of the prison cells, is inexorably drawn into more positive anti-state activity.

Film and novel see him helping to smuggle Jones, disguised as a black peasant woman, into the Pinedas' embassy for temporary sanctuary. Philipot's nephew Henri is a secret guerrilla leader and when he hears of Jones's former heroics is anxious to get the old warhorse to come and train up his ragged band in the hills. Brown, who by now has had a beating-up (warning dose of what could happen to him if he goes on defying authority) spirits Jones out of the embassy and away up to the hinterland to join Philipot's outfit and, while they wait for the revolutionaries, Jones confesses himself the sham soldier we had always really suspected.

At this point novel and film depart from each other dramatically. In the book, Concasseur and his henchmen suddenly turn up at the rendezvous and are summarily dispatched by the guerrillas. Jones, we learn later, has maintained his façade to a devoted band of outlaws up to his eventual death. Brown, who has moved to the neighbouring Dominican Republic to work as an undertaker's assistant, also hears of the death of the dignified Dr Magiot, a close friend of his mother and an important Marxist dissident.

In the film, Jones is shot dead by Concasseur's men shortly before the captain and his cohort are cut down by Henri Philipot's raggle-taggle band. We see Brown's former servant Joseph, who has now joined the guerrillas, grind the Tonton sunglasses into the ground, a symbolic gesture of what is perhaps the ultimate rebellion. Brown, who has never espoused any cause before, is persuaded to take Jones's place at the head of the outlaws. It was Greene's idea to change the ending of the film:

> Brown is a beachcomber-type character. That he had had a religious vocation and lost it is part of his beachcomber personality. He is a person who would like to be better than he is but cannot. The novel is a black comedy. Brown had been washed up on the beach in Haiti and at the end when he becomes an undertaker he has just been washed up on another shore. In the film the ending is different but the point is the same. He does not want to join the guerrillas and he has no experience in guerrilla warfare, but he makes the best of the situation.[14]

Bearing in mind that the film, like the novel, is told from one character's point of view as far as possible (taking into account Greene's own earlier thoughts on the matter) it was almost inevitable that such a drastic character substitution had to take place. Dramatically it was necessary, and philosophically the result is the much the same, for Brown is, to all intents and purposes, as much a sham as Jones.

The film ends with the Pineda family leaving by air for the United States. Apparently before the film was finally cut for general release there was one rather neat ironic touch that has since been lost. The voice of a stewardess was heard telling passengers on board the flight that they could now unfasten their safety belts, adding that the flying time to Miami was just one' hour and ten minutes. Between hell and some sort of deliverance was a mere seventy minutes!

Greene had visited Haiti twice in the fifties and then for a third, and final, time in 1963 by which time Duvalier was ensconced and at the height of his excesses. Greene was clearly shocked by what he saw compared with his earlier visits when, although poverty was extreme (under President Magloire), tourism was plentiful and the atmosphere lively. The various elements for the novel and subsequently the film were beginning to take shape. A doctor and philospher (but not a communist) Greene met and liked would be the model for Magiot; the Hotel Oloffson became the Trianon; fellow guests resembled Mr and Mrs Smith; there was a brothel like Mère Catherine's, a Petit Pierre, voodoo and televised public executions. And there was always a Captain Concasseur and his malevolent attendants forever hovering ominously on the sidelines. Haiti, Greene concluded, 'really was the bad dream of the newspaper headlines'.[15]

Duvalier was furious about the novel. First he denounced it in his own morning paper thus: 'The book is not well written. As the work of a journalist, the book hasn't any value.' And then in an elaborately prepared brochure which was circulated through Europe, Greene was pilloried as a 'liar, a cretin, a stool pigeon, unbalanced, sadistic, perverted . . . a perfect ignoramus . . . lying to his heart's content . . . the shame of proud and noble England . . . a spy . . . a drug addict a torturer'. 'The last epithet,' muses Greene, 'has always a little puzzled me.'[16]

The fury continued as the novel was adapted to film and when the film was first shown on American TV, via CBS, the Haitian Embassy in Washington felt moved to issue the following statement:

The author claims the plot of the story is based in Haiti. Such is not the case. Haiti is a land of smiling, singing, dancing, happy people with a joy of living. It is not a country of crime, of witchcraft or of diabolic excesses of any kind . . . the Haitian Government is convinced that this television programme is propaganda intended to adversely affect tourism and its efforts to improve its economy and the lives of its people . . . It is an affront to the dignity of the Haitian people, to all black communities and to all the Third World.

Peter Glenville was anxious to shoot the film on location. Obviously Haiti itself was a non-starter and the Haitian Government made noises attempting to dissuade other countries from co-operating with the film-makers. Eventually the rather unlikely double of Dahomey (squeezed between Togo and Nigeria on Africa's west coast) was selected. Greene said:

I had the shock of my life when I landed in Dahomey. Driving from the airport, I saw a big banner strung across the roadway saying 'Welcome to Haiti'. For an awful moment I thought that we had possibly landed in Haiti instead of Cotonou and 'what's going to happen to me?' The scenes in the mountains were shot here behind St Raphael. During the filming, I had a visit from Fred Baptiste who was the leader of the guerrillas in Haiti. With him was a very sinister character, an ex-major in Duvalier's army who apparently was now a dissident. Actually I thought he was spying on Baptiste who was a simple, honest peasant. Anyway, I drove them up to see the shooting of Jones in the mountains and as we were winding up the road to find the film unit, Fred Baptiste said: 'But this *is* Haiti.' So I think we had chosen pretty well as far as locations were concerned.

There was authenticity too when it came to filming the frenzied voodoo ceremony involving Henri Philipot and witnessed by Brown and Joseph. Greene said:

We found a real voodoo priest in Dahomey (imported from Paris where he was in exile). Now this is interesting. He would consent to rehearse with a dummy cock and the dummy cock was always carefully preserved in case there was any comeback from the Society for the Prevention of Cruelty to Animals. The dummy cock was filled with red liquid and so when the priest bit off its head at the climax of the ceremony, the blood flowed. However, for the actual shooting, he refused to use the dummy cock. He would do it only with a live cock – it would have been a kind of blasphemy for him to do otherwise. So, in the film, you actually see a live cock having its head bitten off.

Just one of the gruesome excesses in the film that may have been more tolerable in black and white. Greene added: 'We felt, before we started, that it should have been shot in black and white but, at that period, you couldn't get the major film companies to do it. In a sense, colour helped falsify the film. Now, people like Woody Allen and Martin Scorsese have proved that black and white can be far more beautiful than colour.'

That falsification was compounded with the quite revoltingly gratuitous murder of Magiot. In the book he is reported shot dead. In the film we see him having his throat cut in lingering close-up as he is interrupted by the Tontons in the midst of conducting a rather less explicit surgical operation. The only possible point of interest about this might be for film buffs in that it predated the famous throat-slitting at the climax of Peckinpah's *The Wild Bunch* by fully two years.

With the exception of Elizabeth Taylor, the playing is uniform-ly good. Burton has all the right sort of world-weariness and cynicism as Brown, Guinness is just right as the global equivalent of a brash second-hand car salesman, Ustinov is unusually low-key as the cuckolded ambassador. Lillian Gish and Paul Ford as the rapidly disillusioned Smiths descend with dignity. The main black actors – James Earl Jones as Magiot, Raymond St Jacques as Concasseur and, particularly, Roscoe Lee Browne as the impish Petit Pierre – are excellent.

However, Taylor's ineptness as the German Martha almost tends to devalue the other performances. It is suddenly as if Hollywood has intruded in what was very respectable drama-documentary and curdles the mixture with artifice. Greene agrees that Taylor was a mistake. 'She had, though, just made *Who's Afraid of Virginia Woolf* and certainly when I saw her in that I thought to myself "My God, she *can* act". Anyhow it was a disaster having her in *The Comedians*, and she was also a very difficult person too.' Greene's overall verdict on the film is that it is not 'bad', merely 'disappointing'.

Peter Ustinov felt that it was 'too strange and too long – two and a half hours with those characters is too much. It was one of those mysterious films that look marvellous in the daily rushes and everyone gets terribly excited but when you string the whole thing together, there is a certain feeling of imbalance.'[17]

Sir Alec Guinness's verdict was that:

Something happened which was theatrical instead of filmic. It was too slow-moving. The voodoo stuff went on for ever. It was also all rather sickening.

There are though things I do like. I'm mad about Peter Ustinov's performance – it was frightfully underrated and I think it is one of the most distinguished pieces of work he's done. I also rather liked the graveyard scene with Burton and me. To do a great lump of one person speaking at that stage of the film was rather brave. The trouble was the scene didn't *look* frightfully convincing. It was rather curiously lit. I didn't think I was right casting although, overall, I don't think I got in the way.

There were scenes we shot which were cut out. A rather good one was of my playing jungle warfare with the ambassador's son indoors in among potted palm trees. People playing games. I'm sorry they lost that. Blood and feathers obviously got in the way.

Critically, the reaction was extremely mixed. John Russell Taylor in *The Times* said: 'It is just loaded with production values. Unfortunately, loaded is the operative word. Under there somewhere is perhaps quite an interesting little film trying to get out, but if so, it is smothered at birth.'[18]

Time was more generous:

Ironically, the film's most stirring moments are not its overheated love scenes but the brief encounters between Burton and Guinness. In one, Guinness, a short day's journey from death, recounts his wasted life of lies in a graveyard retreat. Priestlike, Burton answers the tortured confession with a symbolic absolution. At such moments of transcendent drama – and there are enough to make it worthwhile – *The Comedians* is casually forgiven its other sins.[19]

One may feel able to forgive the film its sins. What is more difficult is to forgive a potential masterpiece its lost opportunities.

PART FIVE

The Seventies

10
Past Remembered

Distance lends considerable disenchantment to both the book and subsequent film of *Travels with My Aunt*. Both, more than any other Greene original and adaptation, have dated fatally. Geriatric and middle-aged incursions on the swinging scene of the late sixties must have seemed like a good idea at the time, but as with much of the art of that particularly ephemeral moment, which seems to have been conceived on speed, the effect is a momentary buzz followed by a splitting headache.

Greene says that it is the only book of his written 'for the fun of it' and his own enjoyment seems evident on every page. It is packed with in-jokes: Aunt Augusta's great love, the disreputable Mr Visconti, is named after Gian Galeazzo Visconti, *The Viper of Milan* in Marjorie Bowen's book, which had so profoundly influenced Greene as a teenager; Detective Sergeant Sparrow is called after the ex-Warden of All Souls, and the Bowen *hommage* is complete when Sparrow refers to Visconti as a 'viper'; Visconti's son, Mario, has echoes of another past friend, the flamboyant director Mario Soldati with whom Greene had collaborated on that Venetian bunfight, *The Stranger's Hand*, fifteen years earlier.

More revealingly, Greene tells how its writing represented the 'manic' side of a manic-depressive writer (the depressive had been demonstrated in *A Burnt-Out Case* eight years before). The problem, I have always found, is that the more manic the cause, the more depressive the effect. Which is why the relentlessly mad, mad world of Aunt Augusta palls all too quickly. However, it was, Greene told me, 'a book made for films', and certainly his picaresque, global tale must have appeared a natural for a free-wheeling translation. The key to a successful adaptation would necessarily be the casting of Augusta.

Greene says: 'I put Katharine Hepburn on to it because I happened to know she was looking for something, and she accepted at once to play in it.' Greene had been a long-time fan of Hepburn's, ever since he had written of her in *Break of Hearts*, in 1935, 'Very great talent . . . Miss Hepburn always makes her young women quite horrifyingly lifelike with their girlish intuitions, their intensity, their ideals which destroy the edge of human pleasure.'[1]

That might also have served as a summary of the new film's intentions, in part anyway, for Jay Presson Allen and Hugh Wheeler's script would be calling for a much more literal interpretation of Augusta's verbal flashbacks to her colourful past of the novel. While I would dispute the necessity of the device – the novel seemed to have more than enough material in the contemporary narrative – the film-makers seemed determined on their course.

Judging by the delays that ensued one can only speculate that Miss Hepburn, then aged sixty-three, was quailing at the prospect of this cinematic rejuvenation – a supposed fear, subsequently paralleled, then realized, in her TV movie *Love Among the Ruins* when she signally failed to be convincing as a younger self.

Under the aegis of her old mentor, director George Cukor (seventy-three at the time, about the same age as the fictitious Augusta), she had been given a great deal of freedom to rewrite – rewriting which became progressively, and to Metro Goldwyn Mayer's chagrin, more and more protracted.

Greene says: 'I think she must finally have got fed up with the script. There were immense delays and finally MGM said that Hepburn had to go and Cukor would have to find someone else. I think she was probably fighting the script because she's an intelligent woman.'

At just a week's notice, the role was given to Maggie Smith, with good reason, for three years earlier she had won the Oscar for the best actress as the maddening Edinburgh schoolteacher in *The Prime of Miss Jean Brodie* produced by Robert Fryer, who was one of the co-producers this time round. Recalls Maggie Smith: 'They were in trouble, and it was Bobby Fryer who went out on a limb for *Jean Brodie* – if it had not been for him I would not have done the film – and I would have been out of my skull not to work with Cukor.'

Henry Pulling, a retired bank manager, never happier than when he is nursing his suburban dahlia beds, is whisked off on an odyssey of adventure and intrigue by his elderly Aunt Augusta whom he meets for the first time at his mother's funeral. Before he embarks on the Orient Express, he is questioned by the police about his mother's ashes which turn out to be pot as the result of a switch made by Augusta's black lover Wordsworth to avoid a police 'bust'.

Her plan, of which Henry is unaware, is to smuggle illegal currency into Turkey to help free the great love of her life, Mr Visconti. On the train, Henry is initiated into the joys of sex and dope-smoking by a transient hippie girl, Tooley. In Istanbul, the money is confiscated and they are deported back to Paris. Having secured a Modigliani by rather dubious means from another, and rather rapidly ex-, lover Dambreuse, they sell it to raise the ransom. It seems, however, that Visconti had engineered his own kidnapping and makes off with the money.

Henry, by this time made aware that Visconti is his father and, he deduces, Aunt Augusta his real mother, beats the con man at his own con game. Now on an island off the North African coast, Henry suggests to Augusta that with the money they buy back the Modigliani and return it to Madame Dambreuse. She argues, so they toss a coin to decide.

In these bare bones of the film's plot, it is clear that Cukor had opted for Mediterranean bound limits to his story, a story which, Greene says, stopped 'before the one I wrote really gets going'. He was referring, in particular, to the omission of the book's long finale in South America which culminates in the death of Wordsworth and a rather touching scene as the old couple, Visconti and Agatha, waltz together at sunrise with Henry, who is now a real man of the world, if belatedly, as a wry observer. 'Two old people dancing together in the empty house, with the dead Wordsworth lying outside – it was a perfect film ending. Instead, they had this absurd thing about tossing a coin or something . . .' Greene was not amused.

Cukor told Gene Phillips:

Greene . . . created some very rich and marvellous characters in

his story. The warmth and range of both the elderly aunt and
her nephew attracted me to the story. I think it is a rare
combination of robust adventure and really funny comedy.
When I acquired the rights, I went through it and cross-
referenced all of the episodes. Of course we couldn't put in
everything that is in the book into the film, but every incident
of importance in the story turned up somehow in the picture.

Greene has never seen the entire film. 'Somebody smuggled the
script to me from Spain, and it was horrifyingly bad, I thought. It
came on television the other day so I went downstairs to a friend
who has a big colour television. We watched the funeral at the
beginning and I thought it was so awful – the over-acting of
Maggie Smith, in particular – that we turned it off after about four
minutes.'
Ironically, the parts of the film which worked best were the
very same youthful flashbacks that had deterred Hepburn from
taking the role. The thirty-eight-year-old Maggie Smith was
obviously much more at home in what one critic has described as
'stylish flashbacks in the style of Colette, Labiche and Noël
Coward'[2] than in the heavy elderly drag of, in her own words,
'that real old cow'. Poor Maggie Smith, though nominated for an
Oscar (which she did not win) received a fearful drubbing from
the English critics – 'I couldn't grasp the contradiction. There I
was being nominated by the Americans and getting some of the
worst notices I have ever had all on the same day!' In spite of her
'septuagenarian' excesses, I suppose one could at least be grateful
for the fact they had not cast Ruth Gordon in one of her notorious
wacky impersonations.
Never less than elegant, the film could also be forgiven minor
liberties like introducing the Dambreuse couple from Augusta's
memory into the contemporary narrative and spelling out Henry's
loss of virginity, which is ambiguous, even unlikely, in the book.
What finally, for me, sinks Cukor's adaptation of Greene's piece
of unalloyed, if self-indulgent, fun is a correlative that permanently smacks of a sense of self-satisfied permissiveness. In an early
scene Alec McCowen, as Henry, tells Maggie Smith, as she is
reclining on an enormous gold baroque bed in her pink bedroom,
'I believe, Aunt Augusta, you get exactly out of life what you put
into it.'

'Balls!' she replies. One's sentiments about the film entirely.

England Made Me was Greene's fifth published novel (in 1935) but it took more than thirty years for it finally to reach the screen, certainly the most tardy of all Greene's book-to-film transfers. Quite why it should have taken so long is rather hard to fathom. 'The subject – apart from the economic background of the thirties and that sense of capitalism staggering from crisis to crisis – was simple and unpolitical, a brother and sister in the confusion of incestuous love.'[3] Greene's own retrospective summary seems almost irresistible as a potential scenario.

Writer and critic Philip Strick suggests that:

Part of the answer is that Greene was well aware of what can remain when film companies have ploughed their indifferent ways across a novelist's landscape, and he guarded the film rights with the intention of constructing any screenplay himself. His caution is understandable: with its shifting viewpoints and unexpected flashbacks, the novel is delicately phrased. It has an undercurrent of personal fervour, and its allusions to the British educational system are so ironic as to suggest autobiography from the very title onwards.[4]

Greene admits that he has 'always had a soft spot' in his heart for the novel, written in 'the middle years for my generation, clouded by the Depression in England, which cast a shadow on this book, and by the rise of Hitler'.[5] With this background in mind, Greene chose to set the novel in Sweden, presumably because he had decided to base the shadowy financier Erik Krogh on the real-life Evar Kreuger, the notorious Swedish Match King. Greene says that it is probably the only time that he has 'deliberately chosen an unknown country as a background and then visited it, like a camera team, to take the necessary stills'.[6] Greene remains content enough with his evocation of Sweden and yet I tend to feel that, in the same way as the author has his own considerable reservations about the characterization of Krogh – 'who obstinately refuses to live, who is there only for the sake of the story'[7] (along with, Greene brackets, Ida in *Brighton Rock*, Wilson in *The Heart of the Matter*, Smythe in *The End of the Affair* and Parkinson in *A*

Burnt-Out Case) – so the novel's setting obstinately refuses to live or particularly retain interest. One cannot see Sweden in the thirties proving much of a lure for film-makers either.

Extraordinarily, when writer-director Peter Duffell became involved with the subject in 1971 he was first confronted with a Wolf Mankowitz script that had kept the Swedish *milieu* but, explained Duffell: 'The story had been updated to the seventies and had a sort of swinging, permissive setting. There was lots of pot-smoking and copulation. I really didn't reckon it at all. I thought it a terrible injury to Greene's novel for though it was still set in Sweden it was using all those received ideas about Swedish sexuality and permissiveness.'

Duffell, with one previous feature film behind him, the rather stylish horror comic *The House that Dripped Blood*, had been invited on to the project by an American producer, Jack Levin. Levin had tried to get the film moving some three years earlier, first with Swedish director Lars Magnus Lindgren – who directed *Dear John* – and then, when that did not materialize, in association with a Broadway director Alan Schneider. Other commitments then forced Schneider to withdraw.

Duffell recalls: 'I had a call from a writer friend of mine who told me that Levin had the property and was looking for a director and that my name had been mentioned. I got the book out again and reread it – and I was amazed how things had stuck in the mind – both its atmosphere and the mood. It just shows you how powerful Greene is. His writing stays with you.' Duffell told the producer he was not happy with the script and that he felt they should go back to the book and start again.

Apart from its fairly unpromising *milieu*, the novel poses a number of other major hazards for the unwary film-maker. Combining a complex narrative structure with a liberal use of the 'stream of consciousness' technique, it might seem to defy adaptation. And yet, as in all Greene, there is a strong underlying story – of an incestuous relationship between twins, Anthony and Kate Farrant, set against a larger backcloth of political and financial skulduggery – a story, as one writer has described it, 'of debts, short-term and long-term, financial and psychic'.[8]

Before Duffell came 'on board', a preliminary arrangement had already been made by producer Levin to make the film as a co-production in Yugoslavia, so 'knowing that the existing script was a stinker and stuck too with the given fact of knowing where a deal could be made' the film-makers went off to recce in Yugoslavia.

'We met some of the people from Central Studios and they showed me some of the places where they thought we could film. I said I thought we needed a big villa – there was just the place at Lake Bled and then we saw Opatija on the Adriatic coast and thought that could be used for something.' And there was Belgrade itself, hit heavily during the war by German bombers and rebuilt in a functional and rather characterless style but still with quarters and buildings that reflected the country's long domination by Austria.

Duffell asked an old friend, Desmond Cory (who wrote the novel *Deadfall* filmed by Bryan Forbes with Michael Caine) if he would help work with him on the script:

I told Desmond we were in trouble, we needed a new script, that I didn't think I had time to do it and that I desperately needed someone to bounce ideas off. 'What,' Desmond eventually said to me, 'about changing the scene to Nazi Germany?' It would work, he said, and give the piece more meaning. I was a bit reluctant at first. Yet neither of us knew anything about Sweden in the thirties whereas one tends to know a great deal about Germany in the same period. And we felt there was a clue to it from Greene himself with his own introduction to the novel about the thirties being overshadowed by the rise of Nazism in Germany and the Depression in England. Having been to Yugoslavia I certainly thought I could re-create Nazi Germany. Certainly I was damned if I could do Sweden – and who cared anyway!

Duffell opens his film with a prologue sequence where Anthony and Kate, as youngsters, meet in a barn in the rural English setting. Tony has run away from school but his sister, clearly the stronger of the two, persuades him to return. Time then moves forward a number of years and we are on the French Riviera (cleverly simulated at Opatija) where Tony, a feckless, rootless charmer meets up once again with Kate, now the personal secretary and mistress of the mysterious German financier Krogh. She persuades Tony to return to Germany and with her prompting, Krogh, who warms to Tony's open personality, offers him a job in the organization.

Tony is as restless as ever in Germany despite a romantic fling with pretty Liz Davidge, who is on holiday there. He is also cultivated by a down-at-heel expatriate local newsman, Minty, who is anxious to glean juicy items on the eminently newsworthy Krogh. Meanwhile the financier is setting up an elaborate stock-market fraud in anticipation of moving his operation out of Germany, which he believes, by its present policies, is a major threat to his global operations. He holds a lavish party at his lakeside villa (the building used at Lake Bled for filming had, ironically, been built by the Nazis during wartime occupation, and was later Marshal Tito's home) for a visiting Reichsminister to try and cover up his tracks. The party swiftly degenerates into an orgy, counterpointed by a number of key incidents.

One of Krogh's employees, Fromm, arrives to plead for the financier to save his son and is badly beaten up. Tony witnesses this and is shocked. Kate declares her love for her brother. And eventually, Krogh's assistant Haller, concerned that Tony will now prove a stumbling-block to the organization's advanced plans – and that he might have leaked key information to Minty – kills Tony and pays off Minty. Kate and Krogh part.

Noting the initial decision totally to switch setting, Les Keyser, in a remarkably perceptive essay about the film, remarks:

> On another level, however, the shift to a Germany beset by nascent Nazism provides the same density of meaning that Greene provided in his acute observations of and about his characters. In the novel, individual peccadilloes were tied to larger value structures; Tony and the journalist Minty were tied to the past, to nationalist England, and to prep school moralities, just as Krogh and Kate were associated with modernism, internationalism and opportunism. In the film, Minty and Tony and Tony's naïve girlfriend Liz Davidge clearly represent the order, the enduring values and the sentiments of Mother England, while Krogh and Kate, and their cold, calculating world of business, foreshadow the ruthlessness and amoral fascism of the Fatherland. Even Krogh's attempts to dupe the Nazis and flee to England are a form of self-deception; he seems blind to the fact that he (like

Krupp) is one of the damned. His inhumane scheming and his role in the treachery that destroys Tony and alienates Kate is an embryonic form of the national horrors to come.[9]

Duffell says:

When Gavin Millar reviewed it later, he said our shift 'provided handy signposts' which is certainly what we felt it would do. We did, though, have the feeling that perhaps Nazi Germany was being a bit exploited. Visconti's *The Damned* had come out a year or so earlier and *Cabaret* was in the cutting-room. Otherwise, we were concerned, as far as possible, to stay close to the book. We were in the position of having to write a lot of dialogue that wasn't in the book simply because of the change of scene and having to alter the structure to suit the medium. And we slaved mightily to try and write Graham Greene-style dialogue.

A sacrifice, admits Duffell, was the twins element of the book:

One of the key things of the novel is that it is about siblings. Yet one had seen so many disastrous attempts to do twins on the screen. Oddly enough when we got Michael York as Tony and had then gone for, say Susannah York, they might have looked like twins. We made no attempt to establish him as twin to Hildegarde Neil (the South African born actress who had played Cleopatra a year earlier in the film of *Antony and Cleopatra* opposite Charlton Heston). They were just brother and sister and we tried to make a virtue out of necessity by having her as not only the elder of the two but also the stronger.

The character of Krogh may have 'obstinately refused to live' for Greene in the writing. In order to get a film financed, Krogh was not only going to have to 'live' but also be portrayed by a 'bankable' name. 'It was only when we got Peter Finch that the film became a reality,' says Duffell. According to Trader Faulkner, one of Finch's biographers:

Duffell needed a box-office draw to get financial backing for the film and Barry Krost (Peter's agent) suggested Peter Finch.

Duffell asked Jack Levin whether a definite offer could be made to Finch . . . Peter was approached and, as an admirer of Greene's work, accepted. He also accepted because he had not had the opportunity before to play the character demanded of him: to dominate with self-imposed dignity, as a man who was ruthless, lonely, never able to let himself go, awkward socially . . .

The character as conceived by Greene meant that Peter had to portray a German inflexibility and stolidness that was alien to his character. Cory and Duffell omitted from their screenplay certain sympathetic characterizations Greene had included to balance Krogh's single-minded pursuit of personal survival, which Peter had to supplement in his performance . . . He admired Greene enormously as 'an amusing Jacobite' and had enjoyed the challenge of playing Robert Louis Stevenson's (Greene's great uncle) Jacobite, Alan Breck Stewart in *Kidnapped* eleven years before. Peter also had a healthy respect for Greene's cool nonconformity; his curiosity to learn through travel; and what Finchie felt was Greene's common-sense Catholic atheism.

He wasn't really concerned so much about whether he would be a success as Krogh, as he was about convincing himself that to suggest Teutonic, implacable efficiency and strength was well within his range. All through the shooting of the picture, he was deep into William Manchester's *Life of Krupp*, to find out the background and what the character was all about . . . Greene was very impressed with what Peter had done with Krogh. He told me as Father Rank in *Heart of the Matter*, Peter had left no impression on him at all. But, he added, that could have been the fault of the film.[10]

Although quite complimentary about the film overall – 'a good little film . . . I liked Duffell's direction and a lot of the acting' – Greene was concerned about the shift of setting which he felt also caused problems with the Krogh characterization – over and above his own original novelistic reservations. 'Altering the scene to Nazi Germany,' he told me, 'in a way altered the whole balance of the piece. It was based on the Match King in Sweden who was a crook. But a man who is trying to get his money illegally out of a Nazi Germany is a kind of hero, as it were. And that affects the whole picture. Krogh becomes a good character instead of the bad character he was in the book.' This ambivalence, and our perception of the characters, was underscored by Christopher Hudson in the *Spectator*:

> Our sympathy ought to lie with the Englishman. He finds out that the industrial tycoon his sister works for wants to get out to England, double-crossing his government and some of his workers in so doing, and he decides to stop him even though it means sacrificing his sister's happiness. But in Germany, its Nazi brutalities evident from the outset, the moral 'right' may equally be with the tycoon, who is withdrawing his capital from a corrupt and vicious regime. Individual wickedness is overweighed by state wickedness. The result? We are confused, our sympathy lapses, and with it our interest in what, in other respects, is a competent and serious, if somewhat stilted film.[11]

Duffell says he wanted to have Krogh as a 'rather gross Citizen Kane figure; my original casting was, in fact, Joss Ackland, who, in the event, played the sidekick. Once you get a leonine figure like Finch, then you've got a different ballgame – but that's what made the film go.'

Michael York's casting is what probably caused the film to gain initial critical reservations, following as it did in the wake of the fabulously successful *Cabaret*.

Certainly York had some of his own reservations before agreeing to play Tony. 'After *Cabaret*, I thought it was really not for me. It would have been just a repeat performance and in fact I turned it down. But then it kind of haunted me.' Later, 'something inside me stirred. I realized I'd made a stupid, superficial judgement. I was very uncomfortable about the choice I'd made – I really do believe you have to seize on these little warnings.'[12]

York's natural blandness, so often a stumbling-block in other more heralded roles, works perfectly for him here. I tend to go along with a reviewer who wrote:

> [Duffell] kept it a character study of a British arrested adolescent who is upset by what he sees around him yet has no means but a schoolboy's tricks for dealing with it. Tony the innocent –

callow, fun-loving, bright-eyed – is perhaps the quiet Englishman, an early cousin to Greene's appallingly callow quiet
American. Evil offends Tony – he can't believe people are
breaking the rules – but he doesn't even have any way of
expressing himself beyond a schoolboy's arch-slang.

In retrospect, York is a great deal more satisfactory than
Michael Hordern who, at first glance, 'steals' the film as the
shabby Minty, just as the character had, in a sense, stolen the
novel from Greene. 'Suddenly the boat listed because Minty
stepped on board,' writes Greene:

> He was entirely unexpected when he emerged from the
> preconscious . . . I suppose, for the purposes of Anthony's
> story, I had required, as a minor figure, some fellow outsider
> who would recognize – as only a fellow countryman can – the
> fraudulent element in Anthony, who could detect the falsity of
> the old Harrovian tie, but I had no intention of introducing into
> the story a sly, pathetic Anglo-Catholic; a humble follower,
> perhaps, of Sir John Betjeman, who would steal all the scenes in
> which he played a part and have the last word, robbing even
> Kate of her curtain at Anthony's funeral. Oh yes, I resented
> Minty, and yet I couldn't keep him down.[13]

Hordern had a field-day with all his usual mannerisms.
  Greene had no connection with the film during the time it was
made; indeed Duffell, though a great admirer, met him for the
first time only when Greene was invited over to attend a preview
of the film in Wardour Street. Duffell recalls: 'We were introduced
and I then fled: I was just too worried to stay and watch the film
with him. I had a nice note later which said "Pleased enough".'
  Despite a near poverty-line budget of less than a million dollars,
Duffell mustered his resources with great skill. Ray Parslow's
photography and Tony Woolard's production design combined to
give a look of real opulence, and the director's skill with the actors
(even if the character of Krogh still remains as shadowy and
insubstantial as it was in the novel) presaged the kind of success
Duffell would be achieving a few years later.
  The truth is that despite a clutch of good notices, the film
achieved little or nothing at the box office. Duffell saw it as

'another sad story of poor distribution and marketing. It was a typical victim of the system. And what it did for me professionally was absolutely nothing. Soon after it I was working in children's television for one of the smaller commercial stations.'

Four years later, the film was reissued with some success and confirmed what the critics had almost universally extolled earlier; that *England Made Me* remains one of the most intelligent film adaptations of Greene's work.

11
Spy in the Cold

One of the many qualities of *The Human Factor* is its relentlessly low-key approach. The perfect antidote to James Bond, the novel concerns itself with the bureaucracy of the Cold War, less minutely than does Le Carré but with more humanity. Considering how well Le Carré has translated to both the big and small screens, it is still more extraordinary that Otto Preminger's film, undertaken just a year after the book's rosy reception in 1978, so signally fails in every department. And it is a failure of such staggering dimensions – artistically, technically and logistically – that it seems to transcend the bounds of mere criticism. Preminger's *Human Factor* was low-key, indeed almost muted to the point of terminal inertia. Yet with the help of an extremely literate Tom Stoppard screenplay, the film could also plead a high degree of literal fidelity to the original. So where did it all go wrong?

Friends for more than twenty years – a friendship that had grown out of, and survived, the débâcle of *St Joan* – Greene and Preminger found themselves on the telephone at two o'clock one morning shortly before *The Human Factor* was due to be published. Greene says:

> I was woken up and it was Otto saying, 'Graham, I want to buy your book.' And I said, 'But it's not published yet.' 'No,' said Otto, 'but I want to buy it. I want to make a film of it.' Anyway I told him that he'd have to go through my agent. Well, you know how quickly the American telephone works. Quarter of

an hour later it was New York back again. My agent. And she said, 'He's not offering enough money.' 'Good,' I told her, 'ask him for twice what he's offering, because I don't want him to make it.'

Friends they might have been but Greene was convinced that Preminger was not the right man to adapt his novel: 'I liked the old boy [Greene is actually two years older than Preminger] and that made it very difficult over *The Human Factor*; and I liked some of his films though I think that *Carmen Jones* (1954) was probably his last good film.' Preminger had had a string of failures in the preceding decade – *Skidoo*, *Tell Me You Love Me*, *Junie Moon* and *Rosebud* – and most likely saw *The Human Factor* as something of a quality comeback opportunity. He remained persistent in his pursuit of the project. Greene goes on:

He had an option, paid the option money and the whole thing just seemed to drag on and on. Then I heard that Joseph Losey was interested and thought to myself that Losey would certainly be better than Preminger. Preminger called me again, saying, 'Well, Graham, I have a feeling that you do not want me to make it still.' And I said, 'But Otto, I don't think it's quite up your street; it's just not right for you.' He said that he had given me a list of scriptwriters and that I had 'approved' Tom Stoppard. 'Yes, but all the same . . .' I told him. And I thought to myself that at least the option was running out; so I tried to encourage Losey. But the day the option expired, Preminger walked into the office, paid the money, and there was nothing more that could be done.

Greene's book was the result of a long-held ambition

to write a novel of espionage free from the conventional violence, which has not, in spite of James Bond, been a feature of the British Secret Service. I wanted to present the service unromantically as a way of life, men going daily to their office to earn their pensions, the background much like that of any other profession – whether the bank clerk or the business director – an undangerous routine, and within each character the more important private life.[1]

He started writing it more than ten years before it was eventually published, abandoning it first time at around about 20,000 words, principally because of Philby's final defection to the Soviet Union.

> My double agent Maurice Castle bore no resemblance in character or motive to Philby . . . but I disliked the idea of the novel being taken as a *roman à clef*. I know very well from experience that it is only possible for me to base a very minor and transient character on a real person. A real person stands in the way of the imagination. Perhaps a trick of speech, a physical trait may be used, but I can write no more than a few pages before realizing that I simply don't know enough about the character to use him, even if he is an old friend.[2]

It is a deceptively simple story. Castle, fiftyish and suburban, has been feeding the Russians trivial information purely as a thank-you for past communist aid in helping to spirit his black, pregnant (not by him) girlfriend out of South Africa, where he was once posted. Castle, Sarah and the bastard son, Sam, live very happily in Berkhamstead. When a department 'new broom', Colonel Daintry, starts investigating these minor leaks, various human tragedies unfold.

Castle's younger colleague, Davis, is the initial target for suspicion and, perhaps a shade improbably, is liquidated by the department boffins. Castle, realizing that matters are closing in, wants to arrange for his family's flight to Russia. In the event, only he can get out and his wife and son are left stranded with Castle's unsympathetic mother in England. From Castle's bleak apartment in Moscow, his only link with home is a temperamental telephone. Preminger says:

> I wanted Graham Greene to write the screenplay but he said he was too tired of the subject and suggested I get another writer. Several people were mentioned and I met with them. Tom Stoppard seemed the most enthusiastic. Also I liked his personality very much, and the things he had done; *Every Good Boy Deserves Favour* was wonderful, so was *Night and Day*, in fact *all* his plays. I chose him above the others, but everything in our profession is also partly luck. You cannot just logically say

'this is the best writer'. There must also be luck. A writer is not a machine. He might be very good and for some reason or another, he doesn't work out so well. This worked out very well.

Stoppard, despite having enormous reservations about the finished film, could not have been happier in his writer–director relationship with the formidable Preminger. With only sporadic work for the cinema – Losey's *The Romantic Englishwoman* and Fassbinder's *Despair* – he wanted to adapt *The Human Factor*, he told me, because:

> I am an admirer of Greene and because I thought the book would make a good film. Preminger couldn't have treated me better. He was scrupulous about consulting me about even minor changes to the script – never any of that frightening Hollywood stuff of changing your script without telling you, or getting someone else to rewrite it. He wanted to keep very closely to the book, with one exception – to have a substantial flashback to Africa to show how Castle met his wife and so on. Greene wasn't in favour of this and personally I didn't think it was a good idea either. But this is where movies get to be different from writing for, say, the stage. There is really no other way of putting this: here the writer wasn't working for Graham Greene, he was working for Otto Preminger, so I did what seemed to be required and the sequence was in the film.

Apart from this long and, in the event, turgidly realized sequence (filmed in Kenya, doubling for South Africa) and the odd verbal embellishment or omission, Stoppard's script was precise almost to Greene's letter and phrase. He did, though, write a first scene that was not in the book. Says Stoppard: 'It was Doctor Percival (the department's avuncular, but murderous, boffin) trout-fishing, foul-hooking a fish – very symbolic! I think it probably was a tactical error to present Preminger with an original scene at the very top of the script. Anyway, he didn't want it, and didn't use it.'

In view of Greene's own comments about the role of James Bond in Secret Service mythology, I am rather sorry that another piece of original Stoppard did not stay in the final cut: the plump

Buffy is bemoaning the fact that he never goes to the cinema, 'Ian (Fleming?) took me to one of his once. Couldn't make head nor tail of it – feller kept killing people with extraordinary gadgets and being kissed by amazing-looking girls who then tried to kill *him* – and all the time he was trying to save the world from some foreigner in a submarine I think it was.'[3]

There was nothing yet to suggest the future calamities. Until it came to casting. Michael Caine was desperately keen to play the role of Castle but let it be known that he would only do it if the film was made in Ireland, for tax reasons. Richard Burton was another to declare his interest but, says Preminger, 'because of the way we were going to film the book, it was totally impossible to have Burton as a thirty-seven-year-old man. Instead, I offered him Daintry but he still wanted to play Castle. We just couldn't see eye to eye.'

Quite why Preminger wanted to portray Castle as a man in his late thirties is not clear but in settling for Nicol Williamson he had, at least, hit the right age-group.

Williamson had been given the book to read by John Osborne during the revival of *Inadmissible Evidence* – probably the actor's most celebrated performance – and recalls: 'It was so good I rationed myself to a few pages a day . . . it had such an incredible feeling of that sadness for England now which I absolutely share . . . Castle is not really involved in the secrets business. He has no political ideology, he has not been compromised sexually, he has no motive of financial gain. He is just a victim of the Cold War.'

Fine words which a fine actor was simply unable to translate into anything much more than doleful looks. Williamson is an explosive actor on a slow fuse, who needs, as Derek Malcolm so aptly puts it, 'a head of steam to get him going'. Castle is a dull old commuter with a past, world-weary, kind and patently lacking the sort of danger that fires Williamson's best work. In retrospect, how right Burton would have been.

If Williamson was miscast (Greene disagrees, believing Williamson to have given a 'good' performance 'which would have been magnificent if the direction were all right') then the casting of Sarah and Muller, the sinister South African security chief, was plain ludicrous, completely off-balancing the real professionalism of such seasoned performers as Richard Attenborough (Daintry), Robert Morley (Dr Percival) and Derek Jacobi (Davis). With echoes of Jean Seberg, Preminger opted for a beautiful, thousand-dollar-a-day, New York-based Somali model called Iman to play Sarah. She was, like Seberg, a complete acting beginner. Stoppard's script called for a Bantu woman, 'attractive but unkempt'. Iman looked as though she had stepped straight from the catwalk into her Berkhamstead villa – which, in a sense, she had – and contrived to deliver her lines with the same strained formality.

To give him credit, Preminger was consistently loyal to his actress, despite her shortcomings. He even threatened to switch his production to Ireland when British Actors' Equity attempted to block Iman's casting. As for Joop Doderer, described at the time as 'Holland's top actor', his Muller was virtually incoherent. It is one of the best-written roles in the piece, full of dark humour and hypocrisy. I kept thinking of a scene-stealing performance as a clipped BOSS man in another movie, *The Wilby Conspiracy*, played by none other than . . . Nicol Williamson.

It is a very literal adaptation, a curious mish-mash of casting and had no backing from a major studio. Instead, by his own powers of persuasion, Preminger obtained the promise of a seven-and-a-half-million dollar budget, courtesy of three bankers on behalf of Saudi Arabian oil interests. As has so often happened in the mercurial world of independent film financing, the money never materialized.

The film was already a couple of months into shooting when first rumours of the film's cash problems were then confirmed via a series of garish newspaper headlines: 'Otto and the Bounced Cheques'; 'Otto's Film is Stolen' (when a disgruntled editor 'kidnapped' reels of the film against payment), 'Picasso to the Rescue' (as Preminger sold some of his modern paintings to bail out the bankrupt production). Equity, probably with fire still in its nostrils after being foiled over Iman, served writs for non-payment to actors. It was a veritable shambles.

According to Preminger: 'I was the victim of three European bankers who promised to put up money for the film. The money never came. I was let down. I had to spend two million dollars of my own money to get the film made. Some cheques to the cast and technicians were not covered. I'm too old for experiments like this again.' By November 1979 (the film had started shooting in May) *Variety* reported that Metro Goldwyn Mayer had acquired the American and Canadian rights to the film, which would, it said, get a brief North American release before the year's end in order to qualify for Academy Award consideration the following spring: 'Speculation is that Preminger is using the MGM distribution advance to square away the financial problems, but an MGM spokesman said: "In actuality, there is no problem right now. Preminger resolved everything himself." '

A little over three weeks later, *The Times* carried a story that actors were still owed around £150,000 out of the £1 million debts left by the production. Equity secured an agreement that a release of the film would be allowed so long as the entire revenue from its showings would be used to pay creditors. 'This agreement,' added Equity, 'is written in such a way that Otto Preminger could actually be sent to prison, by either English or New York courts, if it is broken.' And *The Times* concluded, rather optimistically, that judging by the enthusiasm for the book, the actors should 'escape penury'.

The film crept briefly into cinemas early the following year and died quickly: some of the debts still remain but, as far as I know, Mr Preminger remains at liberty. As for Oscar contention, the film would more likely have been shortlisted for the Golden Turkeys.

The finished piece betrayed at once the film's cash problems which must have dogged the production from the very onset. Stoppard was horrified when he saw the film:

> You could see its bankruptcy all over the screen. One of the actors had warned me earlier that, as far as he could tell, the film was going to be awfully short of 'cutaways' and this proved to be the case. The editor was left nothing to edit with. The film seemed to me to be full of shots held too long to save the expense of a new set-up. I thought that the lighting was primitive, presumably for the same reason, and one or two of the settings, especially the Moscow flat, were ludicrous. I thought the view of the Kremlin was mind-boggling.

Sir Richard Attenborough told me: '*The Human Factor* ought to have been marvellous . . . there was a scene when I visit Nicol at his house and we had no time to cover a scene that ran three and a half minutes. It was all done in a two shot.'

Apart from these aberrations deriving (I hope) from cash restrictions – and I felt particularly sorry for a fine cameraman like Mike Molloy whose work was so clearly, and hideously, hindered – there were still a number of gross artistic miscalculations. Such as the dreadful scene when Percival takes Davis and Castle out on the town. In the book, it is a highly amusing scene at Raymond's Revue Bar, counterpointing a striptease show with the trio's chatter about fishing. The film gives us a perfunctory strip followed by an interminable routine from 'the world-famous Ipi Tombi dancers' accompanied by leering close-ups of Robert Morley:

> This must be like old times for you, Castle, says Percival.
> Castle: Why?
> Percival: Africa.
> Castle: (dryly) – Oh, yes – Africa.[4]

The result is somehow more offensive than meaningful. The cardboard set and painted backcloths of the Moscow finale are, perhaps, forgivable in view of the circumstances but, according to Greene, much of the actual point of the dénouement is lost. 'One's presenting hells – Castle's hell in Moscow and his wife's hell at home. It's very important that Castle's mother, who's producing Sarah's hell, should have had a good part. In fact, she was given nothing to do in the film. So the point was thrown away. The hells should have balanced each other.'

One of the most perceptive reviews of the film came from the *Observer*'s Philip French:

> Tom Stoppard has made a highly respectful job of dramatizing the story, but no one would guess that, while not among the very finest fictions in the canon, this is perhaps Greene's most extensive and subtle meditation on the nature of loyalty, patriotism and treason . . . *The Human Factor* is a sombre, comic ironic fable set in the author's own version of contemporary Britain, which is really an extension of that old Greeneland he mapped out in the 1930s. The cinema may have closed in Berkhamstead, but people there still have buttons on their flies. The moral force and narrative drive of Greene's book are inextricably bound up with its prose style, the clusters of images

and literary allusions creating elaborate patterns of meaning. Much of this has been crudely diluted – the emblematic references to Richardson's *Clarissa* and Ben Nicholson, for example, are changed to *Huckleberry Finn* and Mondrian. Yet Stoppard's script could have been the basis for a sprightly espionage thriller comparable with Pinter's *Quiller Memorandum*.[5]

From Antibes, the following week, winged a fan letter to French but with, inevitably, a jocularly contradictory pay-off: '. . . but what is all this fuss about buttons on flies. All my suits have buttons as they are all around fifteen or sixteen years old. I don't suppose the man in the inn yard at Berkhamstead had a newer suit than I have.'[6]

Interestingly, Greene had sent a copy of his book to Philby in Moscow, who replied with the criticism that he had painted too bleak a portrait of Castle's circumstances. It was a criticism that Greene considers valid. He also finds himself profoundly dissatisfied with the book overall. 'I had betrayed my purpose. There *was* violence – the death of Davis – and Doctor Percival was hardly a typical figure of the British Secret Service. It wasn't as realistic a picture as I had intended, and the novel was saved only by the human factor of the title. As a love story – a married-love story of an elderly man – I think it may have succeeded.'[7] Not even the human factor could save Preminger's film.

PART SIX

The Eighties

12
Down Argentine Way

In the autumn of 1983, posters outside more than 700 cinemas around the United States proclaimed a new film, *Beyond the Limit*, starring Richard Gere and Michael Caine. The posters themselves were luridly designed with a topless Gere stretched on a bed as a rather disapproving Caine gazes down from a wall portrait. Standing before Gere is a long, dark-haired girl provocatively clad in a tight-fitting petticoat with a shoulder-strap slipped. Superimposed over this tantalizing tableau is the legend: 'The first time he saw her, she was a prostitute. The second time, she was his best friend's wife, the third time, she was his.'

Somewhat further down the same poster, squeezed between the co-star and the screenplay-producer credits is the revelatory line: 'based on the novel *The Honorary Consul* by Graham Greene'.

It seems that Paramount Pictures, the film's releasing company in the States, had undertaken 'research' which appeared to indicate that since the term 'honorary consul' was not usage in the world's most potent cinemagoing market, its employment as a film title would actually legislate against people flocking to theatres. And as if to compound that particular piece of Hollywood-style lunacy, a bland, and even more meaningless, title was substituted (without the producer's approval).

It was a final frustration in what had been a ten-year tale of two obsessions – one abortive, the other realized – to bring arguably Greene's best novel to the screen. The first five years of that dual obsession were set in motion by Peter Duffell, whose version of *England Made Me* reached the cinemas the year *The Honorary*

189

Consul was published, 1973. Duffell loved the book and later that year wrote to Greene asking if he could have a crack at writing a screenplay with a view to filming it. Greene, who had admired *England Made Me* (with reservations) welcomed Duffell's query, saying he would be only too happy to discuss the scripting with him and his collaborator, Desmond Cory. He also told Duffell that a once-interested Fred Zinnemann had faded from the scene, leaving Duffell's path clear, for the time being at least.

Ever-helpful, even at this embryo stage, Greene was already indicating the right kind of geographical setting for a truthful translation – 'a great deal of the film takes place in a very constricted surrounding, after all, of a studio set. The only daunting expense perhaps is the outside setting, but a great South American river might possibly be shot in the estuary of the Tagus . . . no ordinary European river would be possible. And the river is very important,' he wrote to Duffell, adding that major companies had, to date, shown a marked lack of interest in the project due to its high anticipated production cost. 'Personally,' said Greene, 'I think it would be a much better film if it could be made inexpensively than if the Americans spent millions of dollars.'

The novel had been born out of a dream which dealt with a sort of playboy American ambassador but otherwise had no connection with the events that he had described in the course of writing. As had so often happened before with Greene, his subsequent plotting would anticipate future events; the story dealt with the kidnapping of a British consul in Argentina by Paraguayan guerrillas in mistake for an American ambassador. The first day Greene was in the Northern Argentine town of Corrientes to begin his research, he opened his paper to find that a Paraguayan consul from a nearby town had been snatched in error; that country's ambassador had been the real target. As he was completing the book came news of diplomat Geoffrey Jackson's kidnapping by Tupamaros guerrillas in Uruguay. One could understand Sir Alec Guinness's sentiments when he told Gene Phillips:

Take any of the world's trouble spots from Cuba to Haiti and you will find that Greene has been there two or three years beforehand and accurately dealt with the tensions there through

the medium of the novel. I have often said jokingly that when I
hear that Graham is going off to visit some part of the globe I
will avoid the place like the plague because that means that a
revolution or a war is bound to break out there soon.[1]

The book, says Peter Duffell, 'is really about the capacity to
love'. Charley Fortnum, the permanently sozzled cuckolded old
consul, is the ultimate winner because he has the capacity; Dr
Plarr, half-Paraguayan, half-British and half Fortnum's age, who
casually impregnates Clara, the consul's ex-whore wife, is
blindingly jealous of Charley because of his own incapacity to love
and so is the ultimate loser.

Shedding Cory – 'We agreed to disagree on our approach to this
subject' – Duffell moved to the South of France to begin work on
the screenplay. 'Graham had given me a free option for a year or
so. Every four or five days, I would take pages round to him, talk
to him about them and get his ideas and reaction.' By June of that
year (1974) Greene was able to tell Duffell that he thought his first
screenplay was 'very impressive' and read 'almost like a final one'.
Duffell set out for New York with his approved script, some
interest from Trevor Howard in playing Fortnum and a mission to
find an American star for Plarr ('I've no objection to Robert
Redford if you have to have an American,' Greene told him) as
well as production cash.

Before he left, Duffell had expressed concern that some others
who had seen the script felt that there was not sufficient action.
Greene admonished him:

> I wouldn't worry at all . . . People like this consider action is
> either bedroom scenes or tomato scenes. They don't realize that
> action can be psychological and the better for that. I suspect
> audiences will soon tire of the tomato sauce. One of the good
> things about *The Conversation* was that one could say in their
> terms that the film lacked action – to disguise this there had to
> be one scene of tomato sauce and one in bed.

Apart from a diversion to Canada to talk to Donald Sutherland
about Plarr, the North American trip proved fruitless. Both
Redford and Al Pacino, a thought for the guerrilla-priest Leon
Rivas, were unavailable. Duffell says: 'I went to America to try

and get some contact and I failed miserably; I just didn't know the scene.' In between other chores, he embarked on a second, and third, rewrite of the script.

Almost exactly a year later, in July 1975, Duffell received a letter from Greene, encouraging as ever about his script and with some thought on Plarr: 'Plarr will make or break the film. He is the character who "grows". A sexual cynic who is trapped by love and jealousy. One needs an actor who can, at the beginning, convey the sense of emptiness, but a *superficial* emptiness – one must be aware of an inner life.' Ideally Greene envisaged Jack Nicholson for the role – 'I can't think of anyone who could play the character more nearly to our conception.'

Yet another year came and went. In May 1976 Duffell sent his third version to Greene, at 138 pages, more than thirty pages shorter than the previous draft. 'With some reluctance,' Duffell told Greene,

I changed Plarr to an American. It was put to me that you couldn't have an American star with Charley saying, 'you are as English as I am'. I think it is inevitable, and given an American star, not really disastrous . . . in view of the current political upheavals in Argentina, I thought it better not to be specific about the country now; a loss of focus, I suppose, but as the situation there makes it out of the question to shoot on the real location anyway.

Another twelve months on, in 1977, Duffell's script was read and much admired by both the prolific entrepreneur, John Heyman, (of *The Go-Between, The Hireling* etc.) and Heyman's close friend, Richard Burton, who, in the wake of his stage success *Equus*, had become 'hot' again. Burton seemed keen to play Fortnum.

Duffell told me:

At that point my option lapsed once more but I had a kind of loose working arrangement with Greene's agents that, if they got interest in the project, they would pump my script because Graham had approved it. I told the Heymans (John and his ex-wife Norma, who was working as a producer-consultant with John's company World Film Services) this. Almost immediately I got a call to say that now Orson Welles had an option on the book. I rang up Graham who confirmed that Welles had bought a month's option but didn't seem to think it would amount to anything. I then heard that Orson had got his backers to buy the rights outright. So that, for me, really seemed to be the end of the story.

The best part of a year later, the Minema cinema in London decided to revive *England Made Me*. Duffell wrote to Greene about this, also spelling out how disappointed he had been about *Consul* as well as thanking him for all his past support:

He wrote back saying that Welles hadn't, in the event, paid up and that he, Graham, had instructed his agents to tell Orson either pay up or shut up. He shut up. I was now directly responsible for Norma Heyman getting the rights. I found out though that my script had been offered first to Fred Zinnemann, who felt he couldn't cope with the location problems, and then to Louis Malle. I then discovered they had asked Christopher Hampton to write another script, so I assumed the usual thing – they had lost confidence in my script.

So after nearly five years of on-off activity but a continuingly obsessive interest with the subject, Duffell finally bowed out of *The Honorary Consul* to go on and increase his own stature with first a British Academy Award-winning television film *Caught on a Train* and then a multi-million-pound mini-series, *The Far Pavilions*, based on Molly Kaye's best-seller.

A former actress and model, Norma Heyman took over the 'obsession' from 1978 until she finally got the film into production in 1982. She had read the book when it first came out and loved it too but she was deflected as the various options ensued over the years. Now, with Duffell's script, she apparently found herself stymied: 'It was wonderfully written but an extremely literal translation – I'd rather have sent copies of the novel to friends. It also seemed as if it had been with every major and minor company, every financier and about fifteen leading actors during the past five years. It was just no go. I thought, "well, we're going to have to start again, but who does one go with?" '

Having seen the play *Savages*, and thought it 'remarkable',

Norma Heyman decided to invite its young playwright, Christ-opher Hampton, to meet her and discuss his adapting the novel. Hampton was delighted to undertake the assignment. Hampton says:

> I was rather influenced by an interview Tom Stoppard gave at the time of writing *The Human Factor* when he said that Graham Greene was startled that he had been so faithful to the book. This for me was the green light. *The Honorary Consul's* a very long, and complicated, book and encouraged by this and what Greene had written in his *Ways of Escape* about the rules for writing fiction being quite different from the rules for writing for the screen, I decided to be rather radical with the novel. I began by throwing out my favourite character, Saavedra (the novel's noble, if faintly absurd, literary apostle of *machismo*). What I landed up with is a kind of distillation of the central story of the book, slightly differently emphasized.[2]

Happy with Hampton's first draft, Norma Heyman proceeded to hawk it around with about as much success as Duffell had had: 'Frankly, I couldn't get it arrested. I didn't know what to do though I suppose it was everyone turning it down that made it that much more important to me.' Her first real breakthrough was when she met the American actor Richard Gere in New York after seeing him in the controversial play *Bent*:

> I remember him coming through the door and my thinking immediately, 'he's Dr Plarr'. I sent the script to his agent and six weeks later heard back that Gere thought it extraordinary. He committed then, that was nearly three years before we'd get the film finally together, and, of course, in the meantime he became a huge star with *An Officer and a Gentleman*, after which he was offered everything under the sun. Yet he stuck with us through thick and thin.
>
> Michael Caine was another matter. We couldn't think of an actor for Fortnum. When Plarr dies who could we, in filmic terms, have who'd make an audience want to stay in their seats. By rights, when Plarr dies, it should be the end of the film – in a way, everything after that is a sort of epilogue.

In the book, Plarr, who has become inexorably entangled with the terrorists who have kidnapped Fortnum, believes that he can mediate with the troops surrounding the hut. He is shot down and killed. Fortnum survives, fortified by his love for Clara, and even prepared to call his child-to-be Eduardo after Plarr – 'you see I loved Eduardo in a way'. Caine was suggested by director John Mackenzie (who had been secured by Norma Heyman with the rent money from hiring her house out to Elizabeth Taylor during the London run of *Little Foxes*).

Mackenzie, whose work had included *The Long Good Friday* for the cinema and plays like *A Sense of Freedom* and the Italia prize-winning 'Just Another Saturday' for British television says:

Caine is actually a lot younger than the character in the novel but I liked the idea of creating more of a rivalry, a tension between him and Richard Gere . . . it was tense and believable to have them a little closer in age. I think that Caine has a gentle, humorous quality, a sort of potential for showing love, which isn't often exploited. Certainly those were the qualities I wanted for the character.[3]

Norma Heyman felt that Mackenzie, as well as being a good actors' director, could give

an added sense of drive and style to Christopher's script. It already had the sort of drive and energy on the page which I hadn't seen resulting in many of the films from Greene's work. What I wanted to make was a compulsive film with the elements I adored in the book – its story of commitment and betrayal – transposed to film without the over literary-ization which has been one of the problems of Greene adaptations.

With a budget of over seven million dollars, arranged by her ex-husband, the film finally started shooting in October 1982 in Mexico, doubling for Argentina, now specifically named in Hampton's script, which indeed further identified the main centre of action as Corrientes, the town of Greene's own research. Greene had actually left it nameless in the book 'because I wished to take liberties and not to be tied down to the street plan of a particular city or the map of a particular province'.[4]

Just as Peter Duffell had indicated more than six years earlier, Argentina was never going to be likely for location shooting, and this was poignantly so now, with the recent intervention of the short, sharp but bitter Falklands conflict still fresh in the memory (even on this, the old Greene prescience was in evidence within the pages of the novel, 'somebody had started up another Falklands Islands scare: the island cropped up, like Gibraltar, whenever there was nothing else to worry about'.[5]) Norma Heyman told me: 'We have a dichotomy here, in a strange way. We've made a film in 1982–3 of a book written in 1972 when, theoretically, Argentina was a democracy. We were making it at a time of military dictatorship and we wanted to stress that without, necessarily, spelling it out. I think Greene would have written a different book now.'

It would have been marvellous to report that such longevity of effort from first Duffell and then Norma Heyman had finally borne memorable fruit. In a sense, Heyman and Mackenzie's technically fine film had achieved the worst of all possible worlds; in remaining generally faithful to the novel's dramatic line, it somehow still contrived to miss the real drama; in, as one critic pointed out, 'virtually eliminating the subtle religious, moral and political discussions' it failed to convey the substance of Greene's work. There are good things in it: Caine, though too young, and frankly, too wholesome, is genuinely moving and Gere never less than watchable as Plarr. The American critics, however, tore into Gere.

Norma Heyman admits: 'We were slightly hoist on our own petard, for between his committing to us and the film's release he had become a giant media star and was, unfortunately, judged on his previous screen roles. Their views had been predicated by a sense of "there's Gere taking off his clothes again".' Gere was also, rather unkindly, called to task over his English accent. Despite having an American star, the film-makers had, in my view, bravely gone back to the original concept of Plarr as half-British, and Gere obliged nobly.

Whether or not Duffell's script would have made a good film is, of course, pure speculation. He nevertheless had attempted to present many more layers as well as a more concerted development of tension before the final shoot-out. Hampton's final version is a fairly straightforward, chronological narrative, all bones and precious little flesh. Norma Heyman would dispute this:

> I hoped we hadn't stuck to a pure narrative. I hoped, by expressions at least, one understands the moral dilemmas. I think Fortnum comes out as the only true believer of both the novel and the film, while Plarr is the man who can't commit or love in the widest possible sense. Of course we shot a lot more – I suppose in another world I would have preferred to have a shorter script to begin with – for example the scene where Plarr is screwing Señora Escobar. It's one of my favourite scenes in the book which I knew in my bones wouldn't work in the film because I think it would have taken it into the element of farce. We had cut Saavedra right from the beginning. I don't feel his loss in the film; he's too difficult to translate. Anyway his concept of *machismo* is surely summarized by the character of the police chief Perez.

I remain unconvinced and can only wonder what Greene might make of this, his admitted favourite among his own works, the one 'that bothers me the least . . . in *The Honorary Consul* the doctor evolves, the consul evolved, the priest too, up to a point. By the end of the novel they have become different men. That's not easy to bring off, but I think that in this book I have succeeded.'[6]

Norma Heyman sent Greene a script 'and I haven't heard back from him that day to this'. Greene told me he thought it 'very bad . . . but it was a first draft and, well you know, a first draft is never perfect'.

Hampton rationalizes: 'In *Ways of Escape*, Greene says that a novelist who has organized a series of facts in this meticulous way is never going to be pleased whatever one does. Indeed, I think the relationship between adaptor and adaptee is rather a delicate one. In this case, I have no relationship with Greene whatsoever.'[7]

Director Mackenzie would agree with Greene about Hampton's first draft:

> which, frankly, I didn't think was good – but then if you get three good scenes in any screenplay, you're very lucky. We went to three drafts but the changes were not immense in the

structure. The linear thing was always there. I felt there was a nice simplicity about it. Maybe, in retrospect, the script should have been more cleverly contrived with a sense of unfolding events, not necessarily in sequential time order. Perhaps the film lacks that extra tension. I still feel that our film could help to open out Graham Greene to an even wider audience. Of course, if you don't like the film it may turn you off him.

When the film opened outside North America, it fortunately reverted to its proper title but it attracted much the same sort of critical reservations. These, to be fair, were less aimed at the inadequacy of Gere than at what was generally felt to be a fatal distillation of Greene's original. Nevertheless, European box-office takings were shaping up well in the early months of 1984. In the *Sunday Telegraph*, David Castell had concluded a little optimistically that here was 'a film, I suspect, Greene would recognize and respect'. Greene told me, tersely: 'I haven't seen *The Honorary Consul* and I don't want to!'

These travels in Greeneland are, in every sense, a continuing exercise. At the time of writing, a long-overdue television film of Greene's 1980 novella *Dr Fischer of Geneva, or the Bomb Party* was in production with James Mason as the eponymous anti-hero and Alan Bates as the narrator Jones. This was intended for transmission by the BBC late in 1984 (see Appendix I).

Greene's most recent novel, a delightful reworking of Cervantes' *Don Quixote* as *Monsignor Quixote* in modern Spain has reached first draft stage for Thames Television. There is news too of a new version of the fluffy *Loser Takes All*, being financed by Thorn EMI Films and made by Christine Oestreicher and James Scott who fashioned an Oscar-winning short feature from 'A Shocking Accident', out of the *May We Borrow Your Husband?* anthology.

In this age of remakes, prequels and sequels, generally resulting from a dearth of good, original screen-writing, one would not be terribly surprised to see a whole new celluloid generation of Greene Revisited. But as Greene himself warns, the books are likely to be remembered long after the films are forgotten.

Notes

Introduction

1. Marie-Francoise Allain, *The Other Man* (The Bodley Head in association with Simon & Schuster Inc., 1983), p. 144.
2. Graham Greene, *A Sort of Life* (Penguin edition, The Bodley Head, 1971), p. 11.
3. Graham Greene, *Collected Essays* (The Bodley Head, 1969), p. 15.
4. Graham Greene, *Ways of Escape* (Penguin edition, The Bodley Head, 1980), p. 45.
5. Graham Greene, *The Pleasure Dome: The Collected Film Criticism 1935–40*, edited by John Russell Taylor (Martin Secker & Warburg, 1972), pp. 39–40.
6. *Ibid.*, p. 11.
7. Basil Wright, *The Long View* (Paladin edition, Martin Secker & Warburg, 1974), p. 94.
8. Evelyn Waugh, 'Felix Culpa?' from *The Tablet* (5 June 1948). Reprinted in *Commonweal* (16 June 1948) © Commonweal, 1948).
9. *Ways of Escape*, p. 179.
10. Graham Greene, 'The Novelist and the Cinema: A Personal Experience', *International Film Annual*, ed. William Whitebait (New York: Doubleday, 1958), pp. 56, 61.
11. *The Other Man*, p. 80.

Chapter One

1. *The Pleasure Dome*, pp. 78, 79, 97, 117.
2. *Ways of Escape*, p. 50.
3. John Mills, *Up in the Clouds, Gentlemen Please* (Weidenfeld & Nicolson), p. 138.
4. *Ways of Escape*, pp. 51–2.

5. *The Pleasure Dome*, p. 262.
6. Basil Dean, *Mind's Eye* (London: Hutchinson, 1973), pp. 250, 251.
7. *Ibid.*, p. 253.
8. *The Pleasure Dome*, p. 262.
9. *Ways of Escape*, p. 22.
10. Graham Greene, *Journey without Maps* (Heinemann, 1936).

Chapter Two

1. Charles Barr, *Ealing Studios* (Cameron & Tayleur in association with David & Charles, 1977), pp. 32–3.
2. *The Long View*, p. 195.
3. *Ways of Escape*, p. 54.
4. Gene D. Phillips S.J., *Graham Greene: The Films of His Fiction* (Teachers' College Press, 1974), p. 24.
5. Carlos Clarens, *Crime Movies – An Illustrated History* (Martin Secker & Warburg, 1980), p. 178.
6. Beverly Linet, *Ladd* (New York: Arbor House, 1979), p. 61.
7. Veronica Lake, *An Autobiography* (W.H. Allen, 1969), p. 85.
8. *Ladd*, p. 60.
9. *An Autobiography*, p. 85.
10. *Commonweal*, 29 May 1942.
11. *The Pleasure Dome*, pp. 84–5.
12. *Ways of Escape*, p. 74.
13. *The Pleasure Dome*, pp. 195–6.
14. Charles Higham, Joel Greenberg, *The Celluloid Muse* (Angus & Robertson, 1969), p. 112.
15. Graham Greene, *The Ministry of Fear* (Penguin edition, Heinemann, 1943), p. 128.
16. *Ibid.*, p. 236.
17. David Thomson, 'Lang's Ministry' (*Sight & Sound*).
18. *Ibid.*

Chapter Three

1. *Ways of Escape*, p. 68.
2. Graham Greene, *The Confidential Agent* (Penguin edition, Heinemann, 1939), p. 194.
3. Ted Sennett, *Masters of Menace* (New York: Dutton, 1979), p. 163.
4. Lauren Bacall, *By Myself* (Jonathan Cape, 1979), pp. 144–8.
5. Charles Higham, *Hollywood Cameramen: Sources of Light* (Thames & Hudson in association with the British Film Institute, 1970), p. 89.
6. *The Pleasure Dome*, p. 250.

7. *The Confidential Agent*, p. 26.
8. *Ways of Escape*, p. 14.
9. *Observer* (6 April 1947).
10. *Ways of Escape*, p. 14.

Chapter Four

1. *Daily Mirror* (8 January, 1948).
2. *Daily Mirror* (9 January, 1948).
3. *Ways of Escape*, pp. 61–2.
4. Graham Greene, *Brighton Rock* (Octopus edition, Heinemann, 1938), p. 13.
5. *Ways of Escape*, p. 58.
6. *Ibid.*, p. 58.
7. *Brighton Rock*, p. 45.
8. *Ibid.*, pp. 129–30.
9. *Ibid.*, p. 144.
10. *Ibid.*, p. 177.
11. *Ibid.*, p. 178.
12. Christopher Burstall, 'Graham Greene Takes the Orient Express' (*Listener*, 21 November, 1968).
13. *The Other Man*, p. 176.
14. *Ways of Escape*, pp. 60–2.
15. *Radio Times*, 19 April, 1973.
16. *Graham Greene: The Films of His Fiction*, p. 165.
17. *Manchester Guardian*, 10 January, 1948.
18. *News Chronicle*, 10 January 1948.

Chapter Five

1. *The Pleasure Dome*, pp. 42, 90–1, 265.
2. Graham Greene, *The Fallen Idol* (Penguin edition, Heinemann, 1935), p. 157.
3. *A Sort of Life*, p. 39.
4. Preface to *The Fallen Idol*, p. 123.
5. Preface to *The Fallen Idol*, p. 124.
6. *Graham Greene: The Films of His Fiction*, p. 59.
7. Michael Korda, *Charmed Lives* (Allen Lane, 1980), p. 217.
8. Francis Levison, 'Carol Reed Special Collections' (3).
9. Karol Kulik, *The Man Who Could Work Miracles* (W.H. Allen, 1975), p. 320.
10. *Ways of Escape*, p. 96.
11. *Ibid.*, p. 96.

12. Graham Greene, *The Third Man* (Penguin edition, Heinemann, 1950), p. 25.

13. Preface to *The Third Man*, p. 10.

14. *Memo from David O. Selznick*, selected and edited by Rudy Behlmar (Viking Press, 1972), p. 383.

15. *Ways of Escape*, pp. 51–3.

16. *Memo from David O. Selznick* (16 October, 1948), pp. 384–7.

17. Judy Adamson and Philip Stratford, 'Looking for the Third Man' (*Encounter*, June 1978), p. 44.

18. *Ibid.*, p. 42.

19. Interview with Carol Reed by Charles Thomas Samuels in *Encountering Directors* (Putnam & Sons, 1972).

20. Graham Greene, *The Third Man: Modern Film Scripts* (Simon & Schuster, 1968), p. 114.

21. Preface to *The Third Man*, p. 10.

22. Lynette Carpenter, ' "I Never Knew the Old Vienna": Cold War Politics and the Third Man' (*Film Criticism*, Vol. 3, 1978), p. 34.

23. Preface to *The Third Man*, p. 11.

24. *Charmed Lives*, p. 218.

25. C.T. Samuels interview.

26. Joseph McBride, *Orson Welles* (Secker & Warburg, 1972), p. 8.

27. C.T. Samuels interview.

28. *Memo from David O. Selznick*, p. 391.

29. Ivan Butler, *Cinema in Britain* (A.S. Barnes & Co., 1973), p. 179.

30. *Daily Mail*, 3 April, 1950.

Chapter Six

1. Graham Greene, Prologue to *The Lawless Roads* (Penguin edition, Heinemann, 1939), p. 20.

2. *Ways of Escape*, p. 66.

3. *The Other Man*, p. 154.

4. *Ways of Escape*, p. 66.

5. *News Chronicle*, 3 April, 1948.

6. *Ways of Escape*, p. 66.

7. *Graham Greene, The Films of His Fiction*, p. 107.

8. Andrew Sinclair, *John Ford* (Allen & Unwin, 1979), p. 135.

9. Lindsay Anderson, *About John Ford* (Plexus, 1981), p. 76.

10. Peter Bogdanovich, *John Ford* (Studio Vista, 1968), pp. 85–6.

11. *About John Ford,* p. 76.

12. *Sunday Times*, 4 May 1948.

13. Andrew Sarris, *The John Ford Movie Mystery* (Secker & Warburg, 1976), p. 128

14. Bogdanovich, *John Ford*, p. 85.

15. Graham Greene, *The Heart of the Matter* (Octopus edition, Heinemann, 1948), p. 185.

16. *Ways of Escape*, p. 89.

17. *Ibid.*, pp. 93–4.

18. *Ibid.*, p. 93.

19. 'Felix Culpa?'

20. *Ibid.*

21. *Graham Greene: The Films of His Fiction*, p. 120.

22. *Focus* (Vol. VI, no. 9, September 1953).

23. *Sight & Sound* (January–March 1953).

24. Trader Faulkner, *Peter Finch: A Biography* (Angus & Robertson, 1979), pp. 151–2.

25. *Ibid.*, pp. 151–2.

26. Robert Gessner, *The Moving Image* (Cassell, 1968), pp. 279–81.

27. *Picture Post* (2 April, 1955).

28. *Manchester Guardian*, 2 February, 1955.

Chapter Seven

1. *Ways of Escape*, p. 167.

2. *Ibid.*

3. *Ibid.*, p. 168.

4. George Bernard Shaw, Preface to *Saint Joan*, (Penguin edition, 1946), pp. 65–6.

5. Gerald Pratley, *The Cinema of Otto Preminger* (A.S. Barnes & Co., 1971), pp. 119–20.

6. Otto Preminger, *An Autobiography* (New York: Doubleday & Co., 1977), p. 151.

7. *Time*, 1 July, 1957.

8. *An Autobiography*, p. 153.

Chapter Eight

1. Graham Greene, *Across the Bridge* (Penguin edition, Heinemann, 1947), p. 85.

2. Rudyard Kipling, 'The Power of the Dog'.

3. *Daily Mail*, 30 July, 1957.

4. *Daily Express*, 3 August, 1957.

5. *News Chronicle*, 2 August, 1957.

6. *Films and Filming*, July 1960.

7. Rod Steiger, *Movie People* (Ross Firestone, Douglas Book Co., 1972), p. 117.

8. *The Times*, 29 January, 1957.
9. *Financial Times*, 31 March, 1958.
10. *The Times*, 29 January, 1957.
11. *Ways of Escape*, p. 121.
12. *The Other Man*, p. 94.
13. *Ibid.*, p. 95.
14. *Sight & Sound*, April 1958.
15. *Ibid.*
16. *Ibid.*
17. *The Novelist and the Cinema*, p. 55.
18. *The Other Man*, p. 100.

Chapter Nine

1. *Ways of Escape*, p. 47.
2. *The Pleasure Dome*, p. 75.
3. *Ibid.*, p. 47.
4. *Ways of Escape*, p. 184.
5. *Ibid.*, pp. 184–5.
6. *Ibid.*, p. 191.
7. 'Reunion in Havana' (*Film Literature Quarterly*, Vol. 2, Fall 1974, no. 4).
8. *Daily Express*, 16 April, 1959.
9. *Sunday Express*, 3 January, 1960.
10. *Saturday Review*, 6 February, 1960.
11. Cole Lesley, *The Life of Noël Coward* (Jonathan Cape, 1976), p. 397.
12. *Graham Greene: The Films of His Fiction*, p. 175.
13. Graham Greene, *The Comedians* (Penguin edition, the Bodley Head, 1966), p. 145.
14. *Graham Greene: The Films of His Fiction*.
15. *Ways of Escape*, p. 206.
16. *Ways of Escape*, p. 207.
17. Tony Thomas, *Ustinov in Focus* (Zwemmer, 1971), p. 176.
18. *The Times*, 18 January, 1968.
19. *Time*, 3 November, 1967.

Chapter Ten

1. *The Pleasure Dome*, pp. 20–2.
2. Carlos Clarens, *George Cukor* (Secker & Warburg, 1976), p. 122.
3. *Ways of Escape*, p. 31.
4. *International Film Quarterly* (Winter 1972/73), p. 22.
5. *Ways of Escape*, p. 29.

6. *Ibid.*, p. 29.
7. *Ibid.*, p. 30.
8. *Literature/Film Quarterly* (Vol 2, Fall 1974, no. 4), p. 364.
9. *Ibid.*, p. 366.
10. Trader Faulkner, *Peter Finch: A Biography*, p. 255.
11. *Spectator*, 19 June, 1973.
12. *Over 21* (February 1973).
13. *Ways of Escape*, p. 31.

Chapter Eleven

1. *Ways of Escape*, p. 227.
2. *Ibid.*, p. 228.
3. *The Human Factor* script (c. 1978, Otto Preminger), p. 18.
4. *Ibid.*, p. 36.
5. *Observer*, 3 February, 1980.
6. *Observer*, 10 February, 1980.
7. *Ways of Escape*, p. 229.

Chapter Twelve

1. *Graham Greene: The Films of His Fiction*, p. 85.
2. BBC TV interview, 18 October, 1983.
3. *Screen International* (29 January, 1983), p. 15.
4. Foreword disclaimer in *The Honorary Consul*, Graham Greene (Penguin edition, the Bodley Head, 1973).
5. *Ibid.*, p. 133.
6. *The Other Man*, p. 136.
7. BBC TV interview, *ibid*

Filmography

1933

Orient Express (based on *Stamboul Train*). Distributor: Twentieth Century-Fox. Production company: Twentieth Century-Fox. Producer/Director: Paul Martin. Screenplay: Paul Martin, William Conselman, Carl Hovey, Oscar Levant. Cast: Heather Angel (Coral Musker), Norman Foster (Carlton Myatt), Ralph Morgan (Dr Czinner), Herbert Mundin (Mr Peters), Una O'Connor (Mrs Peters), Dorothy Burgess (Mabel Warren), Lisa Gova (Anna), William Irving (Conductor), Roy D'Arcy (Josef Grunlich), Perry Ivins (Major Petrovitch), Fredrik Vogeding (Colonel Hartep), Marc Lobell (Lieutenant Alexitch). 73 minutes.

1937

The Green Cockatoo aka *Four Dark Hours*, aka *Race Gang*. Distributor: Twentieth Century-Fox. Production company: New World Pictures. Producer: William K. Howard. Director: William Cameron Menzies. Screenplay: Edward O. Berkman, Arthur Wimperis from an original story and scenario by Graham Greene. Cast: John Mills (Jim Connor), Rene Ray (Eileen), Robert Newton (Dave Connor), Bruce Seton (Madison), Charles Oliver (Terrell), Julian Vedey (Steve), Allen Jeayes (Inspector), Frank Atkinson (Butler). 65 minutes.

Twenty-One Days aka *Twenty-One Days Together* (US). Distributor: Columbia. Production company: London–Denham. Producer: Alexander Korda. Director: Basil Dean. Screenplay: Graham Greene and Basil Dean from a short story, 'The First and the Last', by John Galsworthy. Photography: Jan Stallich. Art director: Vincent Korda. Editor: Charles

206

Crichton. Music: John Greenwood. Cast: Vivien Leigh (Wanda), Leslie Banks (Keith Durrant), Laurence Olivier (Larry Durrant), Francis L. Sullivan (Mander), Hay Petrie (John Aloysius Evan), Esme Percy (Henry Walenn), Robert Newton (Tolly), Victor Rietti (Antonio), Morris Harvey (Alexander MacPherson). 75 minutes.

The Future's in the Air. Production company: Strand Film Unit. Producer: Paul Rotha. Director: Alex Shaw, commentary written by: Graham Greene. Photography: George Noble. Music: William Alwyn.

A documentary made to celebrate the inauguration of the Empire Air Mail. The stillness of the first sequence, Waiting in the Outback of Australia, titled 'January 1937', shows an isolated air-strip in the glaring heat, desultory and silent except for a cricket commentary on the radio; a title '4 days later' and, with 'Waltzing Matilda' on the accordion, through the same heat and emptiness we hear at last the drone of a plane; it lands and a chap strolls over to the shed with the letters. On we go with the plane, over mountains and rivers. It is not until here that the commentary begins. Superb overhead shots of sea and air take us on a journey eastwards from Southampton, and then going further on towards the East, with its bazaars and temples. The brilliant light of the Gulf, and craggy Afghans, women at work on the Karachi building-sites, majestic Ankor Val all add up to a travelogue by the best people with the best of reasons, the best of facilities . . . The Strand Film Unit was set up in 1935 to make documentary films which would compete with commercial shorts. It was formed by Donald Taylor (ex of the GPO Film Unit) and Ralph Keene, and later joined by Paul Rotha as Director of Productions. In 1936, they got a £5000 contract from Imperial Airways – *The History of the British Film, 1929–39* (Allen & Unwin, 1979).

1940
The New Britain. Production company: Strand Film Unit. Producer: Alex Shaw. Director: Ralph Keene. Commentary written by: Graham Greene.

A patriotic documentary, produced at a time of national crisis, extolling the material and social achievements of Britain in the two preceding decades.

Went the Day Well? aka *Forty-Eight Hours* (US). Distributor: United

Artists. Production company: Ealing. Producer: Michael Balcon. Director: Cavalcanti. Screenplay: Angus MacPhail, John Dighton, Diana Morgan from a story 'The Lieutenant Died Last' by Graham Greene. Photography: Wilkie Cooper. Art director: Tom Morahan. Music: Sir William Walton. Editor: Sidney Cole. Cast: Leslie Banks (Oliver Winsford), Elizabeth Allan (Peggy), Frank Lawton (Tom Sturry), Basil Sydney (Ortler), Valerie Taylor (Nora Ashton), Mervyn Johns (Sims), Edward Rigby (Poacher), Marie Lohr (Mrs Frazer), David Farrar (Jung), Thora Hird (Land girl), Harry Fowler (George Truscott). 92 minutes.

This Gun for Hire (based on *A Gun for Sale*). Distributor: Paramount. Production company: Paramount. Producer: Richard Blumenthal. Director: Frank Tuttle. Screenplay: Albert Maltz, W.R. Burnett. Photography: John Seitz. Music: David Buttalph. Cast: Veronica Lake (Ellen Graham), Robert Preston (Michael Crane), Laird Cregar (William Gates), Alan Ladd (Philip Raven), Tully Marshall (Alvin Brewster), Marc Lawrence (Tommy), Roger Imhof (Senator Burnett), Harry Shannon (Steve Finnerty). 81 minutes.

1943
The Ministry of Fear. Distributor: Paramount. Production: Paramount. Producer: Seton I. Miller. Director: Fritz Lang. Screenplay: Seton I. Miller. Photography: Henry Sharp. Art directors: Hans Dreier, Hal Pereira. Music: Victor Young. Editor: Archie Marshek. Cast: Ray Milland (Stephen Neale), Marjorie Reynolds (Carla Hilfe), Carl Esmond (Willi Hilfe), Hilary Brooke (Mrs Bellane), Erskine Sanford (Mr Rennit), Thomas Louden (Mr Newland), Dan Duryea (Cost), Percy Waram (Prentice), Alan Napier (Dr Forrester), Helena Grant (Mrs Merrick). 84 minutes.

1945
The Confidential Agent. Distributor: Warner Brothers. Production company: Warner Brothers. Producer: Robert Buckner. Director: Herman Shumlin. Screenplay: Robert Buckner. Photography: James Wong Howe. Music: Franz Waxman. Cast: Charles Boyer (Denard), Lauren Bacall (Rose Cullen), Katina Paxinou (Mrs Melandez), Peter Lorre (Contreras), Victor Francen (Licata), George Coulouris (Captain Currie), Wanda Hendrix (Else), John Warburton (Neil Forbes), Dan Seymour (Mr Muckerji), George Zucco (Detective Geddes), Miles Mander (Brigstock), Holmes Herbert (Lord Benditch). 122 minutes.

1947

The Man Within aka *The Smugglers* (US). Distributors: General Film Distributors. Production company: Production Film Service. Producers: Muriel and Sydney Box. Director: Bernard Knowles. Screenplay: Muriel and Sydney Box. Photography: Geoffrey Unsworth. Music: Clifton Parker. Cast: Michael Redgrave (Richard Carlyon), Jean Kent (Lucy), Joan Greenwood (Elizabeth), Richard Attenborough (Francis Andrews), Francis L. Sullivan (Braddock), Felix Aylmer (Priest), Ronald Shiner (Cockney Harry), Ernest Thesiger (Farne), Basil Sydney (Sir Henry Merriman), David Horne (Dr Stanton), Maurice Denham (Smuggler). 88 minutes.

Brighton Rock aka *Young Scarface* (US). Distributor: Pathé. Production company: Associated British Picture Corporation. Producer: Roy Boulting. Director: John Boulting. Screenplay: Graham Greene, Terence Rattigan. Photography: Harry Waxman. Art director: John Howell. Music: Hans May. Editor: Peter Graham Scott. Cast: Richard Attenborough (Pinkie Brown), Hermione Baddeley (Ida Arnold), William Hartnell (Dallow), Harcourt Williams (Prewitt), Wylie Watson (Spicer), Nigel Stock (Cubitt), Carol Marsh (Rose), Alan Wheatley (Fred Hale), George Carney (Phil Corkery), Charles Goldner (Colleoni). 92 minutes.

1947

The Fugitive (based on *The Power and the Glory*). Distributors: RKO Radio. Production company: Argosy Pictures. Producers: Merian C. Cooper, John Ford. Director: John Ford. Screenplay: Dudley Nichols. Photography: Gabriel Figueroa. Art director: Alfred Ybarra. Music: Richard Hageman. Editor: Jack Murray. Cast: Henry Fonda (A Fugitive), Dolores del Rio (A Mexican Woman), Pedro Armendariz (Lieutenant of Police), J. Carroll Naish (Police Informer), Leo Carillo (Chief of Police), Ward Bond (El Gringo), Robert Armstrong (Sergeant of Police), John Qualen (Refugee doctor). 102 minutes.

1948

The Fallen Idol (based on 'The Basement Room', from the *Twenty-One Stories* anthology). Distributor: British Lion. Production company: London Films. Producer: Carol Reed. Director: Carol Reed. Screenplay: Graham Greene. Photography: Georges Perinal. Music: William Alwyn. Art directors: Vincent Korda, James Sawyer. Editor: Oswald Hafenrichter. Cast: Ralph Richardson (Baines), Michele Morgan (Julie), Bobby Henrey (Felipe), Sonia Dresdel (Mrs Baines), Denis O'Dea (Detective-

Inspector Crowe), Walter Fitzgerald (Dr Fenton), Jack Hawkins (Detective Ames), Bernard Lee (Detective Hart), Geoffrey Keen (Detective Davis), Dora Bryan (Rose), George Woodbridge (Desk Sergeant), Karel Stepanek (First Secretary), Joan Young (Mrs Barrow), Dandy Nichols (Mrs Patterson). 95 minutes.

1949

The Third Man. Distributor: British Lion. Production Company: London Films. Producer: Carol Reed. Director: Carol Reed. Screenplay: Graham Greene. Photography: Robert Krasker. Art director: Vincent Korda. Editor: Oswald Hafenrichter. Music: Anton Karas. Cast: Joseph Cotten (Martins), Trevor Howard (Calloway), Alida Valli (Anna), Orson Welles (Harry Lime), Bernard Lee (Sergeant Paine), Paul Hoerbiger (Porter), Ernst Deutsch (Baron Kurtz), Siegfried Breuer (Popescu), Erich Pontu (Dr Winkel), Wilfred Hyde-White (Crabbin). 104 minutes.

1953

The Heart of the Matter. Distributor: British Lion. Production company: London Films. Producer: Ian Dalrymple. Director: George More O'Ferrall. Screenplay: Ian Dalrymple, Lesley Storm. Photography: Jack Hildyard. Art director: Joseph Bato. Editor: Sidney Stone. Music adviser: Edric Connor. Cast: Trevor Howard (Scobie), Elizabeth Allan (Louise), Maria Schell (Helen Rolt), Denholm Elliott (Wilson), Peter Finch (Father Rank), Gerard Oury (Yusef), Michael Hordern (Commissioner of Police), George Coulouris (Portuguese Captain), Earl Cameron (Ali). 105 minutes.

1954

The Stranger's Hand. Distributor: British Lion. Production company: IFP. Producers: John Stafford, Graham Greene. Director: Mario Soldati. Screenplay: Guy Elmes, Georgio Bassani from an original story by Graham Greene. Photography: Enzo Serafin. Editor: Tom Simpson. Music: Nino Rota. Cast: Trevor Howard (Major Court), Alida Valli (Roberta), Richard Basehart (Joe Hamstringer), Richard O'Sullivan (Roger Court), Eduardo Ciannelli (Dr Vivaldi), Stephen Murray (British consul). 85 minutes.

1955

The End of the Affair. Distributor: Columbia. Production company:

Coronado. Producer: David Lewis. Director: Edward Dmytryk. Screenplay: Lenore Coffee. Photography: Wilkie Cooper. Art director: Don Ashton. Editor: Alan Osbiston. Music: Benjamin Frankel. Cast: Deborah Kerr (Sarah Miles), Van Johnson (Maurice Bendrix), Peter Cushing (Henry Miles), John Mills (Albert Parkis), Stephen Murray (Father Crompton), Michael Goodliffe (Smythe), Nora Swinburne (Mrs Bertram), Joyce Carey (Miss Palmer), Charles Goldner (Savage), Frederick Lister (Dr Collingwood). 105 minutes.

1956

Loser Takes All. Distributor: British Lion. Production company: IFP. Producer: John Stafford. Director: Ken Annakin. Screenplay: Graham Greene. Photography: Georges Perinal. Art director: John Howell. Editor: Jean Baker. Music: Alessandro Cicognini. Cast: Rossano Brazzi (Bertrand), Glynis Johns (Cary), Robert Morley (Dreuther), Tony Britton (Tony), Felix Aylmer (The Other), Albert Lieven (Hotel Manager), A.E. Matthews (Elderly Man in Casino), Walter Hudd (Arnold). 88 minutes.

1957

Saint Joan. Distributor: United Artists. Production company: Wheel Productions. Producer: Otto Preminger. Director: Otto Preminger. Screenplay: Graham Greene, from the play by George Bernard Shaw. Photography: Georges Perinal. Production designer: Roger Furse. Editor: Helga Cranston. Music: Mischa Spoliansky. Cast: Richard Widmark (Charles the Dauphin), Jean Seberg (St Joan), Richard Todd (Dunois), Anton Walbrook (Cauchon), John Gielgud (Warwick), Felix Aylmer (Inquisitor), Harry Andrews (John de Stogumber), Barry Jones (De Courcelles), Finlay Currie (Archbishop of Rheims), Bernard Miles (Master Executioner). 110 minutes.

Across the Bridge (based on the short story in the *Twenty-One Stories* anthology). Distributor: Rank. Production company: Rank Film Productions. Producer: John Stafford. Director: Ken Annakin. Screenplay: Guy Elmes, Denis Freeman. Photography: Reginald Wyer. Art director: Cedric Dawe. Editor: Alfred Roome. Music: James Bernard. Cast: Rod Steiger (Carl Schaffner), David Knight (Johnny), Marla Landi (Mary), Noel Willman (Chief of Police), Bernard Lee (Chief Inspector Hadden), Bill Nagy (Paul Scarff), Eric Pohlmann (Police Sergeant), Faith Brook (Kay). 103 minutes.

The Quiet American. Distributor: United Artists. Production company: Figaro. Producer: Joseph L. Mankiewicz. Director and screenplay: Joseph L. Mankiewicz. Photography: Robert Krasker. Art director: Rino Mondinello. Editor: William Hornbeck. Music: Mario Nascimbene. Cast: Audie Murphy (The American), Michael Redgrave (Fowler), Giorgia Moll (Phuong), Claude Dauphin (Vigot), Bruce Cabot (Bill Granger), Kerina (Miss Hei), Fred Sadoff (Dominguez). 121 minutes.

Short Cut to Hell (based on *A Gun for Sale*). Distributor: Paramount. Production company: Paramount. Producer: A.C. Lyles. Director: James Cagney. Screenplay: Ted Berkman, Raphael Blau, based on screenplay by Albert Maltz, W.R. Burnett. Photography: Haskell Boggs. Art directors: Hal Pereira, Roland Anderson. Editor: Ken McAdo. Music: Irvin Colbert. Cast: Robert Ivers (Kyle), Georgann Johnson (Glory), William Bishop (Stan), Jacques Aubuchon (Bahrwell), Peter Baldwin (Adams), Yvette Vickers (Daisy), Richard Hale (AT). 89 minutes.

1960

Our Man In Havana. Distributor: Columbia. Production company: Kingsmead. Producer: Carol Reed. Director: Carol Reed. Screenplay: Graham Greene. Photography: Oswald Morris. Art director: John Box. Editor: Bert Bates. Music: Hermanos Deniz Cuban Rhythm Band. Cast: Alec Guinness (Jim Wormold), Burl Ives (Dr Hasselbacher), Maureen O'Hara (Beatrice), Ernie Kovacs (Segura), Noël Coward (Hawthorne), Ralph Richardson (C), Jo Morrow (Milly), Paul Rogers (Carter), Gregoire Aslan (Cifuentes), Jose Prieto (Lopez), Duncan Macrae (MacDougal). 111 minutes.

1961

The Power and the Glory (CBS Television). Producer: David Susskind. Director Marc Daniels. Screenplay: Dale Wasserman. Photography: Alan Posage, Leo Farrenkopf. Editors: Sidney Meyers, Walter Hess. Music: Laurence Rosenthal. Cast: Laurence Olivier (Priest), George C. Scott (Lieutenant), Julie Harris (Priest's mistress), Mildred Natwick, Martin Gabel, Cyril Cusack. 98 minutes.

1962

Stamboul Train (BBC Television). Transmitted 11 September. Producer: Prudence Fitzgerald. Adaptation: Christopher Williams. Designer: Tony

Abbott. Cast: Susan Burnet (Coral Musker), Peter Birrel (Carleton Myatt), Richard Warner (Dr Czinner), Anna Burden (Mabel Warren), Ivor Salter (Grunlich). 50 minutes.

Hugh Carleton Greene, younger brother of Graham and then Director General of the BBC, writing to the *Sunday Telegraph* about the corporation's decision to apologize for its production (an apology which had been variously described as 'craven' and 'abject'):

'I have never been able to understand why it should be considered cowardly to apologize when one is conscious of having made a mistake. To my mind an apology is cowardly only when it involves a surrender to pressure against one's better judgement. In this case the BBC considered that it had been responsible for a thoroughly bad production. Graham Greene was in entire agreement with us about this. In my opinion, creative departments are more likely to be encouraged than discouraged by a critical attitude towards their work.

'The old sad story of 50 minutes' compression crumbling the shape and atmosphere of the original and hopelessly distorting the skilful way Greene wove the fortunes of those fellow-travellers on the Trans-European Express' – *Daily Mail.*

'It was one of the best plays I have ever seen on BBC TV' – Audrey Whiting, *Daily Mirror.*

1967

The Comedians. Distributor: MGM Production Company: MGM/ Maximilian/Trianon. Producer: Peter Glenville. Director: Peter Glenville. Screenplay: Graham Greene. Photography: Henri Decae. Art director: François de Lamothe. Editor: Françoise Javet. Music: Laurence Rosenthal. Cast: Richard Burton (Brown), Elizabeth Taylor (Martha Pineda), Peter Ustinov (Pineda), Alec Guinness (Major Jones), Paul Ford (Smith), Lillian Gish (Mrs Smith), Georg Stanford Brown (Henri Philipot), Roscoe Lee Browne (Petit Pierre), James Earl Jones (Dr Magiot), Raymond St Jacques (Captain Concasseur), Douta Deck (Joseph), Cicely Tyson (Marie Therese). 150 minutes.

1972

Travels with my Aunt. Distributor: MGM. Production Company: MGM. Producers: Robert Fryer, James Cresson. Director: George Cukor.

Screenplay: Jay Presson Allen, Hugh Wheeler. Photography: Douglas Slocombe. Production designer: John Box. Editor: John Bloom. Music: Tony Hatch. Cast: Maggie Smith (Aunt Augusta). Alec McCowen (Henry Pulling), Lou Gossett (Wordsworth), Robert Stephens (Mr Visconti), Cindy Williams (Tooley), Jose Luis Lope Vasquez (M Dambreuse), Valerie White (Mme Dambreuse), Corinne Marchand (Louise), Raymond Gerome (Mario), Daniel Emilfork (Hakim), Robert Flemyng (Crowder). 109 minutes.

England Made Me. Distributor: Hemdale. Production company: Atlantic Productions/Central Film Studio Kosutnjak (Belgrade). Producer: Jack Levin. Director: Peter Duffell. Screenplay: Desmond Cory, Peter Duffell. Photography: Ray Parslow. Production designer: Tony Woollard. Editor: Malcolm Cooke. Music: John Scott. Cast: Peter Finch (Erik Krogh), Michael York (Anthony Farrant), Hildegarde Neil (Kate Farrant), Michael Hordern (F. Minty), Joss Ackland (Haller), Tessa Wyatt (Liz Davidge), Michael Sheard (Fromm). 100 minutes.

1973

La Nuit Americaine aka *Day for Night.* Production company: Les Films du Carosse/PECF (Paris)/PEC (Rome). Executive producer: Marcel Berbert. Director: François Truffaut. Screenplay: François Truffaut, Jean-Louis Richard, Suzanne Schiffmann. Photography: Pierre-William Glenn. Music: George Delerue. Editors: Yann Dedet, Martine Barraque. Art director: Damien Lanfranchi. Cast: Jacqueline Bisset (Julie Baker), Valentina Cortesa (Severine), Jean-Pierre Aumont (Alexandre), Jean-Pierre Leaud (Aphonse), Henry Graham and Marcel Bebert (Insurance Representatives). 116 minutes.

Truffaut needed a London insurance representative with just two lines of English dialogue for the film. With the connivance of a friend, Greene met up with Truffaut and his assistant Suzanne Schiffman, and the friend introduced him to the film-makers as Mr Henry Graham, a retired English businessman living in France, adding that perhaps 'Mr Graham' could play the insurance rep. They thought he would be perfect so he was signed up. After some initial butterflies, Greene turned up at the Victorine studios in Nice and was handed his two lines on a piece of paper. The phrase 'three-quarters of an hour' concerned him because he had trouble pronouncing his r's so, with permission, he changed the line to 'half an hour'. As Truffaut shot the scene so Greene's face began to become familiar to him. When Suzanne Schiffman finally revealed the bit-part actor's identity to the director,

Truffaut cried 'Oh, what a marvellous joke' and embraced Greene. 'Henry Graham' is immortalized on film and down among the small credits.

1976

Shades of Greene. Production company: Thames Television. Series producer: Alan Cooke. Story consultants: Sir Hugh Greene, George Markstein. (From *Twenty-One Stories* anthology): *The Case for the Defence*. Adapted by: John Mortimer. Director: Peter Hammond. Cast: Kathleen Harrison, Brian Glover, Michael Gough. *When Greek Meets Greek*. Adapted by: Clive Exton. Director: Alan Cooke. Cast: Paul Scofield, Roy Kinnear. *The Blue Film*. Adapted by: John Mortimer. Director: Philip Saville. Cast: Betsy Blair, Brian Cox, Koo Stark. *The Destructors*. Adapted by: John Mortimer. Director: Michael Apted. Cast: Nicholas Drake, George Hillsdon, Phil Daniels. *A Little Place off the Edgware Road*. Adapted by: John Mortimer. Director: Philip Saville. Cast: Tony Calvin. *Alas, Poor Maling*. Adapted by: Graham Greene. Director: Graham Evans. Cast: John Bird. *A Chance for Mr Lever*. Adapted by: Clive Exton. Director: Peter Hammond. Cast: Freddie Jones, Christopher Benjamin, Shane Briant, James Cossins. *A Drive in the Country*. Adapted by: Philip Mackie. Director: Alan Cooke. Cast: John Hurt, Lesley Dunlop, Ronald Lacey. *Special Duties*. Adapted by: John Mortimer. Director: Alastair Reid. Cast: John Gielgud. (From *May we Borrow Your Husband?* anthology): *The Root of all Evil*. Adapted by: Clive Easton. Director: Alastair Reid. Cast: Donald Pleasance, John le Mesurier, Bill Fraser, Peter Jones. *Cheap in August*. Adapted by: Philip Mackie. Director: Alvin Rakoff. Cast: Virginia McKenna, Leo McKern. *Two Gentle People*. Adapted by: William Trevor. Director: Herbert Wise. Cast: Harry Andrews, Elaine Stritch, Elizabeth Sellars, John Carson. *The Overnight Bag*. Adapted by: Clive Eaton. Director: Peter Hammond. Cast: Tim Brooke-Taylor, Joyce Carey, Eleanor Summerfield, Dudley Sutton. *Mortmain*. Adapted by: John Mortimer. Director: Graham Evans. Cast: Ronald Hines, Susan Penhaligon, Eleanor Bron. *Chagrin in Three Parts*. Adapted by: John Mortimer. Director: Peter Hammond. Cast: Genevieve Page, Zou Zou, Anthony Bate. *The Invisible Japanese Gentlemen*. Adapted by: John Mortimer. Director: Alastair Reid. Cast: Denholm Elliott, Celia Bannerman, Royce Mills. (From *A Sense of Reality* anthology): *Dream of a Strange Land*. Adapted by: Robin Chapman. Director: Peter Hammond. Cast: Ian Hendry, Niall MacGuinness, Graham Crowden. *Under the Garden*. Adapted by: Robin Chapman. Director: Alan Cooke. Cast: Denholm Elliot, Arthur Lowe, Vivien Pickles, Bruce Purchase.

'We wanted to convey the essence of Greene's stories as well as their surface detail. We know that beneath their smoothly readable surface there are undercurrents of menace, mystery, allegory. So we have tried to make sure that the plays not only work as entertainment – which is what Graham Greene intended when he wrote them – but also convey these undercurrents, which is *how* he wrote them . . . we are not making illustrated radio plays.' – Alan Cooke

'*Under the Garden* was a difficult one to do, about a man remembering his childhood, dreams of going underground in the garden . . . it was beautifully done . . . *The Destructors*, about a lot of children who destroy a house, was very good . . . they got innumerable telephone calls of protest about it . . . Curiously, Paul Scofield gave the only bad performance I've ever seen him give in *When Greek Meets Greek* . . . Leo McKern was very good in *Cheap in August* as was John Gielgud in *Special Duties* as a man who goads his secretary to go and get indulgences for him at church . . . Koo Stark was absolutely charming in *The Blue Film* . . . *A Little Place of the Edgware Road* I didn't like and *The Root of All Evil* wasn't awfully good . . . *Two Gentle People* was particularly well done, with Harry Andrews; he's such a good actor . . . *Case for the Defence* was all right . . . *Chagrin in Three Parts* was spoilt by the male actor, but the two lesbians were very good . . . On the whole, there were only two or three I didn't like and a couple I was indifferent to.' – Graham Greene

1979
The Human Factor. Distributor: Rank Film Distributors. Production company: Wheel Productions. Producer: Otto Preminger. Director: Otto Preminger. Screenplay: Tom Stoppard. Photograph: Mike Molloy. Art director: Ken Ryan. Editor: Richard Trevor. Music: Richard and Gary Logan. Cast: Nicol Williamson (Castle), Richard Attenborough (Colonel Daintry), Derek Jacobi (Davis), Iman (Sarah Castle), Joop Doderer (Muller), John Gielgud (Brigadier Tomlinson), Robert Morley (Dr Percival), Ann Todd (Castle's Mother), Tony Vogel (Connolly), Martin Benson (Boris), Richard Vernon (Sir John Hargreaves), Cyd Hayman (Cynthia), Paul Curran (Halliday), Fiona Fullerton (Elizabeth). 115 minutes.

1982
A Shocking Accident. Distributor: Columbia-EMI-Warner. Production company: Flamingo Pictures/Virgin Films/National Films Finance Cor-

poration. Producer: Christine Oestreicher. Director: James Scott. Screenplay: James Scott, Ernie Eban, based on a short story in *May We Borrow Your Husband?* anthology. Photogaphy: Adam Barker-Mill. Production designer: Louise Stjernsward. Editor: Tom Priestly. Music: Simon Brint, Simon Wallace. Cast: Rupert Everett (Jerome Weathersby/ Mr Weathersby), Jenny Seagrove (Sally), Barbara Hicks (Aunt Joyce), Benjamin Whitrow (Headmaster), Tim Seeley (Stephen), Sophie Ward (Amanda), Oliver Blackburn (Jerome, aged 9), Robert Popper (Jerome, aged 13). 25 minutes.

James Scott's beautifully realized little film, shot on location in and around London and Naples won the American Academy award for best live-action short of 1982 (only the second Oscar accorded in the whole Greene filmography – the first was for Robert Krasker's black-and-white photography on *The Third Man*). It is a wonderfully deadpan account of a boy having to live with the knowledge that his father was killed when an overweight pig dropped on him from a Neopolitan balcony. 'What happened to the pig?' the boy asks his headmaster on being told the news. Years later, he is about to be married when his girlfriend, Sally, learns of this bizarre fragment of her intended's past. 'I was wondering,' she says when asked a penny for her thoughts, 'what happened to the poor pig?' The shadow is finally exorcized.

1983

The Honorary Consul aka *Beyond the Limit* (US), 20th Century Fox (UK). Production company: World Film Services. Producer: Norma Heyman. Director: John Mackenzie. Screenplay: Christopher Hampton. Photography: Phil Meheux. Production designer: Allan Cameron. Editor: Stuart Baird. Music: Paul McCartney, Stanley Myers, Richard Harvey. Cast: Michael Caine (Fortnum), Richard Gere (Plarr), Elpidia Carrillo (Clara), Bob Hoskins (Colonel Perez), Joaquim de Almeida (Leon), A. Martinez (Aquino), Leonard Maguire (Dr Humphries), Geoffrey Palmer (Sir Henry).

The Heart of the Matter. Production company: Telemunchen Executive producers: Herbert G. Kloiber, Fritz Buttenstedt, Hans Kuhle. Producer: Peter Weissenborn. Director: Marco Leto. Adaptation: Gerald Savory. Photography: Safai Teherani. Cast: Jack Hedley (Scobie), Erica Rogers (Louisa), Manfred Seipold (Wilson), Wolfgang Kieling (Yusef), Silvio Anselmo (Father Rank), Tim Kwebulane (Ali). 4 x 50 mins.

Producers from Germany, France, Italy and South Africa (where it was shot), a communist director with anti-religious views, four million dollars and syrupy music result in an extraordinary mish-mash. Germans play English ex-public schoolboys, a French woman portrays a Home Counties widow and Zulus double for West Africans. No wonder the pukka representatives from Britain look bemused throughout in this most convoluted of international televi-sion co-productions.

1984

Dr Fischer of Geneva. Consolidated Productions in association with BBC Television. Producer: Richard Broke. Director: Michael Lindsay-Hogg. Screenplay: Richard Broke. Director of photography: Ken Westbury. Art director: Austen Spriggs. Editor: Ken Pearce. Cast: James Mason (Dr Fischer), Alan Bates (Jones), Greta Scacchi (Anna-Louise), Clarissa Kaye (Mrs Montgomery), Barry Humphries (Richard Deane), Cyril Cusack (Steiner), Hugh Burden (Kruger), David de Keyser (Belmont), Jacques Herlin (Mr Kips). 110 minutes.

Since the novella was published in 1980, *Dr Fischer* has had perhaps the most tortuous route to the screen of any of the projects in the Greene canon. This wonderfully entertaining first-person observation of human greed and frailty travelled via two major international directors before ending up finally with, first, producer-writer Richard Broke and then director Michael Lindsay-Hogg.

With a John Mortimer script, it was initially in the hands of Joseph Losey, a choice which concerned Greene because it seemed that Losey wanted to add an extra dose of surrealism to the story's already fantastic quality. It then passed from Losey to the Polish director Krystof Zanussi – still under the banner of the independent film company, Consolidated, which had originally bought the rights. A British–West German co-production was structured when Broke came into the act.

Zanussi was insistent on having his usual Polish crew, which was unacceptable and eventually both Zanussi and the West German connection, Sudwestfunk Baden Baden, departed the scene.

Meanwhile, the role of Fischer, the enigmatic toothpaste millionaire who believes that everyone has his price, was always intended to be filled by James Mason despite press reports that John Gielgud was to play the part with Dirk Bogarde as the narrator Jones, finally played by Alan Bates. Greene worked closely with Broke and Lindsay-Hogg on the new screenplay. He was very anxious there should be some form of voice-over narration as in the book and this was injected into

Broke's script.

The £750,000 co-production between Consolidated and now the BBC got under way late last year in Oxfordshire and Switzerland. The plan was for a British television airing towards the end of 1984 and a possible theatrical release in some other territories.

Unrealized Projects

Brideshead Revisited. In 1950 Greene was sought out by a film consortium to adapt Evelyn Waugh's *Brideshead Revisited*, published 1945 (in 1946, MGM had made its own abortive attempt to put a movie together). Waugh, delighted at the prospect, wrote to Greene (15/7/50): 'I hear you have consented to write script for a film of *Brideshead Revisited*. If true, thanks most awfully. It's more than I ever felt possible.' Twelve days later, he wrote again, 'Please don't try to get out of *Brideshead*, I'm sure you can make a fine film out of it.' In the event, the company ran out of money and the project came to nought.

A Burnt-Out Case. Greene's novel set in a leper colony in the Congo, published in 1961. Greene: 'Preminger bought the option twice for that book. Thank God he never made it.'

May We Borrow Your Husband? The deliciously dark title story of Greene's twelve-tale anthology, published in 1967, was purchased by the late Russian–American composer Dimitri Tiomkin, who also dabbled from time to time in production (*Tchaikovsky* etc.).

The Living Room. Greene's first produced play was an outstanding success on the London stage in 1953. It starred Eric Portman and launched a then unknown Dorothy Tutin. The director was Peter Glenville. Seven years later, Greene and his producer-financier friend, John Sutro, tried to set up a film which would have launched an equally-unknown Samantha Eggar. Greene: 'We

220

wanted a new face, just as Dorothy Tutin had been and John had a feeling that this girl was worth something; she'd been to drama school and she seemed right for the part. As we hadn't set up the film yet, we decided to pay her a small sum every month to be available for a year.' When Greene read an article in the *Daily Mail* that seemed to infer that Miss Eggar was in some way his kept woman, he sued successfully.

'My lawyer said that they were offering £200 to settle and that I ought to take it. And I said, "I don't take it. £2000 – and they'll pay". And they did.'

In 1964, there was news that Greene was scripting *The Living Room* for West German Helmut Kautner to direct. Then, later that year, it was reported that Greene, Anthony Quayle and Alec Guinness had established a Swiss-based company to produce it in Madrid, with Quayle directing and Guinness starring. It was shelved.

The Iliad. One of more than ninety projects announced by Alexander Korda that never proceeded beyond the announcement stage. This was to be scripted by Greene and star Laurence Olivier and Vivien Leigh.

The Tenth Man. A short novel by Greene, which was written three years before *The Third Man* and only just uncovered in a Hollywood vault, may be filmed by MGM.

In a *Sunday Times* article in April 1984, Greene told writer Norman Lebrecht that in a wartime deal with the film company – 'I sold myself to MGM on a slave contract under which they owned everything I did' – he wrote what he had believed was merely a two-page idea for a novel set in France immediately after liberation in 1944. Now that same 'idea', in fact some 60,000 words, has been turned up by MGM archivists and will be published in book form in February 1985. And in Greene's introduction to the novel will also be the synopsis of another film treatment he wrote and which MGM apparently turned into 'an important commercial movie' whose identity remains a tantalizing secret until *The Tenth Man*'s publication.

Index